ODDBALL INDIANA

ODDBALL INDIANA

A Guide to 350 Really
STRANGE PLACES

2nd Edition

JEROME POHLEN

CHICAGO
REVIEW
PRESS

Library of Congress Cataloging-in-Publication Data
Names: Pohlen, Jerome., author.
Title: Oddball Indiana : a guide to 350 really strange places / Jerome Pohlen.
Description: Second edition. | Chicago, Illinois : Chicago Review Press,
    2017. | Series: Oddball series | Includes index.
Identifiers: LCCN 2016042392 (print) | LCCN 2016043086 (ebook) | ISBN
    9781613738498 (trade paper) | ISBN 9781613738504 (adobe pdf) | ISBN
    9781613738528 (epub) | ISBN 9781613738511 (kindle)
Subjects: LCSH: Indiana—Guidebooks. | Curiosities and
    wonders—Indiana—Guidebooks. | Indiana—History, Local—Miscellanea.
Classification: LCC F526.6 .P65 2017 (print) | LCC F526.6 (ebook) | DDC
    977.2—dc23
LC record available at https://lccn.loc.gov/2016042392

Cover and interior design: Jonathan Hahn
Cover image: Couch's Body and Frame Shop; photo by Jerome Pohlen
Interior photos: All photos by Jerome Pohlen, unless otherwise indicated.

Printed in the United States of America
5 4 3 2 1

TO
OLGA, TOM, TAYLOR, KYLE, AND KAT,
MY LONGTIME INDIANA FRIENDS

CONTENTS

INtRODUCtiON

Quick—what do these things have in common: Ben-Hur, the birthplace of the automobile, Oscar the Monster Turtle, the World's Largest Egg, Johnny Appleseed's grave, and the Kinsey Institute for Research in Sex, Gender, and Reproduction? Drawing a blank? What about the invention of the pay toilet, Hollywood's first Tarzan, the original People's Temple, and the World's Largest Stump? Still without a clue? How about the birthplaces of corn flakes, Dan Quayle, square donuts, and Wonder Bread? That's right—they're all in Indiana!

While other travel guides tell you about yet another oh-so-quaint bed and breakfast, one more bike trail through Brown County, or that small-town diner where you can waste away the day with a bottomless cup of coffee while chatting with Flo, *Oddball Indiana* gives you the information you *really* need. What happened when the good folk of Plainfield decided to dump a former president of the United States into a mud puddle? Why is Nancy Barnett's grave in the middle of a county road? How did David Letterman get fired from his first broadcasting gig? Who invented Alka-Seltzer? And where can you go to contact your dead aunt Clara? These are the Indiana questions people want answered. Or at least weird people. People like you.

And there's no excuse for not hitting the Hoosier highways in search of the strange. It's the smallest state west of the Appalachians (except Hawaii), and what's more, it's the "Crossroads of the Nation." Seven interstates pass through its borders, creating more interstate intersections than in any other state. Plenty of roads and even more odd things to see . . . so what are you waiting for? You should be laughing on your vacation, not lounging. Get moving!

But first, a little advice. In this book, I've tried to give clear directions from major streets and landmarks, but you could still make a wrong turn. Don't panic, and remember these Oddball travel tips:

1. **Stop and ask!** For a lot of communities, their Oddball attraction might be their only claim to fame. Locals are often thrilled that you'd drive out of your way to marvel at their underappreciated shrine. But choose your guides wisely; old cranks at the town café are good for information; pimply teenage clerks at the 7-Eleven are not.

2. **Call ahead.** Few Oddball sites keep regular hours, but most will gladly wait around if they know you're coming. Some Indiana sites are seasonal or can close at a moment's notice if the proprietor needs to run an errand. Always call.

3. **Don't give up.** Think of that little old lady who's volunteered her days to keep that small-town museum open; she's waiting just for you. She's not standing out on the corner, hollering at passersby—you have to find her. That's *your* job.

4. **Don't trespass!** Don't become a Terrible Tourist. Just because somebody erected a gigantic monument to a peach doesn't mean you're invited to crawl all over it.

5. **Persevere:** Road-tripping is hard work. If you find yourself out of sorts after hours in the car, remember these Indiana folk cures: for arthritis of the fingers, catch and strangle a weasel barehanded; for a stuffed-up head, sniff a dirty sock nine times; and for stammering, a smart slap in the face with raw liver should do the trick.

Do you have an Oddball site of your own? Have I missed anything? Do you know of an Oddball site that should be included in a third edition? Please write and let me know: Chicago Review Press, 814 N. Franklin Street, Chicago, IL 60610.

NORtHeRN INDiaNa

*I*f all you know about northern Indiana is the toll from East Chicago to Angola, perhaps you should slow down. And while you're at it, show a little respect. First of all, if it wasn't for this admittedly flat and corn-covered region, your vacation might be a whole lot less enjoyable—these folks practically *invented* the Great American Road Trip. The Prairie Schooner wagon, probably the first long-distance "family car," was manufactured for pioneers by the Studebaker family of South Bend. Road technology was perfected on the coast-to-coast Lincoln Highway that still bisects the region. And today, most of this nation's recreational vehicles and motor homes are manufactured in and around Elkhart. When you're touring the back roads of Shipshewana, Winamac, and Napanee, you're driving on hallowed ground.

And not just hallowed ground but *strange* ground. Look around. Where else can you find a 3,000-pound egg, a skinny-dipping ghost, a collection of historic outhouses, and Oscar the Monster Turtle? Where will you find the birthplaces of Alka-Seltzer, heavier-than-air flight, and Michael Jackson? And where can you find the remains of Johnny Appleseed and the World's First Ferris Wheel? Nowhere in the world but the top third of the Hoosier State, that's where.

Angola

Lottery Bowl

Hold on, compulsive gamblers! The Lottery Bowl isn't a new scratch-and-win game from the Indiana legislature. No, in this lottery you play for your life.

Resting in a simple cabinet on the top floor of Trine University's athletic facility is one of the Selective Service System's most recognizable artifacts: the Lottery Bowl. This two-foot-tall goldfish tank was purchased by the government from a Washington, DC, pet store at the outset of World

War I. It was used to select numbers that translated into draft notices to thousands of young American men from 1917 to 1918. Following the Armistice, the draft ended and the glass bowl was mothballed in Philadelphia.

But just before the United States' entry into World War II, FDR sent a limousine to pick up the Lottery Bowl and escort it back to the nation's capital. The Selective Service was reactivated in 1940 and continued drafting young men through 1970. For all but one of those years it operated under the direction of General Lewis B. Hershey, Tri-State University graduate and namesake of this college's gym.

Several of Hershey's personal effects are also on display at Hershey Hall, such as his ceremonial saber, as are other items from the history of the Selective Service—but it's the Lottery Bowl that draws the visitors.

Hershey Hall, Trine University (formerly Tri-State University), Angola, IN 46703
Phone: (260) 665-4141
Hours: Most days; call ahead
Cost: Free
Website: www.trinethunder.com/facilities/hershey
Directions: South off Rte. 20 (Maumee St.) on Kinney St., west on Park St. until it comes to an end.

Auburn
Auburn Cord Duesenberg Automobile Museum

When you first step into this impressive museum, you'll know you've found "a duesy," and not just one but more than a hundred.

The life of the Auburn Cord Duesenberg company was short but brilliant. Started by the Eckhart family in 1902, it closed operations in 1937. Its most remarkable models were created after E. L. Cord was hired as the president in 1924. The top-of-the-line Duesenbergs he designed embodied the spirit of the Roaring Twenties with Art Deco interiors and powerful engines—why else would they be named Speedsters? These babies could max out at 130 mph and were the cars of choice for the rich and famous— Clark Gable, Gary Cooper, Frank Lloyd Wright, and later Elvis, John Lennon, and Michael Jordan.

You'll see more of these classic autos here, in the company's restored 1930 corporate headquarters, than anywhere else. All are in mint condition, yet few would think of driving them at 130 mph anymore. The Model J, introduced in 1929, was the make's most popular high-end model; each vehicle had a unique body and was driven 500 miles on the Indianapolis Motor Speedway before delivery. At the time, the Model J had double the horsepower of every other car on the road.

The museum's six galleries feature the entire Auburn Cord Duesenberg line, as well as other Indiana-manufactured autos, like the homely 1952 Crosley. Each Labor Day the town throws an Auburn Cord Duesenberg Festival, with a Parade of Classics capped off by a car auction. This isn't a repo sale at the auto pound—some of the 5,000+ cars sold here each year are worth more than $1 million.

1600 S. Wayne St., Auburn, IN 46706
Phone: (260) 925-1400
Hours: Monday–Friday 10 AM–7 PM, Saturday–Sunday 10 AM–5 PM
Cost: Adults $12.50, Kids (6–17) $7.50
Website: www.automobilemuseum.org and www.acdfestival.org
Directions: South on Main St. from Seventh St. (Rte. 8) until it ends at Wayne St., then two blocks southwest.

Beverly Shores
The House of Tomorrow

At the end of Chicago's 1933 Century of Progress Exposition, organizers sold off most of the exhibits to the highest bidders. More than a dozen of the futuristic model homes ended up across Lake Michigan in Beverly Shores, where folks were anxious for progress.

The House of Tomorrow, a 12-sided structure with more windows than walls, still towers above its fellow fair refugees on Lakefront Drive. Across the street, clinging to the shoreline, the pink stucco Florida Tropical House looks like it would be more at home in Miami Beach. All the adjacent Cypress House needs, with its swampy cypress shingles and siding, is a fan boat and some alligator traps. Two additional buildings on the same road were intended to demonstrate the future of building technology, which is now part of the past: the Rostone House was manufactured with synthetic cast stone and the Armco-Ferro House with prefab steel.

Still, not everyone in Beverly Shores was interested in the future back in the 1930s; some liked the way things were a century and a half earlier. Another developer brought six re-created historic homes to this dunes community: Wakefield House (the birthplace of George Washington),

Boston's Old North Church, Mount Vernon, the Paul Revere House, Long-fellow's Wayside Inn, and the House of Seven Gables. Only the Old North Church remains, converted to a private residence. The rest have been torn down or burned down.

If you'd like to see the World's Fair homes, you have one chance each autumn—the National Park Service conducts a tour of what's left. Tickets go fast, so plan ahead.

House of Tomorrow, Lake Front Dr., Beverly Shores, IN 46301
Phone: (219) 926-7561
Hours: Always visible; view from street
Cost: Free
Website: www.nps.gov/indu/learn/historyculture/centuryofprogress.htm
Directions: Between E. State Park Rd. and Broadway, on Lakefront Dr.

Old North Church, Eaton Ave. & Beverly Dr., Beverly Shores, IN 46301
Private phone
Hours: Always visible; view from street
Cost: Free
Directions: One block west of Broadway on Beverly Dr.

MUSHROOM TRIP

The House of Tomorrow wasn't the only refugee from the Century of Progress to make a trip to Indiana. The **Krider World Fair Garden** in Middlebury (302 W. Bristol Ave., www.middleburyin.com/departments/park_and_recreation/index.php) was once a nursery demonstration garden at the 1933 fair in Chicago. Refurbished and opened to the public in the mid-1990s, it has a windmill, waterfall, benches, fountain, reflecting pools, and several concrete mushrooms that are tall enough to hide under.

BLUFFTON
➡ Two interurban trains, one empty and one full, collided north of Bluffton on September 21, 1910, killing 41 passengers.

Bremen
World's Fattest Man Death Site

Robert Earl Hughes was touring with the Gooding Brothers Amusement Company in the summer of 1958 when he came down with a case of the measles. For most people, this would have been an inconvenience, but for the World's Fattest Man, it was serious.

Hughes's 1,041-pound body (he once tipped the scales at 1,069) could not fit through the doors of the Bremen Community Hospital, so doctors were forced to treat Hughes in his customized trailer in the parking lot. The 32-year-old sideshow performer was just getting over the disease when he contracted uremia, and he died soon thereafter on July 10, 1958. Several days later he was laid to rest in a piano-sized coffin in his hometown, Mt. Sterling, Illinois.

Little of the Bremen Community Hospital of 1958 remains, but several of the current interior rooms are part of the same structure as Hughes was unable to fit into. A new medical facility has been expanded on the site with, presumably, wider doors.

Doctors Hospital & Neuromuscular Center, 411 S. Whitlock St., Bremen, IN 46506
Phone: (574) 546-3830
Hours: Always visible
Cost: Free
Website: www.neuropsychiatrichospitals.net/doctors-neuropsychiatric-hospital/
Directions: Two blocks south of Plymouth St. (Rte. 106/331), five blocks east of Bowen Ave.

Chesterton
Diana of the Dunes

Indiana's best-known ghost is also a nudist, much to the delight of folks visiting Indiana Dunes State Park. She has been nicknamed Diana of the Dunes, but in real life she was Alice Mable Gray.

Gray hailed from Chicago, the daughter of a prominent Illinois physician and a graduate of the University of Chicago. Forsaking her inheritance for a simpler life, she moved into a shack dubbed Driftwood on the shore of Lake Michigan in 1915. There she would spend long days strolling on the beach and skinny-dipping in the icy waters.

Alice met a drifter and ex-con named Paul Wilson, and the two were married in 1921. They produced a daughter, Bonita. Paul was often absent, usually running from the law. He was accused in 1922 of murdering a vagrant and burning the body near Alice's shack, but he was never formally charged with the crime.

When the Ogden Dunes development was announced, the couple was forced to move into town. Not long after, Alice died of uremic poisoning on the night of February 8–9, 1925, following the birth of her second child. Some think her demise was brought on by injuries suffered at the hands of Paul Wilson. Once again, allegations could not be substantiated. Gray was buried in Gary in a pauper's grave in Oak Hill Cemetery (4450 Harrison St., (219) 884-1762), but her soul remained on the shores of her beloved lake.

Rangers and visitors still see her emerge, naked, from the waters throughout the year. Before she can be detained for indecent exposure, she vanishes.

Indiana Dunes State Park, 1600 N. Rte. 25 East, Chesterton, IN 46304
Phone: (219) 926-1952
Hours: Daily, dawn–dusk
Cost: In-state, $7; Out-of-state, $12
Website: www.in.gov/dnr/parklake/2980.htm and www.indianadunes.com
Directions: At the north end of Rte. 49, at Rte. 12.

Historical Society of Ogden Dunes, Hour Glass Museum, 8 Lupine Lane, Ogden Dunes, IN 46368
No phone
Hours: Third Sunday of month, 4–5:30 PM, or by appointment
Cost: Donations accepted
Website: http://odhistory.org
Directions: Two blocks south of Shore Dr. off Hillcrest Rd.

Churubusco
Oscar, the Beast of 'Busco

In 1948 ducks and fish began mysteriously disappearing from farmer Gale Harris's small lake northwest of Churubusco. Rumors began circulating that a pickup-sized snapping turtle was to blame. Local residents organized a turtle hunt to snare the beast they called Oscar, named for the lake's first owner, Oscar Fulk. After several fruitless days and nights searching Fulk Lake, the often-drunken posse abandoned hope of capturing the 500-pound quacker-killer.

But not Harris. Like Captain Ahab, Gale Harris never gave up the quest for his supershelled nemesis. One night he was able to wrap a chain around the creature, which he then hitched to four workhorses. An epic tug-of-war ensued, and the chain was the loser—it snapped, and Oscar dove for the lake's bottom.

A turtle strong enough to overpower four horses? Certainly it was no average reptile, but the very Beast of 'Busco! Though the renamed monster was never seen again, there's no guarantee it's not still lurking in the mud, waiting for its next meal.

Today Churubusco calls itself Turtletown, USA, and has erected a statue to Oscar in Churubusco Town Park. The town celebrates Turtle Days every June—a fish fry, a parade, beer and food tents, fireworks, and yes, a turtle hunt. A lucky teen is also crowned Turtle Queen.

Fulk Lake, Madden Rd., Churubusco, IN 46723
Statue: Churubusco Town Park, 1 John Krieger Dr., Churubusco, IN 46723
No phone
Hours: Always visible
Cost: Free
Website: www.turtledays.com
Directions: Lake, head northeast on Rte. 205 for two miles, turn left on Madden Rd., head north one mile to the pond just south of County Line Rd.; Park, at the north end of town, west of Rte. 33.

There he is!

Dunns Bridge
Remains of the World's First Ferris Wheel

The world's first Ferris wheel was constructed for Chicago's 1893 Columbian Exposition, yet parts of it have outlived everyone who ever rode it above the Midway. How? Following the suspiciously convenient fires during the closing days of the exposition, the Ferris wheel was disassembled and rebuilt on the north side of Chicago. Operating there, it thrilled riders for several years before being carted to Missouri for the 1904 St. Louis World's Fair.

After its second appearance at a World Exposition, the wheel was sold off in pieces for iron scrap. One buyer was Indiana farmer Isaac Dunn. He wanted to connect his land that straddled the Kankakee River west of North Judson, and welded several pieces of the old ride together to accomplish the task. Exactly which pieces of the wheel he bought is up for debate, but this much is clear to the novice observer: this thing sure didn't start out as a bridge. (Metallurgic tests on the bridge have shown the beams came from the same foundry as the Ferris wheel.)

A tiny burg eventually grew up around the unique structure, and locals dubbed their unincorporated town Dunns Bridge. Cars pass over a new bridge today, but what's left of the Ferris wheel was restored and opened to foot traffic in 2005. There's also a roadside park that can be accessed from the north side of the river.

County Road 400E, Dunns
   Bridge, IN 46392
No phone
Hours: Always visible
Cost: Free
Directions: Off Rte. 10 east of
   Wheatfield, north two miles on
   County Road 400E (Tefft Rd.)
   to the Kankakee River.

Spinning wheels don't always got to go 'round.

Dyer

The "Ideal Section" and the Ostermann Bench

If you've ever wondered, while sitting in bumper-to-bumper traffic on an ugly interstate, searching desperately for a rest stop, whether anyone has ever tried to build a better highway, the answer is yes . . . 90 years ago!

When this nation began its love affair with the automobile, a few visionaries realized that road construction technology would have to keep pace with faster and more numerous cars. This need was made all the more clear on June 7, 1920, when Henry Ostermann, an early booster of the Lincoln Highway, hit a slippery shoulder near Tama, Iowa. His Studebaker spun out of control, overturned, and killed the auto dealer.

Ostermann's friends used the tragedy to convince US Rubber to fund an experiment on a two-mile stretch of Route 30 in Dyer, Indiana. The initial plans for the so-called Ideal Section of the Lincoln Highway were, to say the least, impressive. Wide shoulders. Banked curves with proper drainage. Sidewalks and street lights. Landscaped rest stops and free campsites!

But the reality of the Ideal Section didn't match up with the plan. To start with, the original 2-mile stretch was shortened to 1.3 miles after an adjacent cranky farmer named Moeller refused to sell his right-of-way, opting to hold out for more money.

The project began in 1921, but it would be two years before it was completed. Engineers were flying blind, and the frustration showed. The head contractor for the Ideal Section's only bridge, Fred Tapp, committed suicide on October 5, 1922, in a manner only a contractor might choose: he blew himself up with a stick of dynamite clutched against his chest. The rest stops were never built. Farmer Moeller eventually sold part of his land for campsites, but they too were never constructed. A local energy company agreed to power the streetlights for free but pulled the plug after a year. Nearby residents walked off with the landscaping, the sidewalks were eventually ripped out, and Fred Tapp's bridge was replaced.

All that remains of the Ideal Section is a memorial bench to Henry Ostermann. To get to this humble stone monument, you have to stumble along the weed-choked shoulder, conspicuously free of sidewalks and streetlights, just feet from traffic on a less-than-ideal highway.

Rte. 30 & St. John's Rd., Dyer, IN 46311
No phone
Hours: Always visible
Cost: Free
Website: www.lincolnhighwayassoc.org/info/in/
Directions: Just west of Meyer's Castle (1370 Joliet St.) on Rte. 30, on the south side of the highway.

East Chicago
Park on the Sidewalk, Walk in the Street

Has the whole world gone topsy-turvy? In East Chicago it has, at least in the neighborhood of Marktown. This poorly conceived company community has streets that are so narrow residents must park their cars on the sidewalks. With all the cars on the walkways, everyone must stroll in the streets. When parents in Marktown tell their children, "Go play in the street!" they mean it!

The tightly packed homes in Marktown have a European appearance. If you added a few canals you'd think you were in a Dutch village after the war. This 15-block community was designed by eccentric architect Howard Van Doren Shaw and is shoehorned between a steel plant and a refinery, well off the beaten track, yet still only minutes from Chicago.

Marktown has seen much better days, and though it is listed on the National Register of Historic Places, it may not be around much longer. See it while you can, preferably during daylight hours.

Riley Rd. & Dickey St., East Chicago, IN 46312
No phone
Hours: Always visible
Cost: Free
Website: www.marktown.org/tour.html
Directions: Neighborhood bound by 129th St., Dickey St., Pine St., and Riley Rd.; exit Riley Rd. east from Cline Ave. and head northeast.

Elkhart
Birthplace of Alka-Seltzer

Plop, plop, fizz, fizz, oh what a relief it is . . . but almost wasn't. Were it not for an editor who fancied himself a doctor, and a businessman who fancied himself an investigator, Alka-Seltzer might not exist today.

During the late 1920s, the nation was gripped with one flu epidemic after another. But strangely enough, reporters, editors, and typesetters at the *Elkhart Truth* seemed to be resistant to the nasty bugs. Andrew "Hub" Beardsley, president of Elkhart's Dr. Miles Medical Company, was paying a visit to the local paper and asked the editor in chief why everyone was at work. It was the editor's concoction of aspirin and baking soda that did the trick—everyone on staff took it!

Beardsley recognized the medicine's potential and asked one of his chemists, Maurice Treneer, to make it more appealing to the public. Treneer mixed the two ingredients into an effervescent tablet, and Alka-Seltzer was born. That's right, the fizz is just a marketing gimmick.

Alka-Seltzer hit the shelves in 1931. The Dr. Miles Medical Company (now Miles Laboratories, a division of Bayer AG) is also responsible for inventing One A Day multivitamins and forming them into Flintstone and Bugs Bunny shapes.

Sunday morning in Elkhart.

421 S. Second St., Elkhart, IN 46516
Phone: (574) 294-1661
Hours: Always visible
Cost: Free
Website: www.elkharttruth.com and www.alkaseltzer.com
Directions: At the corner of Marion St. and Second St.

Curly Top and the Toothpick Train

Railroad museums are a dime a dozen. It's not as if you can throw a locomotive in the trash, but park it in an old switching yard—voilà—instant museum! But the National New York Central is not a typical railroad museum because of two special exhibits. The first is a collection of autographs, and the second is the Toothpick Train.

During the Depression, a local girl named Violet Schmidt had a unique hobby. Each day she would wait beside the New York Central tracks and wave to the passengers headed someplace more interesting, like Chicago or New York. Because the Twentieth Century Limited moved so fast ("960 miles in 960 minutes"), riders could only recognize Schmidt by her most prominent characteristic: her curly hair. It soon became a custom for riders to reward the loyal Curly Top by tossing autographed menus at her or, for those with a better pitching arm, notes stuffed in hollowed-out potatoes. Whether or not they were trying to bean her, Schmidt saved the best-known autographs, including Al Jolson, Shirley Temple, Spencer Tracy, and President Herbert Hoover. You can see them at the museum today.

Another amazing exhibit at this museum was a lifelong project of an obsessed New York Central fan. Terry Woodling of nearby Warsaw used 421,250 toothpicks and a lot of glue to build a replica of an early steam locomotive on the NYC line. Woodling's elaborate model is encased in glass, lest a visitor with a popcorn kernel stuck between a couple molars try to make it a 421,249-toothpick train.

National New York Central Railroad Museum, 721 S. Main St., Elkhart, IN 46516
Phone: (574) 294-3001
Hours: Tuesday–Saturday 10 AM–5 PM, Sunday Noon–4 PM
Cost: Adults $6, Seniors (61+) $5, Kids (4–12) $5
Website: www.elkhartindiana.org/department/?fDD=54-0
Directions: At the south end of downtown, where Main St. crosses the railroad tracks.

Hall of Heroes Museum

The Hall of Heroes seen in the 1970s cartoon *Super Friends* was just imaginary, you say? Not anymore—the Super Friends' superest friend Allen Stewart has re-created the building as a two-story museum in the yard of his Elkhart home. Currently the Hall doesn't hold meetings between Aquaman and Wonder Woman and the rest of the gang, but it does hold 60,000+ comic books, 10,000+ toys and action figures, and props from TV and film. Stewart has the red suit and cape from *The Greatest American Hero*, Captain America's shield from *Captain America: The First Avenger*, and Adam West's *Batman* costume.

And there's more! Stewart has re-created the original Bat Cave, which even has a Bat Pole from the second floor to the first. And each Halloween he remakes the building into the Hall of Villains to spook trick-or-treaters. Who will save them from the Penguin and the Green Goblin? Their nerdy parents—Super Friends, unite!

58005 17th St., Elkhart, IN 46517
Phone: (574) 522-1187
Hours: Call ahead; most days, Monday–Friday 2–5 PM, Saturday 11 AM–5 PM, Sunday noon–4 PM
Cost: Adults $6, Kids (9 and under) $4
Website: http://hallofheroesmuseum.com
Directions: East from Rte. 19 on Mishawaka Rd. to Rte. 105 (17th St.), then south two blocks.

Not your average Tuff Shed.

RV/MH Hall of Fame

If road-tripping were a religion, Elkhart would be Mecca. Three-quarters of this nation's recreational vehicles and conversion vans are built in and around this northern Indiana city and always have been. It's also the location of the RV/MH Heritage Foundation, the repository of all manufacturing information pertaining to recreational vehicles (RVs) and motor homes (MHs) from their 1930s genesis to the present.

"You can't take sex, booze, or weekends away from the American people." —John K. Hanson Photo by author, courtesy of RV/MH Heritage Foundation

More than 20 restored recreational vehicles circle fake campfires in this barn-sized museum. Flat, cut-out 1950s families roast cardboard weenies and commune with nature, American-style. Most of the vehicles are open, so you can step inside to check out the amenities and period decorations. The collection includes the World's First Winnebago, a 1967 model, and a 28-foot 1940 New Moon, the model Lucy and Desi pulled across the country in *The Long, Long Trailer*. Though it looked big on screen, it barely compares to another model on display, the 1954 Spartan Imperial. This 8-foot-wide, 41-foot-long behemoth has a master bedroom, a full bath, two children's bunk beds, a kitchen with pantry, and a nice-sized living room.

The museum recently moved and expanded to accommodate the collection of David Woodworth, who specialized in pre-WWII RVs and campers. The collection includes a 1931 Chevrolet Housecar built for Mae West, complete with a back porch for her rocking chair.

For true RV/MH nuts, visit the foundation's library to learn how to restore your Airstream, Fan Luxury Liner, or Magic Carpet Pop-Up. This wonderful resource center is doing its part to preserve part of the sentiments once expressed by Winnebago founder John K. Hanson: "You can't take sex, booze, or weekends away from the American people." Amen!

21565 Executive Pkwy., Elkhart, IN 46514
Phone: (800) 378-8694 or (574) 293-2344
Hours: Monday–Saturday 10 AM–4 PM
Cost: Adults $10, Seniors $8, Kids (6–18) $7
Website: www.rvmhhalloffame.org
Directions: Exit I-80 (Indiana Toll Road) at Rte. 17, just south of the interchange.

Fair Oaks
Climbing Cows and Dairy Adventure

You know you're headed somewhere special as you travel south along I-65. First, two fiberglass cows have climbed atop a milk tanker with a sign that reads WE GOT MILK & MOOOORE! Later, another sign has a very large fork, then another with two big chairs, and finally a colossal corn cob, all announcing the tour at Fair Oak Farms.

This isn't just another petting-zoo-and-cheese-house attraction—you can spend the entire day at Fair Oaks Farms and have plenty to keep you entertained. The high-tech Dairy Adventure takes you on a trip through the modern sustainable farm, where you'll try your hand at prepping and tugging on a robotic cow's teats. Learn other interesting facts from an animatronic tree, rooster, and dairy scientist. Have the kids burn off a little steam at the Mooville outdoor play area with a milk jug climbing wall, string cheese maze, and MooChoo miniature train. Then head over to the milking barn, where 72 cows slowly spin on a giant turntable; by the time they make it around in eight and a half minutes, each has been milked and can be unloaded. And don't miss the Birthing Barn. Between 80 and 100 calves are born at the farm every day, most of which enter the world in a corral surrounded by stadium seats filled with wide-eyed tourists like you.

Fair Oaks Dairy Adventure, 856 N. 600 E, Fair Oaks, IN 47943
Phone: (877) 536-1194 or (219) 394-2025
Hours: Monday–Saturday 9 AM–3 PM, Sunday 10 AM–3 PM; Market, bakery, and Farmhouse
   Restaurant open later
Cost: Adults $17, Couples $27, Seniors (62+) $12, Kids (3–12) $12
Website: http://fofarms.com
Directions: Exit I-65 at Rte. 14, then west to the entrance.

COW-A-BUNCHA!

You might have your fill of bovine beauties after a visit to Fair Oaks Farms, but if they leave you wanting more, here are six additional fiberglass cows you can find on Indiana's byways.

Huge Howie the Hereford

Howard & Sons Quality Meats, 719 Ridge Rd., Munster, (219) 836-8000, www.howardandsons.net

The enormous Hereford bull at this Munster meatery has been here for half a century. He balances on a sign that juts out over the sidewalk.

Rooftop Steer

Piatak Meats, 6200 Broadway, Merrillville, (219) 980-3520, http://piatakmeats.com

Though puny by roadside cow standards, the Piatak steer (a Hereford) atop the entrance of this butcher shop points the way to the massive meat-filled coolers inside, and isn't that what you really want?

Howie the Steer

Kelsey's Steakhouse, 2300 Morthland Dr., Valparaiso, (219) 465-4022, http://kelseyssteakhouse.com

Despite his name, Valparaiso's Howie is no relation to Munster's Howie. Yes, he's a Hereford, so he comes from the same breed, but he's even larger—a solid 10 feet tall at the horns. This fancy steakhouse does not have a Howieburger on the menu—that would be too disturbing for the little ones—but they do offer a Howie-shaped chocolate cake for dessert.

Mr. Happy Burger Bull

Mr. Happy Burger, 900 W. Market St., Logansport, (574) 753-4016,
www.facebook.com/Mr-Happy-Burger-55104232912/

Mr. Happy is an eight-foot-tall Black Angus who guards a
hamburger joint on the west side of Logansport. He has blue
eyes and appears to be cleaning out his left nostril with his
bright pink tongue. (How's your appetite?) He also wears a
white bib and chef's hat.

Digging for gold in all the wrong places.

Bareheaded Mr. Happy Burger Bull

Hap's Old Time Ice Cream Sundae Parlor, 3131 E. Market St., Logansport,
(574) 753-6418, www.facebook.com/Mr-Happy-Burger-55104232912/

A twin brother of Mr. Happy, the Black Angus on the east side
of Logansport, keeps his tongue inside his mouth. He too
wears a white bib, but no chef's hat.

Mobile Home Cows

Cohron's Manufactured Homes, 9623 Pendleton Pike, Indianapolis, (317) 897-1043, www.cohronhomes.com

Finally—a milk cow! It's not entirely clear what this large black-and-white Holstein has to do with prefab homes, but here she is, guarding the display models from atop a brick pedestal. She also appears on the company's logo.

Fort Wayne

"Fish Eaters and Idol Worshipers"

There was a time, not too long ago, when anti-Catholic bigotry ran fairly close to the surface in the American psyche. And the prejudice was not limited to hate-mongering groups like the KKK or the John Birch Society, as you will see if you visit a collection at the Cathedral Museum, compiled by John Francis Noll, the fifth bishop of Fort Wayne.

Take the cartoons published in *Harper's Weekly*. One 1871 drawing by Thomas Nast shows bishops crawling out of the "American River Ganges," their crocodile-toothed miters open to devour American schoolchildren. (You might know Nast as the artist who created the modern, white-bearded image of Santa and the elephant as the mascot of the GOP.) And there's more, including books, caricatures, and modern religious tracts you might be handed on a street corner to this day.

The Cathedral Museum also has a large collection of items related to the local diocese, a full-sized statue of the very small Pope Pius X, nun dolls dressed in dozens of religious orders' habits, and two splinters from the cross on which Jesus was crucified . . . or so says the plaque.

Cathedral Museum, 915 S. Clinton St., Fort Wayne, IN 46802
Phone: (260) 422-4611
Hours: Tuesday–Friday 10 AM–2 PM
Cost: Free
Website: www.diocesefwsb.org/cathedral-museum
Directions: Downtown on southbound Rte. 27 (Clinton St.), three blocks south of Main St.

Johnny Appleseed's Grave

John Chapman was America's first hippie. Better known as Johnny Appleseed, he was looked upon with some suspicion by many he met. Maybe it was his claim that God had commanded him in a dream to plant apple trees along the western migration. Maybe it was his devotion to the Swedenborgian faith, passing out as many bibles as tree saplings. But most likely, it was the tin pot he wore for a hat, or that he made drinking water in the winter by melting snow with his dirty feet.

During his travels, Chapman covered a region of 100,000 square miles, starting nurseries from New England to the Midwest. On a trip to Fort Wayne in March 1845, he contracted pneumonia after walking barefoot through the snow to visit an apple orchard. This would have been a stupid act for a young man, but he was 72 years old at the time. He never made it to 73—he died on March 18, 1845.

Chapman was buried in the Archer family plot, located roughly where the city's power lines run along the river today. His exact burial spot is unknown, but there is a gravestone atop a small hill in the center of a park named after him. For all anyone knows, footings for the transmission towers could have been drilled through his remains.

Today, Fort Wayne celebrates Johnny Appleseed with a festival each September.

Johnny Appleseed Memorial Park, 4000 block of
  Parnell Ave., Fort Wayne, IN 46802
Phone: (260) 427-6000; Festival, (260) 427-6003
Hours: Always visible
Cost: Free
Website: www.fortwayneparks.org/index
  .php?option=com_content&id=173:johnny
  -appleseed-park&Itemid=33 and
  www.johnnyappleseedfest.com
Directions: Just south of Coliseum Blvd. (Rte.
  930) and the Allen County War Memorial
  Coliseum.

The last appleseed to be planted.

THANKS A LOT, JOHNNY!

John Chapman spread not just apples across our new nation but also a plant called dog fennel. He thought the noxious weed cured fevers, so he scattered dog fennel seeds *everywhere*. Today, this botanical nuisance is sometimes referred to as "Johnnyweed."

Karpeles Manuscript Library Museums

The Karpeles Manuscript Library Museums are some of the most under-appreciated private institutions in the United States, and Fort Wayne has *two*. Never heard of them? They just happen to be the world's largest private collections of historic documents, with more than a million artifacts, and they share their holdings through exhibits that rotate among 14 museums around the country. Every four months a fresh collection comes to town, so you'll always find something new.

Recent exhibits at Fairfield Hall have included documents related to Eva Perón—love letters to her husband Juan, a draft of her autobiography, and her dental records—and items related to *The Jungle Book*—Kipling's edited manuscript and Disney's sketches of Mowgli. Piqua Hall just finished a show on ancient maps, including the first atlas map of North America, the Ruysch Map of 1507, and the first map of Iran, from 1478. What will they have when you visit?

Fairfield Hall, 2410 Fairfield Ave., Fort Wayne, IN 46807
Phone: (260) 456-6929
Piqua Hall, 3039 Piqua Ave., Fort Wayne, IN 46806
Phone: (260) 449-9551
Hours: Tuesday–Saturday 10 AM–4 PM
Cost: Free
Website: www.rain.org/~karpeles/ftwfrm.html and www.rain.org/~karpeles/FtWcur.html
Directions: Fairfield Hall, one block south of Creighton Ave., at Pierce Ave.; Piqua Hall, one block west of Rte. 27 southbound (Clifton St.), one block north of Wildwood Ave.

Sliced Bread Sign

Back in 1957, Aunt Millie's Bakery installed a rooftop sign on its Fort Wayne facility depicting a loaf of "Perfection Sunbeam Bread." No big deal, right? But take a closer look and you'll see that this is no ordinary loaf. Every 2.3 seconds another slice falls out of the open bag onto a waiting plate, one after another after another, without end.

That's a lotta bread. Do the math: the sign has been running for 60 years—365 days a year, 24 hours a day, 60 minutes an hour, and 60 seconds a minute. Divide that by 2.3 seconds and you realize roughly 822,678,261 slices have dumped out of this big plastic bag. And now 822,678,262. . . . Wait, now 822,678,263 . . .

Aunt Millie's Bakery, 350 Pearl St., Fort Wayne, IN 46802
Phone: (206) 424-8245
Hours: Always visible
Cost: Free
Website: www.auntmillies.com
Directions: On the south side of the river, north of Main St., between Fairfield and Harrison Sts.

822,678,261 slices and counting.

Gary

Circus Train Slaughter

The Hagenbeck-Wallace Circus train had just left Michigan City, headed for Hammond, on June 22, 1918, when it pulled off on a siding near Ivanhoe, a now-unincorporated neighborhood on the west side of Gary. Unfortunately, four of its sleeping cars and the caboose remained on the express tracks. These four cars were rammed by an empty Michigan Central troop train driven by engineer Alonzo K. Sargent, who was drowsy with kidney pills. Sargent had fallen asleep at the switch and awoke too late to apply the brakes.

Rather than come to the victims' aid, many of the local townsfolk fled amid wild rumors that even wilder animals had escaped from the wreckage and were hungry. This was not true; the animals were on another train. Clowns and strongmen, carnies and dancing girls were all trapped in the rubble that soon burst into flames, ignited by the train's kerosene lamps. With few around to rescue the performers, 86 perished. Today, the site is said to be haunted, and for some strange reason (since none died in the crash), you are supposed to hear the wail of elephants on dark nights.

Cline Ave. & W. Ninth Ave., Gary, IN 46406
No phone
Hours: Always visible
Cost: Free
Directions: Head north from I-94 on Cline Ave. (Rte. 912) until you see the train tracks near Ninth Ave.

Gary, First in Flight

Wright Brothers . . . bah! If you really want to see where heavier-than-air flight originated, skip the pilgrimage to the beaches of Kitty Hawk. Instead, go to Gary's Marquette Park on the south shore of Lake Michigan. It was here at Miller's Beach, on June 22, August 20, and September 11, 1896, that Octave Chanute flew the world's first large biplane gliders. Locals were unimpressed and dismissed him as "the crazy man of the dunes."

Chanute was a naturalized American, born in Paris, who retired young from a career as a civil engineer to pursue his dream of solving the riddle of human flight. Chanute was neither shy nor secretive about his findings, and seven years later he would advise the Wright Brothers on their now-famous 1903 flight in North Carolina.

Few people except aviation nuts even remember Chanute today, but a stone monument outlining his accomplishments sits in Gary's Marquette Park, at the approximate location where his gliders lifted free of the dunes. A full-sized model of a Chanute glider hangs in the Lake County Convention and Visitors Bureau (7770 Corinne Dr., (219) 989-7770, www.southshorecva.com) in nearby Hammond.

Marquette Park, 1 N. Grand Blvd., Gary, IN 46403
Phone: (219) 938-7362
Hours: June–August, dawn–dusk
Cost: Free
Website: http://marquetteparkgary.org/
Directions: A boulder marker lies south of the park pavilion, at the lakefront.

Society for the Restoration of the Gary Bathing Beach Aquatorium and Octave Chanute's Place
  in History, 607 S. Lake St., Suite A, Gary, IN 46303
Phone: (219) 938-1986
Hours: By appointment only
Cost: Free
Website: http://aquatorium.org/
Directions: The Aquatorium is in Marquette Park, at the north end of Grand Blvd., then to the
  right along Oak Ave.

Jackson 5 Sites

Several years ago there was a push to commemorate Michael Jackson on a license plate available for Hoosier drivers. The legislation needed to issue the plates suffered the same fate as a 1995 plan for a Gary-based Jacksons theme park: nobody bought into the idea.

Clearly, if you want to acknowledge the Jackson 5's contribution to this steel city, you have to do it on your own. The first place to start is the former Jackson family home located on Jackson Street, which is named for the president, not the King of Pop. It is easy to find if you look for the large granite monolith of Michael on the front lawn, surrounded by a high fence.

Between 1950 and 1966, Joe and Katherine Jackson had nine children: Reebie, Jackie, Tito, Jermaine, La Toya, Marlon, Michael, Randy, and Janet. By all accounts, life in the Jackson household was no picnic. Joe was the classic stage dad, driving the kids to fulfill his own failed musical dreams. Joe played guitar for the Falcons, a band composed of workers at the Inland Steel Company, to earn extra money. But when Joe was at one of his many jobs, a few of his sons began playing with his guitar. He later heard them, realized they had talent, and the rest is history.

The Jacksons were not allowed to hang out with local kids. Joe made them practice, practice, practice—four hours a day in addition to their schoolwork. He paced in front of the band carrying a bullwhip and would assault them if they flubbed a routine. Joe also loved guns and even "fired" an empty shot from a .38 revolver at Michael when the kid laughed at his father's dancing. At night he would terrorize the youngsters by popping out of closet wearing a Halloween mask or standing at the kids' window holding a butcher knife.

Katherine let Joe run the family six days a week, but on Sunday, *she* was in charge, marching the kids off to the local Jehovah's Witness Kingdom Hall. Today the Jacksons' former church houses the Grace Unity church.

Jackson Family Home, 2300 Jackson St., Gary, IN 46407
Private phone
Hours: Always visible; view from street
Cost: Free
Website: http://meetthefamily.online.fr
Directions: Just south of 23rd St., six blocks west of Lafayette St. (Rte. 27).

Grace Unity, 3435 W. 21st Ave., Gary, IN 46408
Phone: (219) 888-9490
Hours: Always visible; Services, check website
Cost: Free
Website: http://graceunity.com
Directions: One block west of Chase St., at Hendricks St.

Though he was the youngest member of the group, Michael was a standout. He made his first public performance in 1963 at the age of five, just down the street at Garnett Elementary. He sang "Climb Ev'ry Mountain," and those who heard it claimed the crowd went wild. Tears streamed down the adults' faces. A star was born!

Images of Hope (former Garnett Elementary School), 2131 Jackson St., Gary, IN 46407
Phone: (219) 886-1362
Hours: Always visible; view from street

Cost: Free
Directions: Two blocks north of the Jackson home.

Michael had started in the group by playing the bongos, but his Garnett Elementary performance made Joe bump Jermaine as lead singer. The band was named the Ripples and Waves Plus Michael when they won their first amateur music competition singing "My Girl" and "Barefootin'" at the Theodore Roosevelt High School gym. The school is still open today.

Theodore Roosevelt College & Career Academy, 730 W. 25th Ave., Gary, IN 46407
Phone: (219) 881-1500
Hours: Always visible; view from street
Cost: Free
Website: www.edlinesites.net/pages/Theodore_Roosevelt_College
Directions: One block west and two blocks south of the Jackson home.

Renamed the Jackson 5, the group's first professional gig came at Mr. Lucky's Lounge, a Gary bar. All the band members were underage at the time; Michael was only six. Before long, they were playing at saloons and nightclubs all over the region. One of their signature acts was to have little Michael disappear into the audience and reappear beneath a female patron's dress. Eventually they caught the eye of Berry Gordy. After cutting their first album, Joe took the group to California, leaving Katherine behind with the rest of the kids.

Mr. Lucky's Lounge has been closed for some time and will likely be demolished, if the sign offering BUY YOUR LUCKY BRICK is any indication.

Mr. Lucky's Lounge (closed), 1100 Grant St., Gary, IN 46404
No phone
Hours: Always visible; view from street
Cost: Free
Directions: Six blocks south of Rte. 20, at 11th Ave.

Beat it!

Griffith

American Natural Resources

Taxidermy isn't for everyone, but maybe that's because the mounted critters can be so predictable—if you've seen one moose head you've seen them all. But American Natural Resources goes beyond the traditional poses, as you'll see in its fur-, fowl-, and fish-filled store. In one display, five raccoons play a game of poker. In another, four hedgehogs ride in a rowboat. These dioramas aren't for sale, but they do make great photos. However, if you're looking for something for the den, they have plenty of floor models to choose from, depending on your budget, from a $5,700 mountain lion on a tree limb to a $1,460 raccoon couple paddling a birch bark canoe to a $63.99 toilet paper holder made from sawed-off deer antlers.

120 N. Broad St., Griffith, IN 46319
Phone: (219) 922-6444
Hours: Monday–Friday 9:30 AM–6 PM, Saturday 10 AM–5 PM
Cost: Free
Website: www.americannaturalresources.com
Directions: Three blocks east of the intersection of Cline Ave. and Main St.

Hammond

A Christmas Story Town

Fans of the holiday film *A Christmas Story* know it is set in the fictional northwest Indiana town of Hohman. *True* fans, however, know that Hohman is a barely disguised substitute for Hammond, the town where author Jean Shepherd grew up. The Shepherds lived from the late 1920s to 1939 in a bungalow at 2907 Cleveland Street, a home that survives to this day (but is off-limits to visitors—view from the sidewalk). Three blocks to the east you can find Warren G. Harding Elementary (3211 165th St., (219) 989-7351, www.hammond.k12.in.us), a new building that replaced the one Shepherd and his brother Randy attended years ago. Yes, that really was his brother's name.

No need to be discouraged that you can't go inside Shepherd's home or school, because Hammond honors its native son each December at the local tourist bureau. Several years ago the town purchased six mechanical window displays from Macy's, all based on the movie, depicting Black

Bart's bandits, the turkey-stealing Bumpus's dogs, the Triple Dog Dare, and more, and put them up for all to see at Christmastime. Check the website, for it also has Santa picture days—he sits atop a snowy mountain with a slide for the kids—as well as Little Piggie eating contests.

And there's more! Outside the building at the flagpole, you'll find a bronze statue of Flick with his tongue stuck to the pole, unveiled in 2013 with the original actor Scott Schwartz on hand. A sign warns tourists, IF YOU LICK, YOU WILL STICK, but that only applies in winter.

The consequence of accepting a Triple Dog Dare.

Finally, if you find yourself in Hammond after dark between Thanksgiving and New Year's, stop by Peteyville (3033 Crane Pl., www.facebook.com/Peteyville.IN/). Pete Basala decorates his home with an over-the-top light extravaganza worthy of all who appreciate the tackier side of the holiday.

Indiana Welcome Center, 7770 Corinne Dr., Hammond, IN 46323
Phone: (800) ALL-LAKE or (219) 989-7979
Hours: September–May, daily 8 AM–5 PM; June–August, daily 9 AM–6 PM
Cost: Free
Website: www.southshorecva.com/about-south-shore/indiana-welcome-center/
Directions: Exit I-80/94 at Kennedy Ave., south one block to first light and turn right.

Highland
Devil, Be Gone!

Have you been on the road a while and the kids seem, well, rowdier than usual? Don't be so quick to blame it on that junk food you had in Muncie. Did you ever consider that the little ones might be . . . *possessed*? Sure you have. So why not bring them by the Hegewisch Baptist Church to drive out those demons? That's right: exorcism, though they call it Demonic Deliverance.

HBC's late Pastor Win Worley began the practice in 1970, but not until 1992 did this place hold its first open house. The church got more than 500 visitors, most from this world. Today, HBC hosts several Deliverance Meetings a year, or if you promise to sit through an entire Sunday service, they'll cleanse your soul on the way out. To find out about the church's next Deliverance Meeting, check out its website. There you'll find do-it-yourself Deliverance prayers (just fill in the blanks with the possessed's name), HBC's perspectives on rock music (including ABBA), and their Plan of Salvation.

Hegewisch Baptist Church, 8711 Cottage Grove Ave., Highland, IN 46322
Phone: (219) 838-9410
Hours: Thursday 6 PM, Sunday 10:30 AM
Cost: Free
Website: http://hbcdelivers.org
Directions: One block north of Rte. 6 (Ridge Rd.), 10 blocks east of Rte. 41.

SPECIAL SERVICES

Maybe you're not a Baptist or aren't possessed by demons. No problem—there are other strange Indiana churches where you can get your Sunday morning fix.

Drive-In Church

Lake Shore Drive-In, Main St. & Rickey Rd., Monticello, (574) 583-5545, www.monticelloumchurch.org

With the Indiana Beach Amusement Park in town, Monticello churches have to do something special to attract the less-than-entirely faithful waiting for the gates to open. During summer months, the United Methodist Church holds an 8:30 AM service at the Lake Shore Drive-In. Congregants stay in their cars and listen to Rev. Wes Brookshire over the radio.

People are encouraged to honk their horns in place of saying "Amen," which the neighbors surely appreciate.

Boat-In Service

702 E. Lake View Rd., Syracuse, (574) 457-7172,
www.wawaseepoa.org/worship.htm

Since 1969, local ministers have sponsored a "Boat-In Worship" service on Syracuse's Lake Wawasee during the summer season—Memorial to Labor Day. The faithful don't have to dress up (you're welcome "from coat and tie to bathing suit") or even leave their watercraft to attend the service. The service is held at Oakwood Pier from 8:30 to 9:00 AM each Sunday, weather permitting.

"Live Gospel" McDonald's

McDonald's, 3639 169th St., Hammond, (219) 845-8625

Though not technically a church, you can still find salvation in this Hammond McDonald's on Tuesday, Thursday, and Sunday evenings. Local gospel singers are invited to perform on the stage for patrons who come from all over northern Indiana and Chicagoland. Stained glass windows add a holy aura. So grab a Big Mac and fries and enjoy performances of "Amazing Grease" and "What a Friend We Have in Grimace." Just kidding—the songs are legit.

Marion Easter Pageant

Marion YMCA, 123 Sutter Way, Marion, (765) 677-2152,
www.easterpageant.com

Every Easter since 1937, with a few years off during World War II, the town of Marion has staged a blockbuster passion play with a cast of hundreds. It's a unique production, as there are no spoken words—the story is told through "music, pantomime, and pageantry." They've had to scale back a little since 2003, when the permanent venue deteriorated, so the play is now performed at the local YMCA.

The Last Supper

Family Christian Center, 340 W. 45th Ave., Munster, (219) 922-6500, www.familychristiancenter.org

While the services at this megachurch are fairly standard, there is something unique about the church: its four-story front entry has a cross-shaped array of windows, and behind those windows is a life-size re-creation of *The Last Supper* made with department store mannequins. Just below, another Jesus mannequin drags a cross to Calvary. The best time to view them is after sundown, when they are illuminated.

Huntington
Outhouse Collection

How many outhouses could one man need? In Hy Goldenberg's case, 17, and he only stopped collecting because he passed away in February 2000. The first one Goldberg bought cost him two dollars. It came from Monument City, a town that was condemned and flooded as part of a dam construction project. When it was delivered to his farm on the Wabash River, the trucker brought two privies, the one Hy had bought and another, "better" outhouse. This gave Goldenberg an idea: Why not start an outhouse collection?

Most of the tiny structures are simple, traditional models, but he did rescue a concrete outhouse, an octagonal model, and a round crapper with a copper weather vane; for that he had to shell out $17. He even found a family's "three-seater"—one for mom, one for dad, and a baby seat in between that is jusssst right. Awwwww . . .

After Hy passed away, his wife, Lorry, donated their farmland to be a nature preserve, as long as her husband's collection was preserved as well. Thanks to the folks at the Acres Land Trust, it has been.

Tel-Hy Nature Preserve, 1129 N. CR 300 W, Huntington, IN 46750
Phone: (260) 637-ACRE
Hours: Dawn–dusk
Cost: Free
Website: www.acreslandtrust.org/tel-hy
Directions: Take Etna Ave. southwest out of town until it becomes N. CR 300 W, ahead on the left.

Remnants of the good ol' days.

The Quayle Vice Presidential Learning Center

The residents of Huntington felt a museum was the least they could do for their most famous native son, so they converted an old Christian Scientist Church and stuffed it with Dan Quayle-obelia. Upstairs you can see the Quayle clan's family heirlooms: a lock of Danny's baby hair, his Little League uniform, and his Senate golf bag, well used. And be sure to check out the report cards from his stellar elementary school career. Every visitor wants to see what he received in Spelling.

The museum's also got Quayle's IU law degree, chewed by Barnaby, the family dog. (Barnaby was put up for adoption shortly after the incident.) One of the strangest artifacts on display is a hollow ostrich egg with Quayle's 1989 inauguration re-created inside, faithfully depicting Marilyn's blue UFO hat. And be sure to get your photo taken next to a life-size cutout of the Boy Wonder; let your pose reflect your political persuasion.

The ground floor of the museum is filled with items relating to all of the nation's Second Bananas. More US veeps have come from Indiana than any other state, earning it the nickname "Birthplace of Vice Presidents": Schuyler Colfax, Thomas A. Hendricks, Charles Warren Fairbanks, Thomas R. Marshall (who said, "What this country needs is a really good five-cent cigar"), and Dan Quayle. The museum has items related to each and every one up through Joe Biden. Wouldn't you like to see Millard Filmore's hat?

815 Warren St., Huntington, IN 46750
Phone: (260) 356-6356
Hours: Monday–Friday 9:30 AM–4:30 PM
Cost: Adults $3, Kids (7–27) $1
Website: http://historyeducates.org/
Directions: At Warren and Tipton (Rte. 24) Sts., one block east of Rte. 224.

Kendallville
Mid-America Windmill Museum

In the history of the settlement of the Great Plains, the windmill's contribution often gets short shrift. Not in Kendallville. This specialty museum honors the wind-powered workhorses that pumped the water and milled the grain that made American agriculture possible.

The windmill collection was started by Russ Baker and now contains more than 50 restored windmills along a strolling pathway. The largest is a replica of the Robertson Post windmill, the first windmill in North America, built in 1610 in Williamsburg, Virginia.

Kendallville was chosen as the location of this museum because the area was once home to more than 90 windmill manufacturers. If you visit in late June, you may even see a windmill erected and blown for the annual Windmill Festival.

732 S. Allen Chapel Rd., PO Box 5048, Kendallville, IN 46755
Phone: (219) 347-2334
Hours: April–November, Tuesday–Friday 10 AM–4 PM, Saturday 10 AM–5 PM, Sunday 1–4 PM
Cost: Adults $5, Seniors (55+) $4, Kids (6–12) $2
Website: www.midamericawindmillmuseum.org
Directions: West of town on Rte. 6, turn south on County Rd. 1000E, follow the signs.

Knox

Bowling Ball Rosary

The idea came from Fr. Emil Bloch of the nearby St. Thomas Aquinas Catholic Church: an enormous World Rosary of Peace, its big beads painted different colors to honor all the inhabitants of Earth. The heavy lifting, however, fell to parishioners Linda and Bill Stage, who constructed the rosary from old bowling balls in their front yard. The chain linking them all surrounds a gazebo dedicated to the Blessed Virgin Mary, the notorious BVM. Visitors are welcome to visit the site during daylight hours, not just to be respectful to the homeowners but also to keep you from cracking your shin on a bead in the dark.

4215 W. CR 200 N, Knox, IN 46534
Private phone
Hours: Always visible, daylight hours
Cost: Free
Directions: North of town on Rte. 35, then east on CR 200 N for about a block.

SUPERSIZED PINS

The rosary in Knox may be large, but its bowling ball beads are standard size—nothing special. As far as anyone knows, there are no giant bowling *balls* in Indiana. There are, however, a few giant *pins* scattered around the state, usually marking the entrance to a bowling center. You can find one in Fort Wayne at **Pro Bowl West**  (1455 Goshen Rd., (260) 482-4889, www.probowlwest.com) and two in Indianapolis, at **Woodland Bowl** (3421 E. 96th St., (317) 844-4099, www.royalpin.com/woodland/) and **Royal Pin Expo Bowl** (5261 Elmwood Ave., (317) 787-3448, www .royalpin.com/expo).

Che Mah

Che Mah was born in China on April 15, 1838, and though he would eventually become world famous, he never amounted to much. At least not in height—he grew to be only 28 inches tall, shorter than Tom Thumb—and was once described as "a pocket edition of a Mandarin, perfect in every detail, and with his scanty black beard and diminutive stature looked as if he had just stepped off a tea caddy."

P. T. Barnum brought Che Mah to the United States in 1881 to be a part of his traveling circus, which took the tiny man on a tour through Europe. He later joined Buffalo Bill's Wild West Show before retiring, settling in Knox with his wife and son. The couple later divorced, but Che Mah remarried. He died at the age of 87 and was buried under a headstone that is more than twice his height. The local historical society also has a few of his personal effects on display.

Crown Hill Cemetery, Lake St., Knox, IN 46534
No phone
Hours: Daylight
Cost: Free
Directions: On the northeast side of town between Lake and John Sts.

Starke County Historical Society Museum, 401 S. Main St., Knox, IN 46534
Phone: (574) 772-5393
Hours: Call for an appointment
Cost: Donation
Website: www.starkehistory.com
Directions: Two blocks west of Rte. 35, five blocks north of Culver Rd.

LaPorte
Belle Was a Groundbreaker

In many ways, Belle Gunness broke new ground for American women. Long before women achieved universal suffrage, Gunness proved that a determined woman could do anything a man could, at least in her chosen profession, which was serial murder. Born in Norway in 1858, she immigrated to the States in 1886 and settled near Chicago. She married Mads Sorenson in 1893 and adopted several children who, shortly after Belle received money for their care, mysteriously died. Then Mads perished in a fit of convulsions in 1900. Belle bought a pig farm outside LaPorte with her husband's life insurance settlement.

She didn't stay single long. Belle married Peter Gunness in April 1902, but he died eight months later when a sausage grinder fell from a high shelf and crushed his skull. Again, Belle received a healthy insurance settlement. See the pattern?

Worried she might begin to develop a reputation among suspicious insurance agents, Belle devised a new fundraising plan. She advertised in Chicago's Norwegian "lonely hearts" newspapers for a spouse and managed to convince her suitors to liquidate their assets and head to LaPorte, cash in hand. "And don't tell your family where you're headed," she'd add in her perfumed letters, "it would ruin the surprise when we tie the knot!"

Disposing of the bodies became an awful chore, so she had a hired hand named Ray Lamphere dig ditches for her to bury her "trash." Many mornings Lamphere would find the ditches filled back in. He started to become suspicious of the late-night departures of so many of Belle's potential husbands, which were described by Belle but never witnessed by him. *And why did they always leave their belongings?* he wondered.

The brother of one suitor, Andrew K. Helgelein, came looking for his sibling, having written Belle in advance. The day before he arrived, Belle made up a will with a local attorney. That night, April 28, 1908, her home burned to the ground, killing Belle and three additional children she had birthed or collected along the way.

Ray Lamphere was charged with arson and murder, but after 13 bodies were unearthed, Belle looked more like a suspect than a victim. Still, Lamphere was convicted of arson and spent the rest of his life in the Michigan City penitentiary.

Was Belle the headless body found in the burned home? Officials claimed it was considerably smaller than the robust Belle, and its only identifying feature was a charred dental plate found in the rubble. Many historians today believe Gunness escaped by killing a prostitute, beheading her, and leaving her own dentures with the body before lighting a cover-up fire.

The excavation of the victims of "Lady Bluebeard" became a popular pastime in pre-TV, pre-radio LaPorte. Families would come out to picnic, watch the diggings, and carve their initials on an unburned shed on the property. You can view the graffiti-covered siding today in the LaPorte County Historical Society Museum. Inside is a scary, crude mannequin of Belle. You'll see sketches of the farm, the letter and four-leaf clover Gunness sent to Helgelein, and a gruesome photo of victim Ole Budsberg, whose head was brought in on a shovel for Lamphere's trial. (It's available as a postcard at the front desk.) A plaque in the shed repeats a popular rhyme of the time:

Big, bad Belle. Photo by Patrick Hughes, courtesy of the LaPorte County Historical Society Museum

> *Amid roses of red*
> *and violets of blue*
> *She buried not one*
> *But forty-two.*

Forty-two? Fourteen? Exactly how victims many did she off? It's hard to tell, but somewhere between 14 and 40 men bought the farm on the farm Belle bought. A. K. Helgelein was buried in Patton Cemetery in LaPorte (1401 Rumely St., (219) 362-9671), and his tombstone indicates his status as Gunness's final victim.

Gunness Farm Site, McClung Rd., LaPorte, IN 46350
No phone
Hours: Always visible; view from the road
Cost: Free
Directions: North from downtown on Rte. 35/39 until the routes diverge; follow Rte. 39 and take the first right onto McClung Rd., follow McClung south along Fishtrap Lake until you see a gate with No Dumping signs on the left; her home was where the field to the west is today.

LaPorte County Historical Society Museum, 2405 Indiana Ave., LaPorte, IN 46350
Phone: (219) 324-6767
Hours: Tuesday–Saturday 10 AM–4:30 PM
Cost: Adults $5, Seniors (60+) $4, Kids (18 and under) free
Website: www.laportecountyhistory.org
Directions: Head southeast from downtown on Rte. 35 (Indiana Ave.) until just past Crescent Dr.

Logansport
Batmobile Builder

Some people spend their entire lives trying to find their passion, but Mark Racop knew at the age of two. It was 1967 when he got his first look at a Batmobile, and though he was barely old enough to talk, he announced to his parents that he would have one someday. They probably thought he wanted a toy, but they were wrong. At the age of 17, barely street legal himself, he built his first Batmobile using a 1974 Monte Carlo in his parents' garage with the help of four friends. It took three years to finish, and he called it Bat 1.

As you can imagine, Bat 1 led to Bat 2, and so on, though for legal reasons they weren't officially called Batmobiles. And then in 2010 the original patent expired and Racop pounced on the opportunity like the Penguin on a herring, buying the rights from DC Comics to produce the car that has meant so much to him. Today his company finishes a few new ones each year for very rich geeks around the world, and there's a waiting list. Each is customized, depending on the interest and budget of the buyer. You can get a Batphone, Batbeam antenna, parachute pull, Batcomputer switch, Emergency Bat Turn lever, and Detect-A-Scope. Everybody gets the flame-shooting exhaust port.

Racop is open to visitors and is generous with his time; he will gladly show you around the shop where you'll see a half-dozen cars in various stages of construction. His hope is to open an adjoining museum to display his huge collection of Batman artifacts and memorabilia.

602 Erie Ave., Logansport, IN 46947
Phone: (574) 722-3237
Hours: Call for an appointment
Cost: Free; Batmobiles, $124,999 and up
Website: www.fiberglassfreaks.com
Directions: One block south of Market St., between Sixth and Berkley Sts., just northeast of the river.

Catch the Brass Ring

Were it not for lawyers, there might be more brass ring carousels in the United States today. All those riders risking their necks, leaning out and grabbing a brass ring for a free ride, turned ambulance chasers into merry-go-round monitors. But the good folk of Logansport are sticking to their rings.

The Cass County Carousel was built in 1902 (though some animals go back to 1885) by Gustav Dentzel in Fort Wayne, then moved to Logansport in 1919. It was restored in 1993 and is the only surviving brass ring merry-go-round in the state. Most of its 42 hand-carved critters are horses, but it's also got reindeer, giraffes, goats, a lion, and a tiger. The two felines don't move up and down, making it much easier to reach for the round, golden object of your desire.

Lest you think this throwback is entirely unaffected by the litigious who walk among us, check out the animals on the outside track. They all have seat belts.

If riding around in a circle isn't your idea of fun, the park also has a historic miniature train. It's 25¢ cheaper than the merry-go-round, and you ride a lot farther.

Cass County Carousel, Riverside Park, 1208 Riverside Dr., Logansport, IN 46947
Phone: (574) 753-8725
Hours: June–August, Monday–Friday 6–9 PM, Saturday–Sunday 1–9 PM
Cost: $1/ride, or one brass ring; Train, 75¢/ride
Website: www.casscountycarousel.com
Directions: Five blocks east of Rte. 25, four blocks north of Rte. 24, between 10th and 11th Sts.

RIDE A RARE ONE

Have you ever ridden a leopard? Or a giant panda? A dugong or a babirusa or a cassowary? Do you even know what those are? Maybe that's part of the problem—these animals are all nearly extinct but can be found on the Endangered Species Carousel at the Fort Wayne Children's Zoo (3411 Sherman Blvd., (219) 427-6800, www.kidszoo.org). There are 36 wooden creatures representing 17 different species on the merry-go-round, which also includes a manatee, a stork, a Sumatran tiger, a sloth bear, and several Asian elephants.

Another carousel with strange figures (though not endangered) can be found at Davis Mercantile in Shipshewana (255 E. Main St., (260) 768-7300, www.davismercantile.com). It's got plenty of elaborate horses, but also a bulldog, a rooster, a lamb, a corn-stealing pig, and a very horny goat.

Finally, Indianapolis's Broad Ripple Park Carousel has been restored and moved to the Children's Museum of Indianapolis (3000 N. Meridian St., (317) 334-4000, www.childrensmuseum.org). In addition to horses, it has giraffes, deer, goats, a lion, and a tiger.

Mentone
World's Largest Egg

As hard-boiled eggs go, this is one of the hardest—concrete no less. Built in 1946 by Hugh Rickel and weighing a ton and a half, the 11-foot Mentone Egg honors the region's primary agricultural export. Mentone calls itself the "Egg Basket of the Midwest," and if all the hens laid them this large, they'd need some mighty big baskets. Every June, the town throws an Egg Festival, and they recently tried to raise enough funds to construct an egg-shaped water tower. They were unsuccessful, so this old oversized ova will have to do for now.

The classic question that comes to mind while admiring this 3,000-pound monument is one that has puzzled philosophers for centuries: Which came first, the concrete chicken or the concrete egg?

E. Main & Morgan Sts., Mentone, IN 46539
Phone: (574) 353-7417
Hours: Always visible
Cost: Free
Website: www.mentoneeggcity.com/history.htm
Directions: Near the grain elevator at the corner of Main (Rte. 25) and Morgan Sts.

This must have hurt.

Michigan City
Submarine Superstar

If you were asked, "Where would be a good location for a submarine base?" would you answer, "Indiana"? You would if you were Lodner Phillips! When this former cobbler began asking the same question of the US Navy, the answer was more likely, "What's a submarine?" Large underwater craft had yet to be invented, and the navy was not convinced that a submarine was even militarily useful.

Phillips set out to change the navy's mind. Between 1840 and 1850 he built several vessels. The first was a small, one-man craft, but later versions were 40 feet long. The full-sized subs could dive 100 feet below the surface of Lake Michigan, which is exactly what he did with his family on weekends.

Phillips was awarded more than 40 patents for his maritime inventions, which included torpedoes, underwater suits, and diving bells. But due in part to the distraction of the Civil War, he never persuaded the navy to build a port in Indiana. He eventually left town for New York and would be forgotten in Michigan City today were it not for several models of his Hoosier inventions on display at its Old Lighthouse Museum. The museum also has a large collection of ship models, old postcards, and lighthouse gewgaws.

Old Lighthouse Museum, Washington Park, Heisman Harbor Rd., PO Box 512, Michigan City, IN 46360
Phone: (219) 872-6133
Hours: April–October, Tuesday–Sunday 1–4 PM
Cost: Adults $5, Kids (under 14) $4
Website: www.oldlighthousemuseum.org
Directions: Just west of Franklin St. (the continuation of Pine St.), at the lake.

Monticello
MiniMonticello

If you ever want to see Monticello, all you have to do is check the flip side of the nickels in your pocket. Or you could go to Charlottesville, Virginia, to see the original for yourself, but that would cost you a lot of nickels. There is, however, a third option: come to Monticello, Indiana, to see a

Monticello-shaped bank—about half the size of Jefferson's architectural masterpiece.

Lafayette Bank and Trust, 116 E. Washington St., Monticello, IN 47960
Phone: (574) 583-4666
Hours: Always visible
Cost: Free
Website: www.firstmerchants.com/LBT
Directions: On Rte. 24 (Washington St.) two blocks west of the river.

Like a nickel, only bigger.

Munster
Carmelite Shrines

Northern Indiana is, in a word, FLAT. This geographic reality makes it all the more difficult to find a cave to establish a grotto. But the parishioners at the Carmelite Shrine in Munster didn't let the topography get them *down*; they just built their caves *up*.

The exterior of the Main Grotto hardly does justice to the treasures that lie within. Just to the right of the main, exterior altar is a small, candle-filled niche that opens to yet another, larger room, and another, and another, and another. The walls are covered in rough stones embedded in concrete and broken by marble bas-reliefs of biblical scenes. Your holy journey is illuminated by recessed lighting and backlit onyx sconces. Find the stairs to the second floor and you can peep out a secret window aimed at a statue of the Virgin. Don't miss the Flagellation Grotto, if that's what you're into. The final grotto has dozens of scenes carved to show Mary and all her incarnations: Mother Undefiled, Mother Most Amiable, Mother Most Admirable, Mother of This, Mother of That . . .

Another grotto, at the north end of the gardens, is sunken into the ground like a crypt. It acts as a chapel, and the clammy, subterranean aura seems all the more spooky when you come across a statue of Jesus, dead and sprawled out on the altar. Yikes!

1628 Ridge Rd., Munster, IN 46321
Phone: (219) 838-7111
Hours: Daily 8:30 AM–5 PM; Grotto, call ahead to have the lights turned on
Cost: Free
Directions: Eight blocks west of Rte. 41, on the south side of the road.

Nappanee, Middlebury, Shipshewana
Amish Mania

Northwestern Indiana has well-established populations of both Amish and Mennonites, and with them, a large selection of sightseeing possibilities. Don't risk sideswiping a buggy by rushing to visit them all in one weekend—take a hint from the local folk: if you want to maximize your humble, back-to-the-land weekend, choose the Amish attraction that's right for you.

Amish Acres

Amish Acres is like Vegas for folks in black hats and bonnets. Its grounds cover 80 acres, a complete farming community with a bakery, meat and cheese shop, cow shed, barn, and white-clapboard home. Check out the candle dipping, quilting, fudge making, and horseshoeing before you settle down at the Restaurant Barn for a traditional 12-course meal.

But that's not all! Amish Acres has Indiana's only resident musical repertory theater. It's longest running production, *Plain and Fancy*, is a toe-tapping salute to life among the Amish. Had enough of the beards and zipperless outfits? How about *Carnival!* or, racier still, *Gypsy* or *Damn Yankees*?

Go ahead—spend the night! This place has two hotels, the Nappanee Inn and the Inn at Amish Acres. Both offer large swimming pools, full-body massages, and electric lights. They even have a helicopter landing field. Who ever thought simple living could be so scrumptious?

1600 W. Market St., Nappanee, IN 46550
Phone: (800) 800- 4942 or (574) 773-4188
Hours: April–October, dates and times vary—see website
Cost: Adults $12.95, Kids (4–11) $4.95; Buggy rides, Adults $6.95, Kids (4–11) $3.95
Website: www.amishacres.com
Directions: One mile west of Rte. 19 on Rte. 6.

Das Dutchman Essenhaus

Maybe you're not interested in full Amish immersion—you're mostly interested in their multicourse dinners. Das Dutchman Essenhaus offers two gorging options: family-style service for parties of 15 or more, or belly up to the buffet—beef and noodles, chicken and noodles, chicken noodle soup, creamed chicken and biscuits, biscuits and noodles, noodles with noodles, noodles noodles spam and noodles, and just plain noodles. Be sure to leave room for pie. If you're lucky, they'll sit you in a booth shaped like a buggy. It'll make it easier to roll you out later.

240 US 20, Middlebury, IN 46540
Phone: (800) 455-9471
Hours: Monday–Thursday 6 AM–8 PM, Friday–Saturday 6 AM–9 PM
Cost: Meals $7–15
Website: www.essenhaus.com
Directions: At the intersection of Rte. 20 and Rte. 16.

Menno-Hof Mennonite-Amish Visitors Center

If Amish Acres is Vegas to buggy-drivers, the Menno-Hof Visitors Center is the Smithsonian. Here you'll follow the rich history of the Anabaptist tradition, from 1525 to the present, through its three main branches: the Hutterites, the Mennonites, and the Amish.

While their faith stresses simplicity, this multimedia extravaganza is anything but. It all starts with the "Good Fences Make Good Community" slide show; then you're whisked back in time to a Zurich courtyard where it all began. The Anabaptists' breakaway from the Roman Catholic

Church didn't come without a price, as you'll see in the next room, the Dungeon. Be sure to look down the stone shaft to see the poor soul awaiting his fate for his beliefs.

Now it's time to emigrate—move through the Harbor to the Sailing Ship, headed for the American colonies. Finish your tour with displays of modern (if that's the word) Anabaptist teachings and activities. And no trip through the barn/museum would be complete without a visit to the Tornado Theater. This simulator recalls the Midwest's 1965 Palm Sunday tornado outbreak, and then Hurricane Joan, which slammed into Nicaragua, with blowing wind, shaking floor, and flashing "lightning." It's not entirely clear what this has to do with the Amish, but as tornados go, it's a lot of fun.

510 S. Van Buren St., PO Box 701, Shipshewana, IN 46565
Phone: (260) 768-4117
Hours: September–May, Monday–Saturday 10 AM–5 PM; June–August, Monday–Friday 10 AM– 7 PM, Saturday 10 AM–5 PM
Cost: Adults $7, Kids (6–14) $4
Website: www.mennohof.org
Directions: At the south end of town on Rte. 5 (Van Buren St.).

New Carlisle
World's Largest Living Sign

Strange as it sounds, the World's Largest Living Sign promotes a product that is not currently available. In 1938 the Civilian Conservation Corps planted 8,259 white pines on the Studebaker automobile proving grounds west of South Bend. The trees were arranged to form letters spelling out STUDEBAKER when viewed from the air. Each letter is 200 feet wide, 200 feet long, and 60 feet tall.

To fully appreciate the living sign, you once had to fly over the old racetrack, which is part of a park currently known as Bendix Woods, and pick out the brand name in the sculpted treetops. Today you can use a drone or the satellite feature on Google Earth.

Bendix Woods County Park, 32132 State Road 2, New Carlisle, IN 46552
Phone: (574) 654-3155
Hours: September–April, daily 10 AM–6 PM; May–August, daily 10 AM–8 PM
Cost: In-state, $4/car; Out-of-state, $5/car

Website: www.sjcparks.org/bendix.html
Directions: On the south side of Western Ave. (Rte. 2), just east of the county line.

If you had an airplane, why would you drive a Studebaker?

Courtesy of Bendix Woods County Park

Peru

Circus City Museum

Most parents would cringe at the thought of their child running away to join the circus, but not in Peru. Kids here are actually *encouraged* to become circus performers . . . and they don't even have to run away—Peru is already the "Circus City."

Peru's circus tradition began in 1884 when Ben Wallace and James Anderson purchased the W. C. Coup Circus at auction and renamed it "Wallace & Co.'s Great World Menagerie, Grand International Mardi Gras, Highway Holiday Hidalgo, and Alliance of Novelties." Who *wouldn't* buy tickets for that? Season after season, Wallace bought out or merged with other shows, and the whole operation wintered at an elaborate facility on the east bank of the Mississinewa River, two and a half miles southeast of town. (Drive east on Rte. 124 and turn left just after crossing the bridge to see crumbling remnants of the headquarters.)

In 1907 Wallace bought the Carl Hagenbeck Circus to form the Hagenbeck-Wallace Circus, the best-known touring operation stationed in Peru. Over the next 30 years (under a variety of owners) it would employ the likes of Emmett Kelly; Tom Mix; lion tamer Clyde Beatty; the Great Willi Wilno, better known as the Human Cannonball; and Blacaman, the Hindoo Animal Hypnotist.

A small museum located downtown within a former circus building is filled with uniforms, posters, harnesses, cages, trapezes, and lots of photos, not to mention Rattlesnake Annie's maracas. On the third weekend in July each year, local residents put on the Circus City Festival. All of the performers are Miami County residents, many of whom are descendants of former performers.

Circus City Center, 154 N. Broadway, Peru, IN 46970
Phone: (765) 472-3918
Hours: April–September, Monday–Friday 9 AM–5 PM; October–March, Monday–Friday 9 AM–4 PM
Cost: Donation only
Website: www.peruamateurcircus.com
Directions: Downtown where Broadway meets Seventh St.

BLUE MONKEY SIDESHOW

What's a circus without a sideshow? Not very odd, that's what. Trouble is, sideshows are hard to find these days, what with modern advances in medicine and psychology. But there is one freaky troupe in Indiana that still makes the rounds: the **Blue Monkey Sideshow** (www.bluemonkeysideshow .com). See performers lie on a bed of nails and swing bowling balls from their earlobes. Gasp as they walk over broken glass, swallow swords, and drive three-penny nails up their noses. They even pair up with guest freaks from around the nation—every show is different! Check the website for a performance near you.

Cole Porter's Birthplace and Grave

Cole Porter was born in Peru on June 9, 1891, and was by all accounts a precocious child. The son of a druggist and an heiress to one of the richest men in town, J. O. Cole, young master Cole was pampered and indulged from the time he could walk. He returned the attention by composing songs for his mother and staging elaborate performances in the sun porch. When his mother consulted a gypsy about her son's future, she was told that people whose initials spelled out words were prone to greatness; mom immediately gave her son a middle name: Albert. C-A-P spells *cap*!

Porter loved growing up in a town of circus performers and would often take the Fat Lady for rides around town in his donkey cart or seek out the Wild Man of Borneo to get the inside scoop on upcoming big-top events. As he grew older his musical abilities improved, and during the summers he would play the piano for passengers aboard the *Peerless*, an excursion vessel that sailed the waters of Lake Maxinkuckee. At the age of 14, Porter was sent off to Worcester Academy, a boarding school in Massachusetts.

The composer and lyricist didn't spend much more time in Peru until he returned in an urn 60 years later. He died in California on October 15, 1964, after complications from a kidney stone operation. Porter's birth home still stands, today converted into a bed-and-breakfast called the Cole Porter Inn. And each June, Peru celebrates Cole Porter Days.

Cole Porter Inn, 19 S. Huntington St., Peru, IN 46970
Phone: (765) 460-5127
Hours: Always visible; call for reservations
Cost: $99.99/night
Website: www.coleporterinn.com and www.coleporterfestival.org
Directions: Just south of Main St., two blocks east of Broadway.

Porter's Grave, Mount Hope Cemetery, 411 N. Grant St., Peru, IN 46970
Phone: (765) 472-2493
Hours: Daily 8 AM–4 PM
Cost: Free
Website: www.mthopeperu.com
Directions: At the corner of N. Grant & W. 12th Sts.

PORTAGE

➡ Each October, Portage hosts **Elvis FANtasy Fest** for the King's fans.

Freaks of Nature and Cole Porter's Hand-Me-Downs

One good thing about living in a town filled with circus-loving folk is that they're not afraid of freaks of nature. Take the stuffed, two-headed calf on the second floor of the Miami County Museum. Born on a local farm, it lived for a few weeks. It's mild in comparison to the one-headed, two-bodied "Siamese" pig standing next to it. And neither holds a candle to the gruesome white dress hanging nearby. It was worn by a local girl when she fell from her family's wagon and was run over. The parents kept the dead child's bloody dress for years before donating it to the museum for all to see.

The ground floor exhibits have their own wonderful weirdness, including the remains of two circus animals. A crudely removed lion pelt, from the tip of its nose to its tail, is draped over a padded stand. In another case, the remains of Charley, a rogue elephant from the Hagenbeck-Wallace Circus. As the museum's brochure says, "Our school children like to hear the story about Big Charley." To make a long story short, on April 25, 1901, this perky pachyderm drowned his cruel trainer, Henry Hoffman, in the Wabash River and had to be destroyed. The museum has his tusk and bullet-ridden skull. Cute story!

Finally, among the dead animals and arrowheads, you can find "artifacts" from Peru's favorite son, Cole Porter, including his 1955 Fleetwood Cadillac, the carrying case for his dog Hildegarde, and his oversized white sofa.

Miami County Museum, 51 N. Broadway, Peru, IN 46970
Phone: (765) 473-9183
Hours: Tuesday–Saturday 9 AM–5 PM
Cost: Free, suggested donation $3
Website: www.miamicountyhistory.org
Directions: At the corner of Broadway and Fifth St.

PORTER

➡ A Michigan Central and New York Central train collided near Porter on February 27, 1921, killing 37 passengers and crew.

Rochester
Hoosier Tarzan

When you think of Hollywood's first Tarzan, who comes to mind? Johnny Weissmuller? Try Otto Elmo Linkenhelt. Never heard of him? Perhaps you know him better by his stage name: Elmo Lincoln. Still not ringing a bell? Then come on by the Fulton County Historical Society for an ape-man education.

Lincoln was a Rochester native who moved to California in his teens and was later discovered by director D. W. Griffith. He played bit parts in *The Birth of a Nation* and other, less memorable films before being cast as Tarzan in 1918. During filming, Elmo was required to kill a lion named Old Charlie. The process was made all the easier because the aged cat was heavily drugged. Anything to impress Jane.

Tarzan of the Apes, which made more than $1 million, was followed by *The Romance of Tarzan*. It was a flop. Lincoln went on to different roles, and other actors were tapped to play the Lord of the Apes. Surprisingly, two more were also Hoosiers: James Hubert "Babe" Pierce of Freedom, in *Tarzan and the Golden Lion* (1927), and Bloomington's Denny Miller in *Tarzan, the Ape Man* (1959). Pierce even married Joan Burroughs, daughter of Tarzan creator Edgar Rice Burroughs.

You can see plenty of Elmo Lincoln artifacts at the Fulton County Historical Society, as well as thousands of other curiosities from the region. Everywhere you turn there seem to be creepy, midsized dolls carved by Ray Fretlinger. The museum buildings seem to run on forever, and you begin to wonder if the curators ever throw anything away. The answer is simple: they don't.

Fulton County Historical Society, Round Barn Museum, 37 E. County Rd. 375 N, Rochester, IN 46975
Phone: (574) 223-4436
Hours: Monday–Saturday 9 AM–5 PM
Cost: Donation
Website: http://fultoncountyhistory.org
Directions: Four miles north of town on Rte. 31 at County Rd. 375 N.

Roselawn

Hanging Out in Roselawn

Do you long for those childhood days when you were allowed to run naked and nobody batted an eye? Well, perhaps you ought to come to Roselawn, where two nudist resorts are open to the general public: Sun Aura and the Ponderosa Sun Club.

Sun Aura, while under new management, has existed at this location for decades. The camp started as Camp Zoro, then Naked City, and was host to the annual Miss Nude America and Miss Nude Teeny Bopper contests. Back in 1969, it launched the nation's first nude ski area, the See and Ski Resort. For what should have been obvious reasons, chief among them frostbite, it never lasted. Today Sun Aura bills itself as a "family-oriented" nudist colony. It looks like a KOA Campground, but the old folks in the golf carts here aren't wearing any clothes. There's a small heart-shaped lake, a large swimming pool, sand dunes, volleyball courts, and other fun-in-the-sun common areas, as well as an 8,000-square-foot round clubhouse that doesn't look like it has been remodeled since the 1970s. Open year-round, Sun Aura schedules an event every weekend from April through September, including a Mother's Day Dance, Yard Sale Weekend, a Pig Roast, and the late season Oldies Dance. Mark those calendars!

Sun Aura does not require that guests be nude but strongly encourages it. The Ponderosa Sun Club, on the other hand, will only allow you to wear a T-shirt if you've got a *really* bad sunburn . . . but no pants! No sunburn? No clothes! The Ponderosa Sun Club has a large pool with a split-level sun deck, tennis, volleyball, and horseshoe courts, and a central campfire pit—just be extra careful of flying embers.

Sun Aura, 3449 E. State Rd. 10, Lake Village, IN 46349
Phone: (219) 345-2000
Hours: Winter, Sunday–Thursday 8 AM–6 PM, Friday–Saturday 8 AM–midnight; Summer, Sunday–Thursday 8 AM–8 PM, Friday–Saturday 8 AM–midnight
Cost: Daily rates range from $30–45, depending on gender and day of week
Website: www.sunauraresort.com
Directions: West of the railroad tracks on the south side of Rte. 10.

Ponderosa Sun Club, PO Box 305, Roselawn, IN 46372
Phone: (219) 345-2268
Hours: May 15–September 15, Monday–Thursday 9 AM–6 PM, Friday–Saturday 8 AM–8 PM,
Sunday 8 AM–6 PM
Cost: Monday–Thursday $30/day, Friday–Saturday $35/day; campsites extra
Website: www.ponderosasunclub.com
Directions: Turn north off Rte. 10, just west of the railroad tracks, and follow the signs on
County Road 400E.

South Bend
Studebaker National Museum

Most automotive manufacturers got involved in the transportation industry *after* the invention of the internal combustion engine. Not the Stude-
bakers. These five brothers began making vehicles in 1852, and what a time
to get started! The Civil War was looming and the nation needed wagons.
Shortly after the smoke had settled, the brothers established the Studebaker Brothers Manufacturing Company in 1868. Over the next hundred
years, they rolled with the changing market, moving from Prairie Schooner wagons to buggies, to autos, to oblivion.

You can trace the company's century-long story at this unique
museum. The building is fronted by a hedge spelling STUDEBAKER, a
miniature replica of the giant living sign in New Carlisle (see page 44).
Inside you will see four different carriages used by US presidents, including the doom buggy Abraham Lincoln rode to Ford's Theatre. Some of
the more popular vehicles here were never available to the public at large,
like the 1956 Packard Predictor, a Jetsonsesque dreamobile with "Push-
Button Control of Its Ultramatic Transmission"; a push-me-pull-you
vehicle named "Peggy" that shuttled senators underground between their
offices and the US Capitol; a small prototype of a two-person hovercraft,
the Curtiss-Wright "BEE"; and the last Studebaker to roll off the assembly
line on March 17, 1966, a turquoise Timberline.

201 S. Chapin St., South Bend, IN 46601
Phone: (888) 371-5600 or (574) 235-9714
Hours: Monday–Saturday 10 AM–5 PM, Sunday Noon–5 PM
Cost: Adults $8, Seniors (60+) $6.50, Kids (6–12) $5
Website: www.studebakermuseum.org
Directions: One block south of Washington St. on Chapin St., west of downtown.

Where the Gipper Died

Unlike the idealized George Gipp portrayed in 1940 by Ronald Reagan in *Knute Rockne, All-American*, the real George Gipp was something less than a saint . . . a lot less. He is widely believed to have bet on football games, played poker until all hours of the night, and drank like a fish. And it was one of those bawdy, boozy binges that was his undoing.

Coming home late from a night of gambling, stinking drunk, the Gipper decided to curl up on the back steps of Washington Hall to get a little shut-eye. Or perhaps he passed out or was locked outside after curfew—nobody seems to know for sure. Unfortunately, it was snowing that evening, and George caught pneumonia. His lung infection worsened over the next few days, and he died at St. Joseph's Hospital (801 E. LaSalle Ave., (574) 239-5298, www.sjmed.com) on December 14, 1920. The movie version had none of the sordid backstory.

A Gipper tale is almost as believable as the film that surrounds his ghost. George's spirit is said to haunt the attic of Washington Hall and has been seen by drama students since the 1970s. Though it is a theater/auditorium today, it was once used as a temporary residence for students that included—you guessed it—George Gipp. He lived on the upper floor, near the attic, and has been making strange noises ever since.

Washington Hall, University of Notre Dame, Notre Dame, IN 46556
Phone: (574) 631-2805
Hours: Always visible
Cost: Free
Website: http://washingtonhall.nd.edu
Directions: Directly east of the Golden Dome; Gipp fell asleep on the tall staircase in the rear, on the north side of the building.

SOUTH BEND

➡ Actor Chad Everett was born in South Bend as Raymon Lee Cramton on June 11, 1937.

➡ A mysterious shower of fish fell on the northwest side of South Bend in July 1937.

➡ South Bend is the "Major World Tool and Die Training Center."

GIPPERISH SITES

Most Fighting Irish football fans can't seem to get enough of their favorite team—its players, its coaches, you name it. One Gipper death site does not a tour make. So here are a few other South Bend sites to check out if the campus isn't enough.

George Gipp would never have been the icon he is today without the creative storytelling of coach Knute Rockne. During this coach's tenure at Notre Dame, he had a record of 105 wins, 12 losses, and 5 ties. Not too bad! He lived at three different homes in South Bend: 1715 College Street (1914–18), 1006 St. Vincent Street (1918–30), and 1417 E. Wayne Street (1930–31). After dying in a Kansas plane crash on March 31, 1931, he was laid to rest in Highland Cemetery (2557 Portage Ave., (219) 234-0036, www.burialplanning.com/cemeteries/highland-cemetery).

St. John
Millennium Mary

The Virgin Mary is a large figure in the Catholic Church, but seldom as large as she is in St. John. This supersized steel saint stands 34 feet tall, created by Charles Parks in 1999. She was commissioned by a man named Carl Demma, who trucked her around to various Chicago parishes during the 2000s. Millennium Mary, as she was affectionately nicknamed, has since retired to a life in the country, though she'll be happy if you visit her today.

In addition to this Megadonna, the Shrine of Christ's Passion also has a life-sized Stations of the Cross that winds along for a half mile. Forty figures fill the 14 stations, each contained within a grotto, with narration by Bill Kurtis if you hit the buttons. Holy music emanates from speakers all around the property to set the mood.

Shrine of Christ's Passion, 10630 Wicker Ave., St. John, IN 46373
Phone: (855) 277-7474 or (219) 365-6010

Hours: Friday–Wednesday 10 AM–5 PM, Thursday 10 AM–8 PM
Cost: Free
Website: http://shrineofchristspassion.org
Directions: On Rte. 41 (Wicker Ave.) north of the Rte. 231 (109th St.) interchange.

Valparaiso
Orville Redenbacher Statue

Back in 1952, Orville Redenbacher and Charles Bowman developed a hybrid popcorn in Valparaiso, a variety they sold under the brand Red Bow Popcorn, from the first three letters in each of their names. People loved it, but the name lacked a certain something-something. That's when Bowman suggested changing it to Orville Redenbacher Gourmet Popping Corn with his partner as the old face of the new brand. It was a stroke of marketing genius!

The *real* King of Pop.

Valparaiso honors its native sons each September with a Popcorn Festival. During one festival, organizers built a 12-foot-diameter popcorn ball that made it into the Guinness Book of World Records. And in 2012 they unveiled a statue of the bow-tied nerd sitting on a bench in the city's central park. Sculptor Lou Cella was able to create a fairly accurate depiction of the man by studying clips of his appearances on *Hee Haw*.

Lincoln Park, 63 Lafayette St., Valparaiso, IN 46383
Phone: (219) 465-0098
Hours: Daylight
Cost: Free
Website: http://valparaisoevents.com/valparaiso-popcorn-festival/
Directions: One block west of the courthouse, south of Lincolnway.

Wakarusa
Bird's Eye View Museum

If you grew up in Wakarusa or Bonneville Grist Mills, DeVon Rose's matchstick creations will remind you of the good ol' days. If you've never been to either of these towns, you can experience them today through his miniature dioramas. Look! There's the Wayne Feed Mill and the Eby Ford dealership! And the bag factory! Oh, what a fascinating place Wakarusa can be, even when shrunk down to a 1/60th scale.

DeVon Rose started building the Bird's Eye View Museum as a weekend project in 1967, and he kept at it until he died in 2011. The mini-museum was once located in his basement, but after he passed away his 72-piece collection was moved to its own climate-controlled building at the museum complex run by the Wakarusa Historical Society.

Wakarusa Historical Society Complex, 403 E. Wabash Ave., Wakarusa, IN 46573
Phone: (574) 862-1181
Hours: Thursday noon–2 PM, Saturday 9 AM–noon, or by appointment
Cost: Adults $4, Kids $2
Website: http://wakarusahistoricalsociety.com
Directions: Three blocks west of Rte. 19, four blocks south of Waterford St.

WAKARUSA
⇒ *Wakarusa* is a Native American term for "knee deep in mud."

Warsaw
Biblical Gardens

If you thought the Bible was filled with only God-said-this and God-said-that, think again. It's also a botanical record of historic Middle Eastern plants . . . *holy* plants! Biblical Gardens claims to be America's Largest Collection of Biblical Flora with more than 160 species crammed into a plot smaller than an acre. Of course, the climate in Indiana is a bit colder than the Middle East, so not every biblical plant can be found here.

Visitors can stroll along a path that winds through the flowerbeds where small plaques indicate where to find each species referenced in the holy book. Feel free to bring a picnic basket and your Bible to make a day of it. But be careful: if a serpent in a tree offers you an Apple of Knowledge, don't take it! To find out why, consult the Good Book—it's somewhere near the beginning.

Center Lake Park, Canal & N. Indiana Sts., Warsaw, IN 46580
Phone: (574) 267-6418
Hours: April–October, dawn–dusk
Cost: Free
Website: www.warsawbiblicalgardens.org
Directions: Just west of Detroit St. (Rte. 15), on the southeast corner of Warsaw Central Park, north of the McDonald's.

Hallmark Ornament Museum

The Party Shop would be just another knickknack and card emporium were it not for a large display in the back of the store. The Hallmark Ornament Museum is the collection of Jess Prudencio and David Hamrick and includes every Hallmark Keepsake Ornament produced since 1973—more than 4,000—when the company started manufacturing them.

While they may be valuable to those who collect them, the early Keepsake Ornaments are extremely ugly. They were either dull balls with imprinted designs or hideous 1970s yarn art, the kind your cat swatted around, chewed up, and regurgitated years ago. In 1977 Hallmark branched out into fake stained glass, but the results were no more eye-catching than the previous designs. Only when the company started making plastic figurines did things get interesting.

Were they not hung on a pine tree in December, it would be hard to figure out that many of these ornaments are Christmas decorations. You'll find such odd subjects as a bottle of Hershey's Syrup, a Wheel of Fortune wheel, the Jetsons in a Space Car, a coop full of singing chickens, Myra Gulch riding a bike (from *The Wizard of Oz*), a Scooby Doo thermos, and the starship *Enterprise*'s Captains Kirk and Picard. The Party Shop has many of the old ornaments still for sale, so if you have your eye on that reindeer on a Jet Ski, it's yours . . . for a price.

The Party Shop, 3418 Lake City Hwy., Warsaw, IN 46580
Phone: (574) 267-8787
Hours: Monday–Saturday 9:30 AM–8 PM, Sunday noon–5 PM
Cost: Free
Website: www.thepartyshop.com
Directions: In the K-Mart Shopping Center south of Rte. 30, at the east end of town.

WHEATFIELD

➡ By law, women may not wear halter tops, bathing suits, or short-shorts to political rallies in Wheatfield.

WHITING

➡ The town of Whiting hosts **Pierogi Fest** on the last full weekend of July each year (www.pierogifest.net). For details, call (877) 659-0292.

WINAMAC

➡ The 1980 trial regarding the 1973 Ford Pinto was held at the **Pulaski County Courthouse** (112 E. Main St., (574) 946-3313, www.pulaskionline.org) in Winamac. Three local teens had been killed in a gas tank fire, but Ford was found not guilty of reckless homicide after a 10-week trial.

WOODVILLE

➡ Two B&O trains collided in a snowstorm near Woodville on November 6, 1906, killing 43.

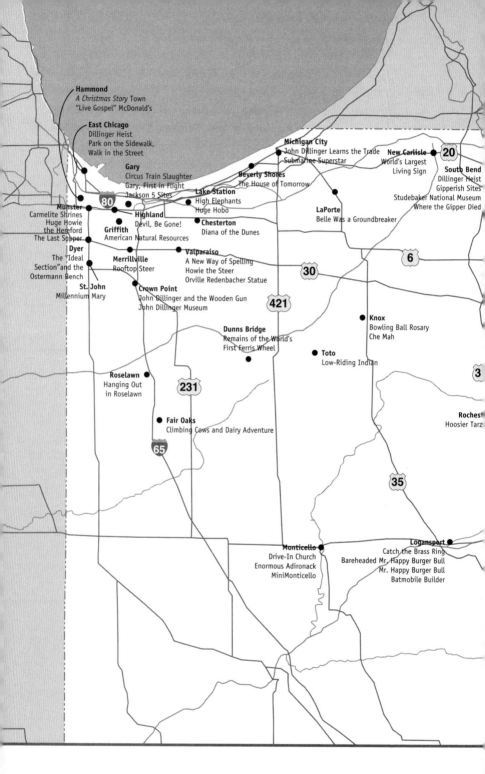

Hammond
A Christmas Story Town
"Live Gospel" McDonald's

East Chicago
Dillinger Heist
Park on the Sidewalk,
Walk in the Street

Gary
Circus Train Slaughter
Gary, First in Flight
Jackson 5 Sites

Munster
Carmelite Shrines
Huge Howie
the Hereford
The Last Supper

Highland
Devil, Be Gone!

Griffith
American Natural Resources

Dyer
The "Ideal
Section" and the
Ostermann Bench

Merrillville
Rooftop Steer

St. John
Millennium Mary

Crown Point
John Dillinger and the Wooden Gun
John Dillinger Museum

Lake Station
High Elephants
Huge Hobo

Chesterton
Diana of the Dunes

Beverly Shores
The House of Tomorrow

Michigan City
John Dillinger Learns the Trade
Submarine Superstar

New Carlisle
World's Largest
Living Sign

South Bend
Dillinger Heist
Gipperish Sites
Studebaker National Museum
Where the Gipper Died

LaPorte
Belle Was a Groundbreaker

Valparaiso
A New Way of Spelling
Howie the Steer
Orville Redenbacher Statue

Dunns Bridge
Remains of the World's
First Ferris Wheel

Knox
Bowling Ball Rosary
Che Mah

Toto
Low-Riding Indian

Roselawn
Hanging Out
in Roselawn

Rochester
Hoosier Tarzan

Fair Oaks
Climbing Cows and Dairy Adventure

Monticello
Drive-In Church
Enormous Adironack
MiniMonticello

Logansport
Catch the Brass Ring
Bareheaded Mr. Happy Burger Bull
Mr. Happy Burger Bull
Batmobile Builder

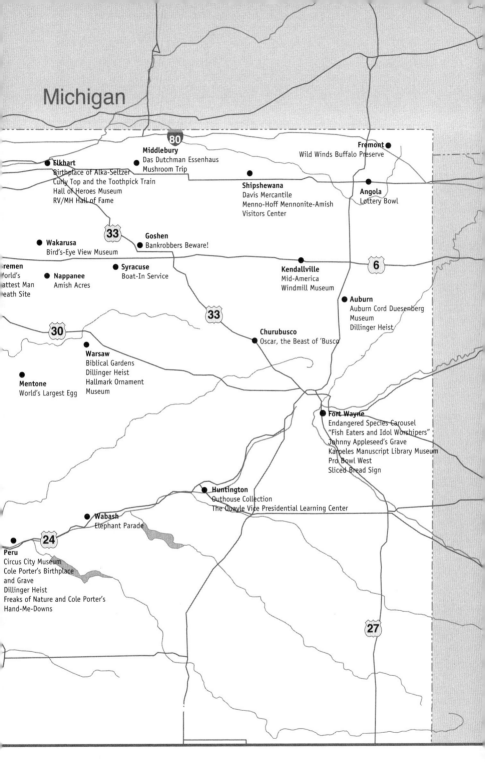

Michigan

80

Middlebury
Das Dutchman Essenhaus
Mushroom Trip

Fremont •
Wild Winds Buffalo Preserve

• Elkhart
Birthplace of Alka-Seltzer
Curly Top and the Toothpick Train
Hall of Heroes Museum
RV/MH Hall of Fame

Shipshewana
Davis Mercantile
Menno-Hoff Mennonite-Amish
Visitors Center

Angola
Lottery Bowl

33

• Wakarusa
Bird's-Eye View Museum

Goshen
• Bankrobbers Beware!

6

remen
orld's
attest Man
eath Site

• Nappanee
Amish Acres

• Syracuse
Boat-In Service

Kendallville
Mid-America
Windmill Museum

• Auburn
Auburn Cord Duesenberg
Museum
Dillinger Heist

30

33

Churubusco
• Oscar, the Beast of 'Busco

• Warsaw
Biblical Gardens
Dillinger Heist
Hallmark Ornament
Museum

• Mentone
World's Largest Egg

• Fort Wayne
Endangered Species Carousel
"Fish Eaters and Idol Worshipers"
Johnny Appleseed's Grave
Karpeles Manuscript Library Museum
Pro Bowl West
Sliced Bread Sign

• Huntington
Outhouse Collection
The Quayle Vice Presidential Learning Center

• Wabash
Elephant Parade

24

• Peru
Circus City Museum
Cole Porter's Birthplace
and Grave
Dillinger Heist
Freaks of Nature and Cole Porter's
Hand-Me-Downs

27

2

CENTRAL INDIANA

*C*ould anywhere be as "Middle America" as the middle region of the middle state in the Midwest? But scratch just beneath the surface of central Indiana's otherwise practical, middle-class skin, and you'll find these Hoosiers have cantankerous interiors, if for no other reason than to give the middle finger to their middle-of-the-road image.

Judge for yourself. Terre Haute is the only place in the universe where you can buy *square* donuts. When a tree began growing on the roof of the 10-story courthouse in Greensburg, citizens didn't chop it down—they pruned it. And then there's Nancy Barnett. Dead for almost two centuries, she is *literally* in the middle of the road—her grave can be found in the center of Camp Hill Road near Amity, and she ain't moving, dagnabbit!

Don't misunderstand—it's not like central Indiana folk are weir-does . . . at least not all of them. Heck, when the US Air Force needed civilian volunteers to sit in an isolated watchtower to watch for incoming Soviet aircraft, almost a hundred Lafayette-area residents said, "Sign me up!" They know when it's time to get serious. Still, you never know when you'll bump into a giant sneaker, a green-eyed concrete dog, or the World's Largest Ball of Paint.

Alamo
America's Least-Dead Revolutionary Soldier

George Fruits's death in 1876 marked the end of a generation of soldiers. Fruits—some say his name was spelled Fruts—was the last surviving veteran of the American Revolutionary War. He served with the Pennsylvania militia and passed on at the ripe old age of 114.

You do the math—he was only 14 when the war broke out. Still a teenager when the conflict ended, he had a lot of life left in him. He eventually married Catherine Stonebraker, who was many years younger than

George. The couple moved west in 1820 and were two of the region's first settlers. When Fruits died, Catherine finally, *finally*, was able to start drawing a widow's pension.

Stonebraker Cemetery, County Road 400 S, Alamo, IN 47916
No phone
Hours: Daylight hours
Cost: Free
Directions: Half a mile west of County Road 600 W, east of town.

Alexandria

World's Largest Ball of Paint

Let's hear it for dedication, a quality all too lacking in today's world of instant gratification. Few people have the fortitude to stick with a project beyond a weekend, but not Michael Carmichael. In 1976 he got the brilliant idea to create a paint ball, and not just any paint ball but the World's Largest Paint Ball! The project was launched on New Year's Day 1977. He had his three-year-old son Michael paint one thin layer of latex on the outside of an old baseball, the first coat. From that day on, virtually every day, the ball gets another layer of paint, though often two or more.

In the early years it was mostly Michael and his wife, Glenda, who did the work. But as the ball grew, so did its reputation. People started showing up from other Indiana towns, then other states and countries, hoping to put their own coat on the ball. Carmichael eventually built a separate building for his growing creation and got Sherwin-Williams to sponsor it. The bumpy, egg-shaped blob currently measures more than 14 feet around and weighs 2½ tons. It is suspended from a ceiling beam to make it easy for you to add a new layer with a roller Carmichael provides. And you'll want

Ready to tackle Layer Number 25,120.

to, because when you're finished he'll give you an official certificate honoring your contribution. How cool is that?

10696 N. 200 W, Alexandria, IN 46001
Phone: (765) 724-4088
Hours: Call ahead for appointment
Cost: Free
Website: http://ballofpaint.freehosting.net
Directions: Head west out of town on Washington St. (W. 1100 N), then south on N. 200 W.

Amity
Nancy Barnett Isn't Moving!

In 1831, long before the first automobile was invented in Kokomo (see page 92), Nancy Kerlin Barnett was buried in a small cemetery along the banks of Sugar Creek. She rested in peace for about 70 years before the modern world began knocking on her door. County officials were planning a road and determined that the best route followed a trail that cut through the center of Barnett's cemetery.

This obstacle didn't bother the engineers; they just moved the bodies to another location. But it did bother Barnett's grandson, Daniel Doty. Though he was born 15 years after Barnett died, he felt an obligation to protect her grave—by force, if necessary. So while the exhumations continued, he sat atop her mound with a gun across his lap. Doty was still there when the road crew laid a gravel bed on both sides of her plot. And when the road was finished, he had one more job left to do: in 1912 he saw to it that a concrete slab was placed atop her grave to protect her bones from those who might not notice the rather significant speed bump in the center median. You'll still find Barnett there today.

Hill's Camp Road, Amity, IN 46131
No phone
Hours: Always visible
Cost: Free
Directions: Head south from Amity on Rte. 31, turn east on County Rd. 400S (Hill's Camp Rd.) and follow it just past Sugar Creek.

Nobody messes with Nancy Barnett!

BIZARRE BURIALS

Nancy Barnett's grave is certainly weird, but it didn't start out that way. Blame it on the county commissioners. There are, however, a number of Hoosiers who chose to be buried in strange style.

Cadillac to Heaven

Riverview Cemetery, 3635 E. Laughery Creek Rd., Aurora, (812) 926-1496, http://aurora.in.us/river-view-cemetery.html

Aurora Schuck loved her 1976 Cadillac Eldorado convertible, but her husband Ray loved Aurora even more. When Aurora's fight with cancer was coming to an end, she made one final request: she wanted to be buried in the Eldorado. Ray said OK, bought 14 plots in the local cemetery, and had a 27-by-12-foot concrete vault constructed. Aurora died November 7, 1989, and true to his word, Ray gave the car a nice wax, had it lowered into the vault by crane, and laid Aurora's casket across the trunk and rear seats. When Ray died in 2002, he was cremated and a hole was drilled into the vault, where his ashes were interred beside the wife he would do anything for. (There's not much to see at the cemetery today, just a headstone and a very large plot.)

Dead on His Feet

Burton Gap Cemetery, Burton Cemetery Rd., Mitchell, No phone

John Plesent Burton was a stand-up guy—still is, as a matter of fact. He was born in Virginia in 1758 and was a soldier in the Revolutionary War. In honor of his service he was given a parcel of land out west, "west" being the frontier of Indiana, and the Burton family moved to Lawrence County in 1826. Ten years later, on his deathbed, Burton made a request that he be buried standing up. This required that the grave be 11 feet deep to keep his head from sticking out. His sons dutifully followed his wishes, even though their father did not explain why. When his wife, Susannah, passed away in 1845, she was buried lying down. Today the Burton family celebrates their odd ancestor each year on the first Sunday of the first full weekend in August with a gathering at the Burton Gap Cemetery. But you can visit whenever you like.

Dueling Chiefs

Route 47 just west of I-65, Thorntown

In 1828 two Miami chiefs, Chief Dixon and Chief Chapodosia, did not agree on the Thorntown Treaty, in which the tribe surrendered their small reservation on Sugartree Creek to the incoming settlers. Dixon and Chapodosia argued about it until their respective deaths, and when that wasn't sufficient, they were planted in a Miami burial ground in full ceremonial dress, sitting upright, defiantly facing one another into the hereafter. That's where these stubborn guys still sit today, though the exact site is known only to the Miami.

Old-Time Hearse

Dove-Sharp & Rudicel Funeral Home, 420 S. State St., North Vernon, (812) 346-3977, www.dovesharprudicel.com

Maybe strange burial plots are not your style, but strange funerals are. You should consider the services of the Dove-Sharp & Rudicel Funeral Home in North Vernon. Parked out front in a covered pagoda is a spooky, horse-drawn hearse from 1914. If you're a customer, they'll pull it out and cart you to your final rest in style, as long as you're buried within walking distance.

Battle Ground

Tippecanoe Battlefield Monument

William Henry Harrison got a lot of political mileage from a battle that took place just north of Lafayette on November 7, 1811. But his military victory at the Battle of Tippecanoe was made possible, in part, by the idiotic advice given to his foe, Tecumseh, by his one-eyed brother Tenskwatawa, better known as the Prophet. Just before his fateful conflict with Harrison's invading militia, the Prophet (a medicine man) claimed to have had visions of the invading army's musket balls passing right through his followers' bodies without harming them.

He was half right. Clad in little more than the Prophet's assurances, the warriors made a preemptive strike against Harrison's encampment of 1,000 men, killing 37 and fatally wounding 24 more. But they suffered far greater casualties than they inflicted. Fleeing the battle, the Native American survivors wanted to kill the Prophet but settled for a curse Tecumseh was said to inflict on the US government that had provoked this conflict: he claimed that every president elected in a year ending in 0 would perish in office. (Before this, no American president had died while serving.)

James Monroe was elected in 1820 and lived out his term. So much for the curse. But in 1840, William Henry Harrison, campaigning under the to-hell-with-the-Indian-curse slogan "Tippecanoe and Tyler, too!", was elevated to the nation's highest office . . . and dropped dead 31 days later. Elected in 1848, Zachary Taylor, who also fought at the Battle of Tippecanoe, died in office in 1850. Abraham Lincoln, first elected in 1860, was assassinated in his second term. And then James A. Garfield (victor in 1880) was gunned down, followed by William McKinley, whose second term began in 1900. Warren Harding, the 1920 winner, died in office three years later, possibly at the hands of his wife. FDR was reelected for a third term in 1940 and perished after his fourth term. John Kennedy in 1960? Everyone knows what happened to him, or thinks they do. Ronald Reagan outlived the curse but not without getting a bullet in the chest. But finally,

---

BOGGSTOWN
➡ Boggstown voted to secede from the Union during the Civil War.

George W. Bush served two full terms and broke the presidential curse, along with just about everything else.

After visiting this historic site, if you have trouble visualizing the battle of two centuries ago, visit the stunning mural of the conflict at the Tippecanoe County Courthouse (301 Main St., (765) 423-9326, www.tippecanoe.in.gov) in nearby Lafayette. The 48-foot-long painting was relocated from the Fowler Hotel when it was torn down.

200 Battleground Ave., Battle Ground, IN 47920
Phone: (765) 476-8411
Hours: March–November, daily 10 AM–5 PM; December–February, Thursday–Tuesday noon–5 PM
Cost: Battlefield, Free; Museum, Adults $5, Seniors (60+) $4, Kids (4–12) $2
Website: www.tcha.mus.in.us/battlefield.htm
Directions: At the southwest end of town on Ninth Rd.

Wolf Park

Ignoring lessons learned from the Three Little Pigs and Little Red Riding Hood, some Hoosiers have established a wolf sanctuary in the American heartland. The folks at Wolf Park believe the lovable lupines have gotten a bad rap and, given the informative presentations at this nature center, they might be right.

The wolves here are not allowed to hang around and wait for a sirloin handout, but must work for their food. Friday and Saturday evenings are Howl Nights when the wolves sing for their supper. And on Sunday afternoons, the pack is encouraged to develop their tracking and hunting skills on a herd of penned bison. You're invited to all the demonstrations, and all the proceeds go to preserve this endangered species.

4004 E. County Road 800N, Battle Ground, IN 47920
Phone: (765) 567-2265
Hours: May–November, daily 1–5 PM; Wolf Howl Nights, May–November, Friday–Saturday 7:15 PM, December–April, Saturday 7:15 PM
Cost: Adults (14+) $8, Kids (6–13) $6; Howl Nights, Adults (14+) $8, Kids (6–13) $6
Website: www.wolfpark.org
Directions: Head north out of Battle Ground on Harrison Rd., then turn right on 800N.

BRAZIL

➡ Orville Redenbacher was born in Brazil on July 16, 1907.

COUNTRY CRITTERS

Are wolves not your thing? Well, there are three other animal rescue operations in Indiana that you might enjoy visiting instead.

Exotic Feline Rescue Center

2221 E. Ashboro Rd., Center Point, (812) 835-1130,
www.exoticfelinerescuecenter.org

Joe Taft founded the Exotic Feline Rescue Center in 1991 to take in abused and abandoned large cats. Most are former circus and private zoo animals, or pets that got too big for their owners. Unable to be released back into the wild, they live out their days on this 108-acre facility in southeast Indiana. Currently the center has more than 230 large cats, and your $10 admission fee goes to feed these hungry beasts. If you'd like to fall asleep to the roar of lions, the center has a B&B for $200 per night.

Wild Winds Buffalo Preserve

6975 N. Ray Rd., Fremont, (260) 495-0137, www.facebook.com
/wildwindsbuffalopreserve.net

Looking for animals once indigenous to the state? Try the Wild Winds Buffalo Preserve, the third-largest private herd in North America—about 200 altogether. The working ranch offers $10 tours for day visitors and overnight accommodations—in a teepee, if you prefer. They would have 201 buffalo, but as you'll see if you spend the night, buffalo sausage is on the breakfast menu.

Red Wolf Sanctuary

3027 SR 262, PO Box 202, Rising Sun, (812) 438-2306, www.redwolf.org

The Red Wolf Sanctuary was founded by Paul Strasser in 1979 with a single red wolf, but today it includes bears, bobcats, coyotes, raptors, buffalo, and more. Most of the animals found on this 450-acre preserve were being raised illegally as pets and were confiscated by authorities. Others have been brought here because they were injured; some can be rehabilitated and returned to the wild. Strasser offers tours of his operation, but by appointment only.

Berne
Switzerland Central

In the 1830s, Swiss immigrants began settling in east central Indiana (after a brief stopover in Ohio) and in 1852 established a town named for their native capital, Bern, but with an extra *e*. As the epicenter of all things Swiss, it's only logical that you would find the state's only re-creation of a Swiss village here.

The place has much of what you'd expect—a cheese house, a one-room schoolhouse, a cow barn, wandering yodelers—but one thing you wouldn't expect: the World's Largest Cider Press. Built by Swiss immigrant William Hauenstein in 1864, its press beam is 30 feet long and weighs 2 *tons*. It can squish 30 bushels of apples into 100 gallons of cider in a single pressing. Which is good—after lifting a 2-ton beam, you'll be thirsty.

Swiss Heritage Village, 1200 Swissway Rd., Berne, IN 46711
Phone: (260) 589-8007
Hours: May, Saturday 10 AM–4 PM; June–October, Monday–Saturday 10 AM–4 PM
Cost: Adults $6, Seniors (55+) $5, Kids (6–12) $4
Website: www.swissheritage.org
Directions: East of Rte. 27, north of Parr Rd., on the north side of town.

If Swiss Heritage Village leaves you wanting more, Berne's got it. In 2010 the town christened a 160-foot-tall Zytglogge, a $3.5 million replica of the famous clock tower in Bern, Switzerland. Each hour a robotic Bernard the Bell Ringer comes out and bangs his clanger to let you know another hour has passed, and at 3, 6, and 9 PM, 12 Glockenspiel characters emerge to re-create scenes from the founding of Berne. The best time to visit is during Swiss Days (www.bernein.com/swiss-days), held here each July.

Muensterberg Plaza, N. Church Ave., Berne, IN 46711
Phone: (260) 589-5139
Hours: Always visible
Cost: Free
Website: www.berneclocktower.org
Directions: At the corner of Main St. (Rte. 218) and Church St. (Rte. 27).

Bethel

Get High in Indiana

If you want to get high, you're better off in Colorado than Indiana. No, I'm not talking about marijuana—I'm talking about *elevation*. Sheesh! Still, there is a spot in this state where you can get higher than anywhere else: Hoosier Hill. This wooded bump encircled by cornfields is barely 20 feet above the surrounding land, but it's 1,257 feet above sea level, Indiana's Everest. Not that you can tell; you'll just have to take the surveyors' word.

As high as you can get in Indiana.

Hoosier Hill is accessed from a turnout on a rural road, and the "hike" is about 40 feet up into the trees. There you'll find a mailbox with a visitor's log in a ziplock bag. Be sure to chronicle your accomplishment. Then sit down and have a beer, or something else, because out here, all alone in the middle of nowhere, it's easy to get really, really high.

Hoosier Hill, 11404 Elliot Rd., Bethel, IN 47341
No phone
Hours: Daylight
Cost: Free
Website: www.peakbagger.com
Directions: Head north out of town on Rte. 227 to Bethel Rd./County Line Rd., turn west and go one mile to Elliot Rd., turn north for ¼ mile to the turnout, park and walk 40 feet into the woods and look for the mailbox.

Cairo
Eyes to the Skies!

The Russians were coming! The Russians were coming! . . . or so the folks of Cairo were encouraged to believe. Back in the early 1950s, before the military was able to install a national radar system, the US Air Force came up with a low-tech solution called Operation Skywatch. Patriotic citizens were asked to volunteer to sit in watchtowers all across the nation and keep their eyes and ears peeled for enemy aircraft or missiles. They were known as the Civilian Ground Observation Corps.

The Cairo Tower, also known as Delta Lima 3-Green (DL3-G), was commissioned on August 16, 1952, the first Operation Skywatch tower in the nation. Built in the backyard of local grocer Larry O'Connor, it was staffed by a group of 90 volunteers on rotating two-hour shifts.

Today, the tower (a reproduction) stands empty, its stairs collapsing, while a vigilant limestone statue of a *Leave It to Beaver* family gazes skyward. A plaque reads, THEY ALSO SERVE WHO STAND AND WATCH. So true.

County Road 850N, Cairo, IN 47923
No phone
Hours: Always visible
Cost: Free
Directions: Just east of County Road 100W on County Road 850N in the center of town, just south of the I-65 overpass.

Let's see the Ruskies get past THIS!

Centerville
World's Largest Candle

Two stories tall and very fat, the World's Largest Candle anchors a store that sells—you guessed it—candles! The colossal candle was built in 2006, along with the rest of the store, because it is part of the store. Sorry to reveal its shortcomings, but it's not a candle deep down, just a candle-shaped room filled with more candles. The flame on top is not real, either, but it does light up and flickers at night. From the interstate it looks almost real.

Warm Glow Candle Outlet, 2131 N. Centerville Rd., Centerville, IN 47330
Phone: (765) 855-2000
Hours: After dark; Store, daily 9 AM–7 PM
Cost: Free
Website: www.warmglow.com
Directions: Exit southbound from I-10 at Centerville Rd.; store is southeast of the intersection.

Burn, baby, burn!

Chesterfield
Spiritualist Camp

Long before there were Psychic Hotlines, spiritualists were the folks people turned to for answers to otherworldly questions. And what is spiritualism? According to this place's literature, it is "the Science, Philosophy, and Religion of continuous life, based on the fact of communication, by means of mediumship, with those who live in the spirit world." Translation? You can talk to the dead, and they'll be glad to help.

This Spiritualist Camp was founded by Dr. J. Westerfield in 1890. During the years following the Civil War, spiritualism was very popular with Americans who wanted to contact loved ones lost in battle. The practice of contacting the dead suffered a tremendous setback when the Fox sisters, who singlehandedly started the religion, confessed that they were not receiving "raps" from beyond the grave but were popping bones in their feet in answer to questions.

That hasn't stopped the true believers. Spiritualism survives to this day in a few places around the country, like Chesterton. Built as a commune for mediums, with small huts surrounding a central park, you can pick up a listing of those accepting clients at the main office. On a nice day, the mediums sit out on their porches, waiting for business, with their prices clearly posted. To avoid a price war, all have agreed to standard fees: $50 for a Private Clairvoyance or Healing, $40 for a Private Trumpet or Trance Séance, etc. You can save money by arranging for a larger group séance, but you'll have to share your communication time with your aunt Clara.

The grounds of the Spiritualist Camp are filled with statues, totem poles, a cave, a labyrinth, and creepy, moss-covered benches. If you call ahead, you can have them unlock the Hett Art Gallery and Museum. It's filled with paintings rendered while channeling spirits through an artists' brushstrokes.

Camp Chesterfield, 50 Lincoln Dr., PO Box 132, Chesterfield, IN 46017
Phone: (765) 378-0235
Hours: Wednesday–Saturday 10 AM–4 PM, Sunday 10 AM–2 PM; Museum, first Saturday each month (Psychic Fair Saturday) 10 AM–2 PM, or by appointment
Cost: Free; Séances, $40–45/person
Website: www.campchesterfield.net
Directions: Off Rte. 32 in the center of town, two blocks north of the Rte. 232 intersection.

Cloverdale
House of Bells

Some in the community of Cloverdale might call the Kennedy family a bunch of ding-dongs. The Kennedys would probably reply, "Thank you very much!" Because while most folks are satisfied with a lawn gnome or two, the Kennedys have filled their rural yard with bells, bells, and more bells—about 230 in all. They call it the Texas Mouse Trap, and it includes some nonringing items, such as windmills, anchor chains, giant axes, and large bear traps. You'd think noise would be a problem for the neighbors, but the Kennedys live way out in the country and can clang away to their hearts' desires. Stop by for a concert on a windy day.

4291 County Road 900E, Cloverdale, IN 46120
Private phone
Hours: Always visible
Cost: Free
Directions: West of town five miles on Rte. 42, turn left on County Rd. 900E when Rte. 42 makes a sharp turn north at the county line.

Converse

Two-by-Two, Children!

If global warming gets as bad as predicted, there might be a lot of people flocking to the Rainbow Christian Camp north of Converse, less for spiritual salvation than for what they've got moored outside their main building: an ark. Unfortunately, it's not big enough to hold every last human, and certainly not two of every creature on earth, so latecomers will be out of luck. The ark is a quarter-scale version of the structure supposedly discovered by Roger Wyatt on Mt. Ararat in Turkey.

This could come in handy in 2050.

The Converse ark is today used as a classroom for kids and, truth be told, is no more seaworthy than the Wyatt ship. If the oceans rise this high, you're probably better off praying anyway.

Rainbow Christian Camp, 3522 N. 1000 W27, Converse, IN 46919
Phone: (765) 395-3638
Hours: Daylight
Cost: Free
Website: http://thearkcm.org
Directions: At the east end of town, head north on Rte. 1000 W27.

Crawfordsville
Ben-Hur Museum

When you think of Ben-Hur, you probably think of Rome. Or chariot races. Or Charlton Heston's overacting. But do you ever think of Crawfordsville, Indiana? You should, for it was here that most of the book was written under a beech tree near the Hoosier home of Major General Lewis "Lew" Wallace.

Wallace was a soldier, an artist, a violinist, an inventor, and a territorial governor of New Mexico, but he is remembered best for writing *Ben-Hur*, first published in 1880. The book was a hit even before it landed on the silver screen. Wallace's Crawfordsville study is surrounded by a frieze depicting the exploits of his heroic character, and displays two costumes from Hollywood's interpretations of his tale. Outside, a statue of Wallace stands on the museum grounds.

Wallace was born in downstate Brookville on April 10, 1827. When he died in Crawfordsville in 1906, he was buried in Oak Hill Cemetery.

General Lew Wallace Study & Museum, 200 Wallace Ave., Crawfordsville, IN 47933
Phone: (765) 362-5769
Hours: February–December, Tuesday–Saturday 10 AM–5 PM
Cost: Adults $5, Students (7–18) $1
Website: www.ben-hur.com
Directions: One block south of Main St. on Elston Ave., at Wallace Ave.

Oak Hill Cemetery, 598 Oak Hill Rd., Crawfordsville, IN 47933
Phone: (765) 362-6602
Hours: Daily 9 AM–5 PM
Cost: Free
Directions: Head north on Rte. 231 from downtown, once over the bridge turn left (west) on Oak Hill Rd.

Rotary Jail Museum

Around and around the criminals go, and where they stop determines if they go. Welcome to the Montgomery County Jail, home of the world's first rotating circular jail.

Construction on the unique building was started in 1881 and completed a year later. It was the brainchild of William H. Brown and Benjamin F. Haugh as a means of reducing the number of law enforcement officials needed to guard a jailful of ne'er-do-wells. The concept was simple: build a two-story set of 16 cells, each shaped like a wedge, that could be turned by an external crank. This oversized coffee can rotated within another set of bars, this one with a single exit. Spin an interior cell's door to match up with the external door, and the inmate could move in or out. All the rest would have to wait.

This design had obvious drawbacks, particularly in a fire, but it didn't concern the county too much; they used it from 1882 until 1939. But then the 27-ton drum was welded to keep it from rotating, and multiple doors were cut into the outer cage. This stationary jail was used until 1973. Two years later the empty structure was put on the National Register of Historic Places and eventually restored.

225 N. Washington St., Crawfordsville, IN 47933
Phone: (765) 362-5222
Hours: March–May & September–November, Wednesday–Saturday 10 AM–3 PM; June–August,
    Wednesday–Saturday 10 AM–3 PM
Cost: Adults $5, Kids (6–17) $1
Website: www.rotaryjailmuseum.org
Directions: On Rte. 231 (Washington St.) just north of Rte. 136 (Market St.).

Crete & Lynn
Jim Jones, That Lovable Tyke!

Everyone's got to start somewhere, and for the Reverend Jim Jones, that somewhere was the dinky town of Crete near the Indiana-Ohio border. He was born here on May 13, 1931, to Jim and Lynetta Jones, both of whom would launch young Jim on the road to kookdom. Lynetta believed she was the reincarnation of Mark Twain and told family and friends that her departed mother had come to her in a dream to proclaim she would give birth to the World's Savior. Talk about pressure!

Jones's father worked for the railroad, if "worked" meant "collected a paycheck." For the better part of his life he was plagued by alcoholism and depression, and not without reason; he returned home from World War I with his lungs nearly destroyed by mustard gas. Jones spent his free hours at the local watering holes, wheezing out war stories with the local drunks. He was also a member of the local KKK.

Jones Birthplace, 8400 S. Arba Pike, Crete, IN 47355
Private phone
Hours: Private property; view from street
Cost: Free
Directions: The first house on the right, heading south from Rte. 36 along Arba Pike.

Everyone's got to start somewhere.

The Jones family moved after the railroad rerouted through Lynn in 1934. There, the family moved into a small house along the tracks on the south side of town. Little Jim became known as Lynn's version of St. Francis, always followed by a menagerie of stray dogs, cats, and other critters. At first he was content to let them roam free, but later he built cages for his animals in the family barn.

Residents recall how Jim liked to run around naked, or at least pantless, until it was time to enter school. He could also be coaxed to deliver profanity-filled diatribes for a five-cent honorarium. The local ne'er-do-wells always had a spare nickel for the weird kid who cursed on command.

Early on, Jones attended religious services with his family at the too-tame Church of the Nazarene (232 Eastern Ave., (781) 593-5742, http://lynnchurch.com). But soon he began attending a holy-roller congregation on the west side of Lynn, the Gospel Tabernacle, where they spoke in tongues and actually stood up in the pews. The minister later capitalized on Jim's swearing talent, turning his foul-mouthed rants-for-pay into fire-and-brimstone sermons from the new child preacher.

Outside church, Jim would baptize his friends in a nearby creek and preside over funerals for rats and other dead animals. Jim set up an altar in the family's barn and would preach to his playmates, attracting his congregation with lemonade and punch (hmmmm . . .) during the hot summer months. And while it didn't seem too odd at the time, he once locked his friends in the loft when they threatened to leave his group.

Jones also had a passion for science and converted the barn into a laboratory between services. Jones would set up a microscope with insect specimens, or perform experiments, like the time he tried to graft a chicken leg onto a duck with string. Sometimes he would combine science and religion, reviving supposedly ailing rabbits and chickens.

The Jones home, barn, and outhouse are long gone, replaced by a small supermarket. The Gospel Tabernacle, where Jones first preached, is today used as an office for Kabert Industries.

Lynn Grocery & Meat Market (Jones home site), 202 S. Main St., Lynn, IN 47355
No phone
Hours: Home torn down
Cost: Free
Directions: At the corner of Grant and Main St. (Rte. 27), south of Church St.

Kabert Industries (Gospel Tabernacle site), 511 W. Church St., Lynn, IN 47355
Private phone
Hours: Always visible; view from street
Cost: Free
Directions: Five blocks west of Main St. (Rte. 27).

Danville

Mayberry Cafe

Fans of *The Andy Griffith Show* know that the TV series was set in a fictional town based on Griffith's birthplace, Mount Airy, North Carolina. And today, people who have never been to Mayberry still have affection for the place, especially Brad and Christine Born.

The Borns opened the Mayberry Cafe in 1989, which means they've been in business 20 years longer than the series, 17 if you count *Mayberry RFD*, and nobody counts that show. In addition to its Southern small-town decor, the Mayberry Cafe has themed menu items—Aunt Bee's Fried Chicken, Barney's Burger, Andy's Tenderloin, Floyd's Fish Sandwich, Goober's Chicken Sandwich, Otis's Whiskey Burger, Clara's Cobbler, and, for some reason, a Roast Beef Manhattan Dinner. Most days you'll find a 1962 Ford Galaxie squad car parked out front and an endless loop of *The Andy*

Griffith Show playing on the overhead TV screens. Come and set a spell . . . no, wait . . . that's *The Beverly Hillbillies.*

78 W. Main St., Danville, IN 46122
Phone: (317) 745-4067
Hours: Sunday–Thursday 11 AM–9:30 PM, Friday–Saturday 11 AM–10 PM
Cost: Meals $8–12
Website: www.mayberrycafe.com
Directions: In the center of town, one block east of Cross St. on Main St.

No, you're not in North Carolina.

Fairmount

James Dean's Boyhood Home

Few Hoosiers have left as lasting an impression on the outside world as James Dean, and no community in the state has gotten as much mileage out of this long-dead rebel as Fairmount, the town in which he grew up.

Dean was born in nearby Marion (see page 97), but his family moved to California when he was an infant. After his mother died of cancer, his father sent the 9-year-old back to Indiana to live on the farm of Ortense and Marcus Winslow, Jimmy's aunt and uncle. The family attended the Back Creek Friends Church (7560 S. County Rd. 150 E, (765) 948-5640), and Jimmy was enrolled at West Ward Elementary (torn down), also known as "Old Academy."

There aren't too many interesting stories about Dean's childhood, mostly because his life at the time was typical and uneventful; Jimmy did his chores, obeyed the Winslows, and played a lot with his young cousin Marcus. Dean knocked out four front teeth while goofing around in the Winslows' barn (which still stands) and learned to play basketball with a wooden basket hoop nailed up by his uncle.

After Dean's death, the Winslows were initially very open to talking to visitors, at least until they loaned a family photo album to a "reporter" doing a story on their famous nephew. It vanished and has never been returned. The farm is still owned by the family, Dean's cousin Marcus, to be exact.

7184 County Road 150E, Jonesboro, IN 46938

Private phone

Hours: Always visible; view from road

Cost: Free

Website: www.jamesdean.com

Directions: Drive north past the cemetery on County Rd. 150 E, on the west side of the road, just past County Rd. 700 S.

Fairmount High School

In high school, James Dean began exhibiting the personal traits that would become his trademark. After Dean gave a rousing monologue for the school's annual Women's Christian Temperance Union competition, drama coach Adeline Nall invited him to participate in the school's plays, a request she did not regret, even when he fired a gun into the set wall to give it a realistic look for a mystery play. His first acting lessons took place in room 21 of the now-crumbling building. He was cast in *You Can't Take It With You, Our Hearts Were Young and Gay, Mooncalf Mungford, The Monkey's Paw,* and *Goon With the Wind,* as Frankenstein.

Though Dean was a Quaker, and theoretically nonviolent, he was not above getting into scraps. He was suspended for punching schoolmate Dave Fox after he criticized Dean's reasoning during a debate class.

Dean owned a motorcycle that he rode everywhere, and he spent a lot of time at Marvin Carter's motorcycle shop (just north of the cemetery on County Road 150E). Once, at the Jonesboro High School baseball park, Dean accepted a dare from two young women to ride his motorcycle nude with friend Clyde Smitson; when the naked pair returned to the park, the women had run off with their clothes, so they had to drive back to Fairmount au natural.

During high school, Jimmy established a close relationship with Methodist Reverend James DeWeerd, who taught him yoga, showed him his travel movies, told him about bullfighting, and encouraged him to sculpt. The minister also taught Dean to drive and took him to the Indy 500, where the teenager got his first look at real speed.

James Dean graduated on May 16, 1949, and two weeks later left for California. His old high school stands empty and is in danger of being torn down. Fairmount boosters have been doing all they can to keep it from a date with a wrecking ball, but in 2013 the roof collapsed. Better see it while you still can.

Old Fairmount High School, Jefferson & Vine Sts., Fairmount, IN 46928
No phone
Hours: Always visible
Cost: Free
Directions: Three blocks east of Main St., two blocks south of Washington St.

James Dean's Grave

Following his fatal car accident on September 30, 1955, Dean's body was returned to Fairmount for burial. (Some, including Walter Winchell, had suggested that Dean was alive but horribly maimed and was learning to use his artificial limbs before returning to society.) Services were held at the Friends Church (124 W. First St., (765) 948-5099) on October 8. James DeWeerd gave the eulogy, and Elizabeth Taylor sent flowers.

Dean's grave in Park Cemetery is an ever-changing memorial. Shortly after his burial, a brick monument was erected in the cemetery with a bust of the star, but the statue soon disappeared. At first, fans were suspected, but later evidence revealed that it was sawed off by a local veterans' group who claimed Dean had avoided the draft by saying he was gay. "I kissed the doctor!" he told Hedda Hopper. Hopper later lobbied to have a granite Oscar posthumously awarded to Dean to be placed on his grave. It never happened.

Dean's first headstone disappeared for eight years, then reappeared. It was stolen again in 1983, but when it didn't return, was replaced in 1985. Eventually, the first marker showed up behind a Fort Wayne dumpster in 1987. The second headstone was taken on June 14, 1998, but was found two days later by a sheriff's deputy after he ran over it on a country road, 60 miles away.

Though chipped and battered, the Dean marker is usually coated in lipstick kisses and surrounded by flowers and items from fans. Packs of Chesterfield cigarettes are a popular offering. But remember, this is a cemetery, so visitors are asked to show some decorum. Leaving mementos is fine; wailing and throwing yourself on the grave is not.

Rebel Not Without a Following.

Park Cemetery, 8008 S. Rte. 150 E, Fairmount, IN 46928
Phone: (765) 948-4040
Hours: Daily 9 AM–6 PM
Cost: Free
Directions: North on Main (Rte. 150) heading out of town, on the left.

Fairmount Historical Museum

Dean fans will find plenty in Fairmount to keep them busy, including two museums. The first is run by the local historical society and includes many items not associated with the town's favorite son.

The Fairmount Historical Museum has an impressive collection of Dean artifacts, most donated by his family and friends. (The museum is housed in the J. W. Patterson home, built by Nixon Winslow, James Dean's great-grandfather.) Dean's first motorcycle was discovered downstate, restored, and is now parked back here, under glass. The museum has his conga drums, a yellow sweater left unclaimed at Del Mar Cleaners after his death, the boots and Lee Rider jeans he wore in *Giant*, a speeding ticket he got early in the morning on the day he was killed, his grammar school art, and a soil experiment from his days in 4-H.

The museum also sponsors the annual Museum Days Celebration on the last weekend in September. Dean fans from across the nation descend on the small town for a street fair, classic car rally, look-alike contest, free screenings of Dean's three films, and much more.

203 E. Washington St., PO Box 92, Fairmount, IN 46928
Phone: (765) 948-4555
Hours: April–October, Monday–Friday 10 AM–5 PM, Saturday–Sunday noon–5 PM
Cost: Free (donations welcome)
Website: www.jamesdeanartifacts.com
Directions: Downtown, one block east of Main St. on Washington St. (County Rd. 950 S).

James Dean Gallery

James Dean's former acting teacher, Adeline Nall used a switchblade to cut the ribbon inaugurating the James Dean Gallery several years back, and this fan museum has been busy ever since. The gallery is filled with Dean-obelia, but most of the souvenirs and trinkets were produced after his death. However, they do have some genuine artifacts on display, including a "life mask" created for makeup artists on his films, a dozen pieces of clothing he wore in his brief movie career (including the wool pants he wore during the *Rebel Without a Cause* knife fight and an outfit from *East of Eden*), old posters, high school yearbooks, artworks the actor created, and lots and lots of *bad* art created by his fans. There seems to be a universal error in the pieces: Dean's head always looks too large for his body.

The James Dean Gallery also has the best gift shop in town. You name it, his handsome brooding image is plastered on it—mugs, ties, magnets, statuettes, plates, puzzles, bobble heads, Christmas ornaments. Nothing is too tacky for the man who invented cool.

425 N. Main St., Fairmount, IN 46928
Phone: (765) 948-DEAN
Hours: Daily 9 AM–6 PM
Cost: Donation
Website: www.jamesdeangallery.com
Directions: Four blocks south of Rte. 26 on Main St.

AND THAT'S NOT ALL!

Gaze up at the Fairmount water tower and you'll see not only James Dean but also Garfield the Cat. Why? Cartoonist Jim Davis grew up just outside of town off Route 26 on a 120-acre farm with 25 cats. Today you can take the Garfield Trail tour past 11 jumbo Garfield statues, each with a different theme, located in towns around Grant County: www.showmegrant-county.com/what-to-do/grant-countys-garfield-trail/

It turns out that Fairmount has been the hometown of many celebrities and claims to have 14 times the national average of entries in *Who's Who*, per capita. There's CBS correspondent Phil Jones and Cyrus Pemberton, creator of the ice cream cone. And Bill Dolman, inventor of the hamburger. And Milton Wright, the father of the Wright Brothers. Who knows who the gene pool will produce next?

Fortville

Drunken Pink Elephant

Remember the scene from *Dumbo*, when the young elephant and Timothy Q. Mouse take a bad trip after drinking water spiked with champagne, where they hallucinate about parading pink elephants and wake up in a tree with massive hangovers? They just don't make kid's films like that anymore! No, today you have to go to an adult establishment like Elite Beverages to see one of those colorful creatures.

Standing outside this not-exactly-elite liquor store you'll find a 10-foot-tall, pink fiberglass elephant wearing Elvis Costello glasses and holding a martini glass in its trunk. Though the statue has been has been outside this business for almost a half century, the current father-and-son owners Ray and Adam Cox have been decorating it with different hats for certain holidays—a Pilgrim hat for Thanksgiving, a green top hat for St. Pat's, and so on. The hats are real, not hallucinations.

Elite Beverages, 308 W. Broadway St., Fortville, IN 46040
Phone: (317) 485-6282
Hours: Always visible; Store, daily 9 AM–11 PM
Cost: Free
Website: www.facebook.com/EliteBeverages
Directions: On Rte. 36 (Broadway Rd.), two blocks southwest of Maple St.

Bottom's up!

FOSTER
⇒ A UFO passed over the Foster farm of Robert Moudy on October 15, 1957, causing his combine's engine to die immediately. It started again after the flat, oval craft flew into the distance.

FRANKFORT
⇒ Each year in July, Frankfort holds a Hot Dog Festival (http://frankfortmainstreet.com). The mascot at Frankfort High School (1 S. Malsh Rd., (765) 654-9224, http://fhs.frankfortschools.org) is the Fighting Hot Dog.

PLENTY O' PACHYDERMS

The drunk Fortville elephant might be Indiana's best-known pachyderm, but it isn't the only one to be found on the state's backroads.

Two Elephants

Jim Hipp Nursery, 1013 W. Warrenton Rd., Haubstadt, (812) 867-2892, www.facebook.com/pages/Hipp-Nursery/315356301860631

The Jim Hipp Nursery brags that it is "Home of the Topiary," which is cool enough, but it's also got an alcoholic pink elephant with martini glass on its property—the same model as Fortville's—side-by-side with a smaller gray teetotaler, as well as other oversized statuary: a black panther, a bald eagle, a pair of buffalo, a giraffe, and a few Cyldesdales.

Elephant Parade

Modoc's Market, 205 S. Miami St., Wabash, (260) 569-1281, www.modocsmarket.com

On November 11, 1942, three elephants from the Great American Circus broke loose before a performance in Wabash. Two—Judy and Empress—wandered off and were recaptured in nearby neighborhoods, but 1,900-pound Modoc headed downtown, where she paused after smelling roasted peanuts at Bradley Brothers Pharmacy. Modoc then burst in, ate the peanuts, and bashed out the back door. She was on the run for five days before being captured in Huntington County. Modoc's Market stands on the site of the old pharmacy and has a less dangerous parade of elephant statues on the sidewalk out front.

High Elephant

Green Fields Trading Company, 2235 Ripley St., Lake Station, (219) 962-4578, http://greenfieldstrading.com

A trumpeting elephant and stoic rhinoceros guard the entrance to a hippie emporium selling tie-dyed clothing, incense, and beads in Lake Station.

Fountain City

Grand Central Station on the Underground Railroad

Between 1827 and 1847 (at this location, and before they lived here), Levi and Catharine Coffin helped more than 2,000 slaves escape to freedom in the North, and because of this earned their home its nickname "Grand Central Station of the Underground Railroad." Not one slave who passed through this station during those 20 years was ever lost to the slave trade. In that respect, they had a *better* track record than Grand Central Station.

Levi Coffin was unofficially dubbed the president of the movement. The Coffins were the inspiration for Harriet Beecher Stowe's Simeon and Rachel Halliday in *Uncle Tom's Cabin*, and the story of one "passenger," Eliza Harris, became the fictitious Eliza, who escaped across an Ohio River ice floe with her baby in her arms.

The Coffins' home has been refurbished to its antebellum appearance with period furnishings. On the tour, you will see a hiding place in the attic located behind a headboard and another between the mattresses on the bed, as well as the building's five different exit doors.

Levi Coffin House State Historic Park, 113 N. Main St., PO Box 77, Fountain City, IN 47341
Phone: (765) 847-2432
Hours: June–August, Tuesday–Saturday 1–4 PM; September–October, Saturday 1–4 PM
Cost: Adults $2, Kids (6–18) $1
Website: www.waynet.org/levicoffin/#house
Directions: Where Main St. (Rte. 27) meets Fountain City Pike.

GAS CITY

➡ Many of Gas City's street signs are mounted atop miniature oil derricks.

Greencastle
Buzz Bomb

It was the terror of London, the German V-1 buzz bomb. During German attacks at the onset of World War II, Brits were familiar with the sound of the guided missiles' engines humming overhead. As long as they could hear the buzz, folks on the ground were safe. But when the noise cut off, the V-1s returned to earth with devastating results.

The V-1 that now sits on the courthouse lawn in Greencastle was decommissioned by the US

Skip this site if you're from London.

Army just after the war, purchased by VFW Post 1550, and dedicated to local veterans on Memorial Day 1947—the only one of its kind on public display in the United States. Might those veterans have felt differently had they been British soldiers? Bloody likely!

Putnam County Courthouse, 1 Court House Square, Greencastle, IN 46135
Phone: (765) 653-3100
Hours: Always visible
Cost: Free
Website: http://cityofgreencastle.com
Directions: On the southwest corner of the courthouse, along Rte. 231, at the corner of Washington and Jackson Sts.

Greenfield, St. Leon, & Bloomington
The Old Crow, the Hickory Pole, and Five-Foot Fish

If you think the nation's recent presidential election was strange, you should hear how things used to be. Two odd, little-known customs can be traced back to the Hoosier State, and there's a remnant of a third.

Before the donkey became the symbol of the Democratic Party, it had the rooster. It all began when Greenfield Democrat Joseph Chapman was asked to "crow up" support for William Henry Harrison in the 1840 election, and "Crow, Chapman, crow!" became the party's rallying cry. The rooster remained the Democratic mascot for years until the party adopted the donkey. You can find a monument to Chapman's first squawk at the entrance to Riley Memorial Park in his old hometown.

Another strange tradition began four years later in 1844 when Democrats erected hickory poles around the United States in honor of their former president Andrew "Old Hickory" Jackson. For many years, during election campaigns, it was common for towns to do the same. Somehow St. Leon got into the act in 1892, 55 years after Jackson was dead and buried, by erecting its first hickory pole in front of St. Joseph's Church (today St. Joseph's Rectory). It was hoisted by hand and was topped by an American flag and a fake rooster.

Whether they feel they're making up for all those lost years, or whether they're suckers for tradition, St. Leon is the only community in the nation that still raises a hickory pole every four years. So why doesn't anyone else still do this? Because it's ridiculous, that's why.

And finally, one last extinct political symbol sits atop the Monroe County Courthouse in Bloomington: a five-foot-long, fish-shaped weathervane believed to reference the Jeffersonian Republican Party, whose symbol was a fish. That party morphed into the modern Democratic Party, and the fish gave way to the crow and then the donkey.

Riley Memorial Park, E. Main St. & Apple St., Greenfield, IN 46140
Phone: (317) 477-4340
Hours: Dawn–dusk
Cost: Free
Website: www.greenfieldin.org/recreation/facilities/162-rileypark
Directions: Eight blocks east of State St. (Rte. 9) on Main St. (Rte. 40).

St. Joseph's Rectory, 7536 Church Lane, St. Leon, IN 47012
Phone: (812) 576-3593
Hours: Always visible
Cost: Free
Directions: One block east of Rte. 1, on the west side of the church building.

Monroe County Courthouse, Kirkwood Ave. & Walnut St., Bloomington, IN 47012
Phone: (812) 365-5542
Hours: Always visible
Cost: Free
Website: www.co.monroe.in.us/tsd/Justice.aspx
Directions: North of Seventh St. (Kirkwood Ave.), at College Ave.

Greensburg
Tree on the Courthouse

This is what happens when you don't clean your gutters . . . for 130 years. In 1870 caretakers (to use the term loosely) of the Decatur County Courthouse in Greensburg noticed a small tree had sprouted in a gutter along the highest roofline. They decided to let it grow for curiosity's sake. Over time, the largetooth aspen grew big enough to see from 10 stories below. It grew and grew and grew, until it started to rip the roof off the building.

This is what happens when you don't clean your gutters.

Maintenance crews finally chopped down the 12-foot tree in 1919, but that didn't put an end to it. A sucker sprouted from the original tree's roots, and Greensburg's mascot was back in business. Since then, a series of trees either have been reluctantly removed when they grew too large, or have blown off in windstorms. Remarkably, a new tree always returns.

Today's tree is the 12th generation, having sprouted in 1958. Greensburg calls itself the "Tree City" and each September throws a Tree City Fall Festival to honor its weird, one-tree arboretum. Rest assured, if the suckers don't keep coming back in the gutters, the suckers on the ground will plant a new tree.

Courthouse Tower, 150 Courthouse Square, Greensburg, IN 47240
Phone: (877) 883-8733 or (812) 222-8733
Hours: Always visible
Cost: Free
Website: www.visitgreensburg.com
Directions: At the corner of Broadway and Main St. (Rte. 421).

Kokomo
Koko-mantis!

Anyone who's a fan of late-night creature features knows how it works: nuclear testing irradiates insects that grow to enormous proportions, or the blast opens up an underground colony of superbugs that crawl forth to wreak havoc on the human population. Harmless 1950s sci-fi fantasies, right?

Wrong! Kokomo residents know better. Every day they can see a 22-foot-long preying mantis outside a Subway sandwich franchise near downtown. The gangly green creature was made from scrap material by Scott Pitcher (see Storybook Express to follow) and installed in a walled planter bed at a busy corner, where it stares at passersby with its beady eyes. No, it isn't alive, nor likely to eat you after mating . . . unless . . . has somebody tested the water in Kokomo for toxic waste?

100 N. Washington St., Kokomo, IN 46901
No phone
Hours: Always visible
Cost: Free
Directions: Two blocks north of Wildcat Creek on Rte. 22 (Washington St.), at Sycamore St.

Storybook Express and Star Nails

With the runaway popularity of Harry Potter and *Game of Thrones*, it's becoming increasingly clear that people today would rather live in an imaginary world than the current real one. If you're among the fantasy-loving crowd and need a microwave burrito or Slim Jim, and you find yourself in Kokomo, head on over to Storybook Express, a minimart for Hobbit fans.

The weird structure was built in 2012 by Scott Pitcher of Fortune Companies Inc. Crews used recycled brick, stone, and other junk to create this one-of-a-kind convenience store. Walk around the perimeter and you'll see bowling balls, springs, hubcaps, cast iron medallions, and broken plates fashioned into rocket ships, flowers, a giant electrical outlet, and odd patterns of every shape, color, and texture. Inside, however, you'll find none of it—just aisles of chips, soda, and jerky. And despite its name, no storybooks.

There's also a lesser but still cool version of Storybook Express in Kokomo: the building that currently houses Star Nails. It was also built by Pitcher and has the same whimsical walls.

Storybook Express, 316 E. Sycamore St., Kokomo, IN 46901
Phone: (765) 450-5718
Hours: Always visible
Cost: Free
Website: www.facebook.com/pages/Storybook-Express/252323918230199
Directions: Two blocks north of Wildcat Creek, at Apperson St.

Star Nails, 1500 E. Markland Ave., Kokomo, IN 46901
Phone: (765) 453-0743
Hours: Always visible; Store, Monday–Saturday, 9:30 AM–7:30 PM, Sunday noon–5 PM
Cost: Free
Directions: Two blocks west of Rte. 931 (Reed Rd.) on Rte. 22 (Markland Ave.).

Bilbo Baggins's bodega.

World's First Automobile

Ask any American who built the world's first successful commercial automobile and you're likely to get "Henry Ford" as an answer. But "Elwood Haynes"? Only in Kokomo.

Locals know that Haynes ushered in the age of the automobile when he putted for six miles along Pumpkinvine Pike on July 4, 1894. Town leaders had so little faith in his contraption that they asked him to drive it outside the city's limits, heading *away* from town. They thought it would scare horses, explode, or both. The experimental vehicle averaged 7 mph during its inaugural run.

The car had been built by Edgar and Elmer Apperson under Elwood's direction. The trio formed a company in 1898 called the Haynes-Apperson Automobile Company but split up and formed their own companies in 1902.

Haynes's accomplishments were not limited to the automobile. In 1906 he invented Stellite, a versatile metal alloy, and in 1912 he created stainless steel. You'll learn this and many other facts at the Elwood Haynes Museum, located in his former home. (He lived here from 1915 to 1925.) You won't see his original vehicle, however, because Haynes donated it to the Smithsonian in 1910. But his fourth car can be found at the Kokomo Automotive Museum, along with other classic cars.

Elwood Haynes Museum, 1915 S. Webster St., Kokomo, IN 46902
Phone: (765) 456-7500
Hours: Tuesday–Saturday 11 AM–4 PM, Sunday 1–4 PM
Cost: Donations only
Website: www.cityofkokomo.org/departments/elwood_haynes_museum.php
Directions: On the east side of Highland Park, just north of Kokomo Creek at Stadium Dr.

Haynes Monument, Pumpkinvine Pike (E. Boulevard St.) & S. Goyer Rd. (Rte. 150E), Kokomo, IN 46902
No phone
Hours: Always visible
Cost: Free
Directions: Four blocks west of Rte. 31 on E. Boulevard St.

Kokomo Automotive Museum, 1500 N. Reed Rd., Kokomo, IN 46901
Phone: (765) 450-9248
Hours: Tuesday–Saturday 10 AM–4 PM
Cost: Adults $5
Website: www.kokomoautomotivemuseum.com
Directions: Head east on North St. from Reed Rd. (Rte. 931), then north on the service road.

CITY OF FIRSTS

For most towns it would be honor enough to claim the World's First Automobile, but not go-go-Kokomo, the "City of Firsts." No less than 14 earthshaking inventions were introduced in this town:

→ Automobile (Elwood Haynes, 1894)
→ Pneumatic Rubber Tire (D. C. Spraker, 1894)
→ Aluminum Casting (Billy Johnson, 1895)
→ Carburetor (George Kingston, 1902)
→ Stainless Steel (Elwood Haynes, 1912)
→ Howitzer Shell (Superior Machine Tool Company, 1918)
→ Aerial Bomb with Fins (Liberty Pressed Metal, 1918)
→ Mechanical Corn Picker (John Powell, 1922)
→ Dirilyte Golden-Hued Tableware (Carl Molin, 1926)
→ Canned Tomato Juice (Kemp Brothers Canning, 1928)
→ Push-Button Car Radio (Delco, 1938)
→ All-Metal Lifeboat (Globe American Stove, 1941)
→ Signal-Seeking Car Radio (Delco, 1947)
→ Transistor Car Radio (Delco, 1957)

World's Largest Steer and World's Largest Sycamore Stump

It is special enough to be able to visit the stuffed remains of the World's Largest Steer, but to discover that it sits next to the World's Largest Sycamore Stump? Too good to be true! No, you're not in Road Trip Heaven, you're in Kokomo.

Old Ben was a lot of bull . . . er . . . steer. He weighed 135 pounds when he was born in January 1902 on the Murphy farm in Miami County. At a year and a half, he was up to 1,800 pounds, and by the time he was four years old, over 4,000. Old Ben became a local celebrity and toured county fairs. Then tragedy struck in February 1910, when the eight-year-old bovine slipped on a patch of ice and broke his leg. At the time he weighed 4,720 pounds, stood 6 feet 4 inches tall, and was 16 feet 2 inches from nose

A lot of bull.

to tail. Old Ben had to be destroyed, but when a butcher suggested selling his meat to the local community, the locals responded with an emphatic "NO!" Instead, Old Ben was shipped off to a meatpacker in Indianapolis for processing. His hide was stuffed and returned to the Murphy farm, and in 1919 it was donated to the city and placed in the windowed shed where you will find him today.

The tale of the World's Largest Sycamore Stump is every bit as dramatic as that of Old Ben. This 100-foot-tall tree grew for 800-something years along the banks of Wildcat Creek on Tilghman Harrell's farm, two miles north of New London, before being felled by a violent windstorm. The hollowed-out trunk was moved to town in 1916 and used for some time as a phone booth. Today, the stump with the 57-foot circumference is protected from the public in the same shed in Highland Park as Old Ben.

Highland Park Visitors Center, 1402 W. Defenbaugh St., Kokomo, IN 46902
Phone: (765) 456-7275
Hours: Daily 8 AM–10 PM
Cost: Free
Website: www.cityofkokomo.org/departments/old_ben.php
Directions: Five blocks south of Markland Ave., at the north end of the park.

Lafayette
Pizza King

If you drive around Indiana long enough, you'll think there's a Pizza King in every town with a stoplight. This Hoosier chain started on the south side of Lafayette at a venue that still stands. And it is perhaps the strangest restaurant in the state.

The carpeted booths seem more like office cubicles than restaurant furniture; their backs are so high you won't see any other patrons except those directly across the aisle. This is good, because each booth is outfitted with its own coin-operated television. If your date's a drag, just pop a quarter into the control box in the wall, and you'll get 15 minutes of video entertainment. Magic Fingers for your brain.

To place an order, pick up the tableside phone—no wait staff here! Your drinks will arrive on a toy train that runs along the booths, protected by a Plexiglas window and decorated with scenes from Lafayette-area attractions. Don't worry that another customer can spike your drink; only the trap door at the destination booth can be opened when the train is in operation.

And the pizza? Well . . . the trains and TV make up for a lot . . .

Jefferson Square, 1400 Teal Rd., Lafayette, IN 47909
Phone: (765) 474-3414
Hours: Sunday–Thursday 11 AM–11 PM, Friday–Saturday 11 AM–1 AM
Cost: Meals $5–12
Website: www.theoriginalpizzaking.com
Directions: East of Ninth St. on Teal Rd., across from the Tippecanoe Fairgrounds.

Dinner is served!

Lebanon
World's Tallest Limestone Columns

. . . Made from Single Pieces of Limestone—an important caveat. While you'd think that the world's tallest single-piece limestone columns would be found on the Lincoln Memorial or the Acropolis, they actually grace the Boone County Courthouse in the Indiana town of Lebanon. The problem is logistics—how do you move a 40-ton pillar hundreds of miles from its original quarry? You can't. But if you live in Indiana, where limestone quarries are everywhere, it's doable and *was* done in 1912.

There are eight columns in all. Each is 36 feet tall and more than 14 feet in circumference. They're located on the north and south entrances of the building and really are impressive, especially up close. So impressive, apparently, that they attracted William "Captain Kirk" Shatner and his fourth wife, Elizabeth Martin, who were married here on February 13, 2001.

The structure isn't the only unique feature of this courthouse. Though you can't see it, a resident cat lives on the roof of the building. It's up there to drive away the pigeons that tend to poop on great works of architecture. The feline has its own warm house in which to seek shelter during bad weather, so don't feel too bad for it.

Boone County Courthouse, Courthouse Square, Lebanon, IN 46052
Phone: (765) 482-3510
Hours: Always visible
Cost: Free
Website: www.boonecounty.in.gov
Directions: At the intersection of Lebanon (Rte. 39) and Main Sts., one block north of South St. (Rte. 32).

Marion
James Dean's Birthplace

On February 8, 1931, Winton and Mildred Dean became proud parents of a boy they named James Byron Dean. At the time, they lived in the Green Gables apartments, where they stayed until young Jimmy was three, when his father came up with a harebrained scheme to raise bullfrogs for profit. The trio moved into a house at Washington and Vine Streets in nearby

Fairmount, but as you might expect with a home-based frog farm, the orders didn't come rolling in. Soon, the family left for California so his dad could accept a position at a Los Angeles VA hospital.

As big a star as James Dean is, very little marked his birthplace until recently. Green Gables was torn down long ago, and for years the land was used for a tire store parking lot. A bronze star was embedded in the sidewalk to mark the historic site—dedicated by Martin Sheen, no less—along with a small plaque near a bus stop bench. The land was later made into a small, shrub-encircled park with a *2001*-like black obelisk engraved with a picture of Dean as a baby.

Best One Tire & Auto Care, 302 E. Fourth Sts., Marion, IN 46952
Phone: (765) 664-6460
Hours: Always visible
Cost: Free
Website: www.bestoneofmarion.com
Directions: Two blocks east of the courthouse on E. Fourth St. (Rte. 18), on the southwest corner of E. Fourth and S. McClure Sts.

Metamora
Grannie's Cookie Jars & Ice Cream Parlor

Eva Fuchs, a.k.a. Grannie, is a big-time hoarder . . . which doesn't mean she isn't discerning—just cookie jars and salt and pepper shakers, thank you very much. Over the years she's collected so many, 2,600+ at last count, the *Guinness Book of World Records* has named her porcelain obsession the World's Largest Collection of Cookie Jars.

LAFAYETTE

⇒ Lafayette has sometimes been derided by local towns as "Laugh-at" or "Lay-flat."

⇒ Clown Emmett Kelly, creator of the character Weary Willie, is buried in Lafayette's Rest Haven Memorial Park Cemetery (1200 N. Sagamore Parkway, (765) 447-1797).

⇒ Guns 'N' Roses singer Axl Rose was born William Bruce Baily in Lafayette on February 6, 1962.

Fuchs has jars shaped like gingerbread houses, cartoon characters, Santas and snowpeople, oversized fruit, vehicles, clowns, animals (dogs, cats, pigs, and cows are favorites), decorated crocks, and more. They're all crammed into display cases and shelves, along with the shakers, in Metamora's historic two-room Canal House building, which also doubles as an ice cream parlor. If you're a klutz or a kid, you might want to wait outside and have somebody else fetch your waffle cone—one wrong turn or jutting elbow and you'll be buying a pile of worthless pottery shards.

10107 Columbia St., Metamora, IN 47030
Phone: (765) 647-1708
Hours: May–October, daily 10 AM–6 PM
Cost: Free; Ice cream, $3.50/scoop
Directions: One block south of Rte. 52, on the east end of town.

Montpelier
Hollywood Giants

Watch the opening credits of *Parks and Recreation* and you'll notice a large fiberglass Indian in a full headdress and fringed leather belt, arm upstretched to greet (or hold back) incoming settlers. But this guy doesn't reside in Pawnee, Indiana—nobody does, since the town is imaginary; he lives in Montpelier. He started his public life outside a Pontiac dealership but now honors less commercial pursuits. A sign in front of him claims that he is Chief Francois Godfroy of the Miami nation, who in 1818 signed a treat at St. Mary's, Ohio, which moved the tribe to a 3,840-acre reservation on the nearby Salamonie River. That land was sold off by 1836, and now he's the primary reminder the Miami were ever here.

Another statue of a large man, this one a golfer in a red cap and windbreaker, also appears in the TV show's opening credits. He guards the now-closed Tin Lizzy restaurant west of town with an empty ice cream cone in his hand. Will he ever get a second scoop?

Main & Huntington Sts., Montpelier, IN 47359
Phone: (765) 728-2246
Hours: Always visible
Cost: Free
Website: www.montpelier-indiana.com
Directions: On Rte. 18 (Huntington St.) downtown.

Tin Lizzy Restaurant, 7126 N. State Rd. 3, Montpelier, IN 47359
No phone
Hours: Always visible
Cost: Free
Directions: Five miles west of town on Rte. 3, at Rte. 18.

Not in Hollywood.

THE REST OF THE TRIBE

The Montpelier Indian is certainly the best-known fiberglass chief in the state and has the ceremonial headdress to prove it, but there are others along Indiana's byways.

Camp Tecumseh Indian

12635 W. Tecumseh Bend Rd., Brookston, (765) 564-2898, www.camptecumseh.org

This YMCA camp's mascot balances atop a pergola overlooking a playing field. He was moved here from a Gary auto dealership in 1973 and today has forsaken capitalistic pursuits for religious ones—a large sign at his feet commands, GO IN PEACE, SERVE GOD AND MAN.

Low-Riding Indian

Richard's of Toto, 3060 S. Range Rd., Toto, (574) 772-5923, www.richardsoftoto.com

The giant brave outside a discount mall in Toto has no headdress but, instead, one very tiny feather in his headband. For some reason his leather pants hang dangerously low on his hips. He originally appeared at the Enchanted Forest amusement park in Porter, but when that institution went under, he was moved here. Back in 2015, half of his upraised arm was torn off, but it has since been restored.

Cigar Store Indians

www.cigarstoreindianstatue.com

Let's face it, a 20-foot statue isn't practical for most businesses or homes. If you want to decorate with an Old West theme, check out the creations of Indianapolis sculptor Chie Kramer. He has carved more than 6,000 cigar store Indians during his career, and you can get a six-foot model for just $600.

Muncie
David Letterman, C Student

When David Letterman attended Ball State during the 1960s, his ironic sensibility had yet to pay off, or at least pay off in a positive way. His first broadcasting gig came as a student DJ on the campus classical station, WBST, a 10-watt station. One evening he introduced Debussy's *Clair de Lune* by asking aloud, "You know the de Lune sisters? There was Claire, there was Mabel . . ." Letterman was promptly canned.

His next "job" was at WAGO, a pirate station run from a men's dorm, followed by a position at local outlet WERK. He worked harder at his broadcasting career than his broadcasting major and graduated with a C average. But if Letterman was embarrassed about his academic performance, all that went out the window in 1985 when he established the Letterman Scholarship for telecommunications students with C averages. Brainiacs and apple-polishers need not apply! He also rehabbed the Communication Department's television and radio studios and mounted a plaque that reads, DEDICATED TO ALL THE C STUDENTS BEFORE AND AFTER ME.

Ball Communications Building, McKinley Ave. & Petty Rd., Muncie, IN 47306
Phone: (765) 285-1889
Hours: Daily 9 AM–5 PM
Cost: Free
Website: http://cms.bsu.edu/map/buildings/campus/ball-communication-building
Directions: Two blocks north of Riverside Ave. on McKinley Ave.

MUNCIE

➡ "If Rip van Winkle went to sleep 50 years ago and returned to Muncie today, he would not have too many adjustment problems." — Robert S. Lynd

➡ Fishing tackle is not allowed in Muncie cemeteries.

➡ Many of the opening scenes of *Close Encounters of the Third Kind* were set in Muncie, though they were not filmed here.

National Model Aviation Museum

For all those who never outgrew their childhood fascination with model airplanes, Muncie's the place to go, because in 1994 the Academy of Model Aeronautics moved its headquarters to the Hoosier state, and it brought all its cool toys with it. The AMA's museum is a re-creation of a 1950s hobby store where nothing is actually for sale, but you can stand with your nose pressed against the display cases crammed with classic models and salivate.

The museum is adjacent to an airplane runway—miniature, of course—where on most days from spring to fall you can find RC enthusiasts flying tiny planes, helicopters, and rockets, so long as the weather cooperates.

Academy of Model Aeronautics, 5151 E. Memorial Dr., Muncie, IN 47302
Phone: (800) I-FLY-AMA
Hours: January–March, Tuesday–Saturday 10 AM–4 PM; April–September, daily 10 AM–4 PM
Cost: Adults $4, Kids (8–17) $2
Website: www.modelaircraft.org/museum/museum.aspx
Directions: Exit Rte. 35 at Memorial Dr., then two blocks east.

New Castle
Big Sneaker

Steve Alford has an impressive basketball résumé: Indiana's "Mr. Basketball" in 1983, gold medal winner at the 1984 Olympics, four-year starter at IU under Bobby Knight, second-round draft pick for the NBA's Dallas Mavericks, traded two years later to the Golden State Warriors, then back to Dallas before he retired from play. He went on to be the head coach at Manchester, Southern Missouri State, Iowa, New Mexico, and today UCLA. And though that all sounds soooooo impressive, you might think differently after stopping by the guy's hotel in his hometown of New Castle. Why? The guy couldn't help but win—he's HUGE! Just look at his Volkswagen-sized sneaker—how could any opponent go up against *that*?

Well, it turns out that the powder blue shoe isn't his, at least not to wear. It was created in 1991 by artists Gary Abner and Todd Anders to decorate a billboard advertising Reebok shoes. When the campaign was over, it was given to Alford, and the other half of the pair ended up at the

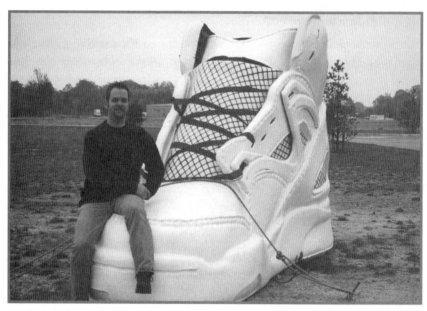

You know what they say about big shoes. Photo by Jim Frost

nearby Indiana Basketball Hall of Fame (1 Hall of Fame Court, (765) 529-1891, www.hoopshall.com). Alford's motel also has a basketball hoop in the parking lot, in case you're looking for a pickup game, as well as a lobby filled with basketball memorabilia.

Steve Alford All-American Inn, 21 E. Executive Dr., New Castle, IN 47362
Phone: (877) 55-STEVE or (765) 593-1212
Hours: Always visible
Cost: Free; Rooms $60–100
Website: www.stevealfordinn.com
Directions: At the south end of town on Rte. 3 (Memorial Dr.), north of I-70.

Oxford
Dan Patch, Gone

Dan Messner thought he had a bum colt. Foaled at Messner's Oxford farm to sire Joe Patchen and dam Zelica on April 29, 1896, Dan Patch had bowed legs, the curse of a harness racer. Messner tried to trade Dan Patch to a local horse trainer named John Wattles, but Wattles turned him down. Dan Patch raced in county fairs, but his promise was never fully realized.

Messner finally sold the pacer to M. E. Sturgis of New York in 1902, who later that year sold him to Marion Willis Savage of Minneapolis. In greener pastures, Dan Patch went on to set a world record for the mile, 1:55, in 1906. This record time stood for 32 years and is still painted on the roof of the barn where the horse was born in Oxford.

Dan Patch never lost a race and came in second only twice during heats. The secret of his success was discovered only after his death on July 11, 1916: his heart was found to be twice the size of a normal horse's heart, weighing a whopping 9 pounds 2 ounces. Owner Marion Savage, whose heart was not as strong as Dan Patch's, died a day after his famous horse.

Rtes. 352 & 55, Oxford, IN 47971
No phone
Hours: Always visible
Cost: Free
Dan Patch website: www.danpatch.com
Directions: Northeast of the intersection of Rtes. 352 and 55.

Pendleton
Mob Town

Pendleton is a mob town—not capital *M* Mob, as in Mafia, but lowercase mob. No less than two famous mob riots have occurred in Pendleton, and both have been commemorated with roadside markers. And they're about 50 feet apart.

The first riot—a slaughter, actually—occurred in 1824. On March 22, seven white men attacked two Seneca families along Deer Lick Creek, site of present-day Pendleton. They murdered nine, four of whom were children, and took their pelts and other items. The incident became known as the Fall Creek Massacre. The first perpetrator captured was put on trial and executed on January 12, 1825, making it the first time in Indiana a white settler was put to death for murdering a Native American. Three others were later tried and convicted of murder. On June 3, 1825, two were executed in Pendleton, but the final killer, 15-year-old John Bridge Jr., was pardoned at the last second by Governor James Brown Ray, who rode up to the gallows on horseback. Today a cement marker in the town park records it bluntly: THREE WHITE MEN WERE HUNG HERE IN 1825 FOR KILLING INDIANS.

Another incident occurred on September 16, 1843. Abolitionists Frederick Douglass, George Bradburn, and William White had come to Pendleton on a lecture tour organized by the Massachusetts Anti-Slavery Society. Midway through Bradburn's speech a mob of 30 locals attacked with stones and brickbats. Douglass was knocked unconscious but was carried to safety by supporters. He returned to speak the next day at the Friends Meetinghouse, without incident. Unlike with the Fall Creek Massacre, nobody was arrested or punished. A historic plaque can be found in the same park today, just up the hill from the hanging marker.

Falls Park, 299 Falls Park Dr., Pendleton, IN 46064
Phone: (765) 788-2222
Hours: Dawn–dusk
Cost: Free
Website: www.fallspark.org
Directions: Both markers are north of the river on the southeast side of Pendleton Ave.; the Hanging Marker is due north of the footbridge, and the Abolitionist Marker is west of Pets & Vets, northeast of the Fall Creek bridge.

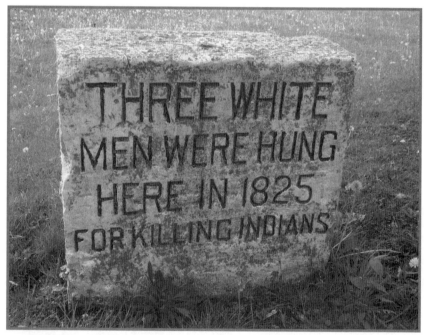

They had it coming.

Terre Haute
Birthplace of the Curvaceous Coke Bottle

For many years, Coca-Cola was sold in a standard glass bottle. Ho hum. Then, in 1913, the company launched a manufacturers' competition to devise a unique bottle. A fellow named T. Clyde Edwards, working for Terre Haute's Root Glass Works, saw a drawing of a bulging, ribbed, cocoa bean pod and modeled what later became known as the distinctive "hobble skirt" or "Mae West" bottle after it. Edwards was assisted by Alexander Samuelson in devising a manufacturing process, and in 1916 Coke launched its new look. Samuelson and Root owned the patent until 1937, when the Coca-Cola Corporation bought them out.

The original hobble skirt was much fatter in the middle than today's bottle, as you will see at the Vigo County Museum. They have one of the Root Glass Works's original molds, a bottle formed inside it, and display cases crammed with Cokeabilia.

Thornton Oil Corp (former site of Root Glass Works), 2330 S. Third St., Terre Haute, IN 47802
Phone: (812) 234-3102
Hours: Always visible
Cost: Free
Directions: On the northeast corner of S. Third St. (Rte. 41/150) and Voorhees St.

Vigo County Historical Society Museum, 1411 S. Sixth St., Terre Haute, IN 47802
Phone: (812) 235-9717
Hours: Tuesday–Sunday 1–4 PM
Cost: Free
Website: www.vchsmuseum.org/#!coca-cola/c18xx
Directions: At the corner of Washington Ave. and S. Sixth St.

Bronze Larry Bird

When you think of Larry Bird you probably don't think "bronze." In reality, he's so white he's almost translucent. But there is one place you can find him in a bronzed condition: outside the Hulman Center on the campus of Indiana State. Byrd played college hoops for the ISU Sycamores from 1976 to 1979, and all his home games were played at this arena.

Erected in 2013, this 15-foot-tall bronze by sculptor Bill Wolfe shows the Hick from French Lick mid–jump shot in his 1970s short shorts and knee-high tube socks. And if you'd like to see a yellow, somewhat uglier version of Byrd, there's a wooden totem, carved with a chainsaw, outside the Boot City Opry complex (11800 US Hwy. 41, (812) 299-8379, http://bootcityopry.com) south of town.

Hulman Center, 200 N. Eighth St., Terre Haute, IN 47809
Phone: (812) 237-3737
Hours: Always visible
Cost: Free
Website: www2.indstate.edu/hctaf/events /events.htm
Directions: Two blocks north of Wabash Ave. at Cherry St.

As bronzed as you'll ever see him.

Square Donuts

First the Coke bottle, and now this? What will those talented Terre Hauteans come up with next? The concept is brilliant in its simplicity. By making a donut square, you can do one of two things: (1) fit *more* donuts on the same-sized tray, or (2) fit *larger* donuts on the same-sized tray. Either way you maximize its donut capacity!

Square donut technology is still in its infancy, for although the outer edges of these delicious dunkers are square, their holes are still round. No doubt somebody is working to crack that challenge in the bakery's backroom laboratory.

Even if the donuts weren't square, they'd be worth a stop—not quite Krispy Kremes, but as close as you'll get around here. The bakery has two locations in Terre Haute: one downtown and one on the north side. It also has seven franchises in four other cities: Indianapolis (6416 W. Washington St. and 1 N. Pennsylvania St.), Carmel (14 S. Rangeline Rd.), Bloomington (1280 N. College Ave. and 3866 W. Third St.), and Richmond (1241 N. West Fifth St. and 3637 E. National Rd.). Still, you'll want to come to Terre Haute—somehow the donuts just taste squarer there.

925 Wabash Ave., Terre Haute, IN 47807
Phone: (812) 232-6463
Hours: Daily 6 AM–3 PM
Cost: 75¢/donut, $8/dozen
Website: www.squaredonuts.com
Directions: Six blocks east of Third St. (Rte. 41) on Wabash (Rte. 40).

2417 Fort Harrison Rd., Terre Haute, IN 47804
Phone: (812) 466-9660
Hours: Daily 6–11 AM
Cost: 75¢/donut, $8/dozen
Directions: Five blocks east of Lafayette Ave. on Ft. Harrison Rd.

It's not just the donuts that are square. Photo by Jim Frost

Stiffy Green, the Stiff Dog

The story has been passed between generations of Terre Hauteans. When he was alive, Stiffy Green followed florist John Heinl everywhere, and when Heinl died in 1920, the distraught loyal bulldog sat outside Heinl's tomb to guard his dead master. Stiffy wouldn't eat, and before long he was found dead beside the mausoleum. Somebody got the bright idea to stuff Stiffy and place him inside the tomb to guard the vault for eternity.

Local teens would head out to the cemetery to peer through the bars where, according to legend, Stiffy would stare back with glowing green eyes or wag his tail. Other visitors have claimed to have spotted the ghosts of Stiffy and Heinl, smoking a pipe, strolling through the graveyard at night. Together again.

Too bad it's all a fabrication. In reality, Stiffy is *very* stiff—he's made of concrete. The dog once stood outside the Heinl home in town and was later placed inside the family crypt. After years of vandalism, Stiffy was removed in 1985 and donated to the local historical society where you can find him today, inside a re-created tomb. And Heinl's tomb in Highland Lawn? Empty . . . except for the Heinls.

Highland Lawn Cemetery, 4420 Wabash Ave., Terre Haute, IN 47803
Phone: (812) 877-2531
Hours: Daily 9 AM–5 PM
Cost: Free
Website: www.terrehaute.in.gov/departments/cemetery/highland-lawn-cemetery-1
Directions: Head east on Wabash Ave. (Rte. 40) from downtown, on the left (north) just past the railroad overpass.

Vigo County Historical Society Museum, 1411 S. Sixth St., Terre Haute, IN 47802
Phone: (812) 235-9717
Hours: Tuesday–Sunday 1–4 PM
Cost: Free
Website: www.vchsmuseum.org/#!local-legends/ce9u
Directions: At the corner of Washington Ave. and S. Sixth St.

FUNKY GRAVES IN HIGHLAND LAWN

So Stiffy's no longer at Highland Lawn. No problem—there are still plenty of interesting monuments and dead folks to see at this scenic cemetery.

First, check out the mausoleum of **Martin Sheets**. It has a chandelier and a telephone inside. Sheets was afraid he would be buried alive, so he had the phone installed to link him to the caretaker's office. Legend says he also put whiskey bottles in the pillars of the tomb so he would have something to drink until the caretaker arrived. Still wilder claims say flowers appear inside the crypt, even when nobody has brought them. According to locals, when Sheets's wife, Susan, died years later she was found clutching a phone receiver. Had Martin given her a call? Perhaps. When the tomb was opened to put her in, they found *his* phone off the hook.

The plot of **John Robert Craig** resembles a bed. The traveling salesman died of a heart attack while having relations with a woman other than his wife in an Indianapolis hotel room on New Year's Eve 1931. Craig's wife commissioned his headstone and coldly observed, "He made his bed. Now he'll lie in it."

Chief Bearfoot (born Benjamin Harrison Myers), a longtime performer with Buffalo Bill's Wild West Show, lies beneath a large granite slab with two silver conch shells embedded in its surface. Open the copper plate on the slab's face and you'll see a color photo of the chief in his war bonnet.

Another dead performer buried at Highland Lawn, **Louis Rudoph Yansky Sr.**, worked the vaudeville circuit for years as a strongman. He was known to challenge audience members to out-strong him, and he always won. Today, not so much.

You probably don't know who **Ellen Church Marshall** is, but she worked for United Airlines from 1930 to 1932. She has the distinction of being the nation's first airline hostess, later known as a stewardess, later known as a flight attendant. Coffee, tea, or embalming fluid?

Just inside the main gate is a globe-shaped marker marking the grave of **Frank Wiedemann**, developer of the X-ray machine. Wiedemann used the profits from his invention to become a world traveler, hence the tombstone.

Anna White was not a famous individual, not in this life anyway. But in a previous life she might have been Egypt's Queen Nefertiti, for in this life (death, actually) White is buried in an oversized pyramid-shaped tomb.

And finally, Socialist and labor leader **Eugene Debs** is interred somewhere in his family's plot—he has a headstone, but it's not over his head. For security reasons, the exact location is a secret.

World's First Pay Toilets

Time to review a few Terre Haute inventions. Curvaceous Coke bottles? Great! Square donuts? Delicious! Pay toilets? Talk about getting you coming and going . . .

Back when there were more railroads running through Terre Haute, Union Station sat at the intersection of north-south and east-west lines near downtown. The station installed what was, apparently, a newfangled luxury at the time: public toilets. The trouble was, so many of the locals were stopping by for a visit that the railroad customers had to wait for a seat. So in 1910, the stationmaster started charging five cents a visit . . . unless you were a ticket-carrying passenger . . . and the modern pay toilet was born.

Union Station, 10th & Wabash Sts., Terre Haute, IN 47807
No phone
Hours: Torn down
Cost: 5¢
Directions: Campus Lot J on Wabash between 9th ½ St. and 10th Sts.

West College Corner
Town Cut in Half

In a world filled with ethnic and regional strife, we should all look to Indiana/Ohio community as an example of civic harmony. West College Corner, Indiana, and College Corner, Ohio, have been getting along for some time. Their states' border runs through the middle of town, which requires that they have different mayors, fire departments, water systems, and taxes, but they have only one post office, united under zip codes 47003 (IN) and 45003 (OH). During daylight savings time, the towns sit in different time zones, so you can leave work in College Corner and arrive home in West College Corner before you punched out. On the downside, you can leave your home in Indiana for a five-minute commute to Ohio and pull into your job an hour late. Still, somehow it all works out.

Back in 1893 the towns built a single high school that straddled the state line. When the building was replaced in 1926, they kept the two-state arrangement. Over the new school's west entrance was a sign saying INDIANA, and over the east entrance was a sign saying OHIO. Inside the building the border runs right down the centerline of the gym's basketball court. Today the building is an elementary school whose office is on the Ohio side.

College Corner Union Elementary, 320 Ramsey St., West College Corner, OH 45003
Phone: (765) 732-3183
Hours: Always visible
Cost: Free
Website: www.uc.k12.in.us/college-corner-union-elementary/college-corner-union-elementary/
Directions: Head north on Stateline St., five blocks north of where the railroad tracks cross Rte. 27.

Hoosiers to the left, Buckeyes to the right.

West Lafayette
Another Small Step for a Man

Purdue University calls itself the "Cradle of Astronauts" because 23 alumni (to date) have gone to outer space, including the first human to set foot on the moon, Neil Armstrong. After serving as a pilot in the US Navy, he attended and graduated from Purdue in 1955 with a BS in aeronautical engineering. You can find a bronze statue of him in penny loafers carrying a slide rule (ask somebody over 60) outside the engineering building named in his honor. Nearby are six Armstrong moonprints striding through the grass. They were cast from Armstrong's original boots but upsized, so it's rather difficult to re-create his bounding lunar gait, unless you imagine yourself under the moon's diminished gravitational field. But if you're a geek, you probably already thought of that.

Neil Armstrong Hall of Engineering, Purdue
    University, 701 W. Stadium Ave., West Lafayette,
    IN 47907
Phone: (765) 494-4600
Hours: Always visible
Cost: Free
Website: https://engineering.purdue.edu/Engr/
    AboutUs/Facilities/ArmstrongHall
Directions: At the intersection of Northwestern
    and Stadium Aves.

Just like the moon, but with grass.

West Terre Haute
St. Anne Shell Chapel

St. Mary-of-the-Woods College started in 1842 as a small convent founded by the Sisters of Providence. A year later, Mother Superior Theodore Guerin went to France to raise funds for the institution and almost perished at sea during the return voyage. Her ship, the *Nashville*, encountered a violent storm, so Mother Superior prayed to St. Anne for deliverance. And deliver she did—the *Nashville* made it safely back to North America.

Guerin decided to build a chapel in honor of her favorite lifesaving saint. It was a simple log cabin and was finished in 1844. But it hardly seemed worthy of such a nautical miracle. So in 1875, Sister Mary Joseph le Fer de la Motte and a group of novices began collecting shells from the Wabash River to embed into the walls of a new chapel. And the altar. And the ceiling. And everywhere, except the floor. Some shells were arranged to form images, like a map of Indiana and the waves from the *Nashville*'s voyage. The chapel was finally dedicated on July 25, 1876.

St. Mary-of-the-Woods College, 3301 St. Mary's Rd., West Terre Haute, IN 47885
Phone: (812) 535-5151
Hours: Call ahead to have it unlocked

Cost: Free
Website: www.smwc.edu/resources/historic-architecture/saint-annes-shell-chapel
Directions: On campus at the east end of Grotto Ln., just west of the cemetery.

Whiteland

Gassy Garden

Amlico, Paraland, El Reco, Sovereign, DX, and Zephyr. Horses in the Kentucky Derby? Nope, they're long-since-bankrupt American gas and oil companies. And unless you're very old, you might not even know they existed were it not for Alan Ray Whitaker. He has collected and displays almost 50 classic metal gas company signs, all mounted atop 18-foot poles like giant porcelain flowers in a gravel-covered garden. Some of them are familiar, like Texaco, Gulf, and Esso, but most will be a complete mystery to you.

649 Brewer St., Whiteland, IN 46184
No phone
Hours: Always visible
Cost: Free
Directions: One block north of Main St., one block west of State St.

WILLIAMSPORT

➡ **Williamsport Falls,** a 90-foot cascade in the town of Williamsport, is the highest free-falling waterfall in the state of Indiana.

WINCHESTER

➡ A Winchester ordinance against pornography was so graphic it could not be published in a local paper.

➡ Each July, the town of Winchester hosts the **Aloha International Hawaiian Steel Guitar Convention** (http://aloha-intl.org/).

WINDFALL

➡ The town of Windfall was named after a large storm blew over trees in the area.

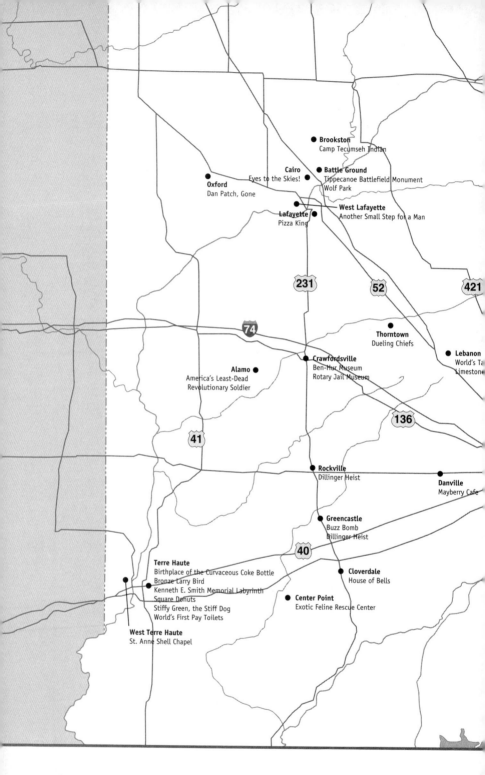

Brookston
Camp Tecumseh Indian

Cairo
Eyes to the Skies!

Oxford
Dan Patch, Gone

Battle Ground
Tippecanoe Battlefield Monument
Wolf Park

Lafayette
Pizza King

West Lafayette
Another Small Step for a Man

231
52
421
74

Thorntown
Dueling Chiefs

Lebanon
World's Ta
Limeston

Alamo
America's Least-Dead
Revolutionary Soldier

Crawfordsville
Ben-Hur Museum
Rotary Jail Museum

136

41

Rockville
Dillinger Heist

Danville
Mayberry Cafe

Greencastle
Buzz Bomb
Dillinger Heist

40

Terre Haute
Birthplace of the Curvaceous Coke Bottle
Bronze Larry Bird
Kenneth E. Smith Memorial Labyrinth
Square Donuts
Stiffy Green, the Stiff Dog
World's First Pay Toilets

Cloverdale
House of Bells

Center Point
Exotic Feline Rescue Center

West Terre Haute
St. Anne Shell Chapel

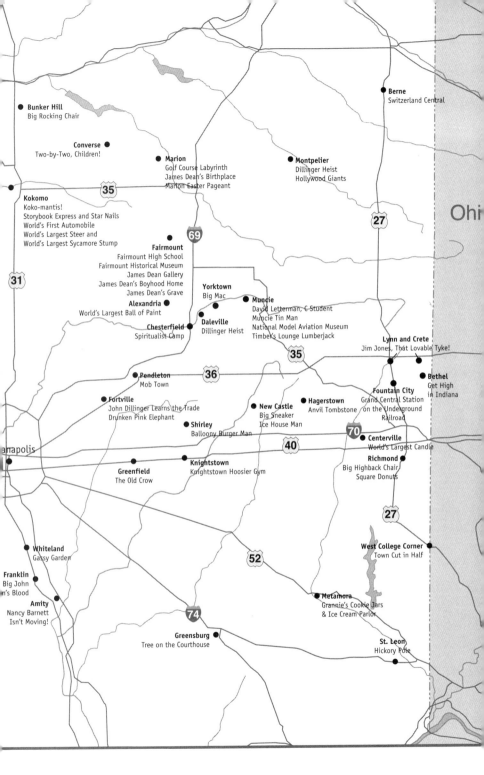

Bunker Hill
Big Rocking Chair

Converse ●
Two-by-Two, Children!

● **Marion**
Golf Course Labyrinth
James Dean's Birthplace
Marion Easter Pageant

35

Kokomo
Koko-mantis!
Storybook Express and Star Nails
World's First Automobile
World's Largest Steer and
World's Largest Sycamore Stump

69

●
Fairmount
Fairmount High School
Fairmount Historical Museum
James Dean Gallery
James Dean's Boyhood Home
James Dean's Grave

31

Alexandria ●
World's Largest Ball of Paint

Yorktown
Big Mac

Chesterfield ●
Spiritualist Camp

● **Daleville**
Dillinger Heist

● **Muncie**
David Letterman, C Student
Muncie Tin Man
National Model Aviation Museum
Timber's Lounge Lumberjack

● **Berne**
Switzerland Central

● **Montpelier**
Dillinger Heist
Hollywood Giants

27

Ohi

Lynn and Crete
Jim Jones, That Lovable Tyke!

35

● **Pendleton**
Mob Town

36

● **Bethel**
Get High
in Indiana

● **Fortville**
John Dillinger Learns the Trade
Drunken Pink Elephant

● **Shirley**
Balloony Burger Man

● **New Castle**
Big Sneaker
Ice House Man

● **Hagerstown**
Anvil Tombstone

Fountain City
Grand Central Station
on the Underground
Railroad

70

40

● **Centerville**
World's Largest Candle

● **Knightstown**
Knightstown Hoosier Gym

Greenfield
The Old Crow

Richmond
Big Highback Chair
Square Donuts

anapolis

27

● **Whiteland**
Gassy Garden

Franklin
Big John
n's Blood

52

West College Corner
Town Cut in Half

Amity
Nancy Barnett
Isn't Moving!

74

● **Metamora**
Grannie's Cookie Jars
& Ice Cream Parlor

Greensburg ●
Tree on the Courthouse

St. Leon
Hickory Pole

3

SOUTHERN INDIANA

Something strange happens when you reach southern Indiana. As the state's cornfields turn upward into gentle hills, the region takes on a Kentucky sensibility. The land of Wonder Bread and Dan Quayle turns to creepy limestone monuments, hillbilly campgrounds, and pig brain sandwiches. They've got museums dedicated to old steamboats and human hair, statues of Joe Palooka and a very large rubber ducky, trees draped in discarded shoes, and the World's Largest Toilet.

And southern Indiana has more than just hillbilly attractions; they've got international places to visit that would take years to see in their original locations. On a three-day weekend you can explore a town named after Santa Claus, a Tibetan Culture Center, a crumbling Egyptian pyramid, and the footprints of the Angel Gabriel—yet never leave the state. So forget snowshoeing to the North Pole, trekking through the Himalayas, jetting to the Middle East, or flying off to heaven. Southern Indiana has it all, and more!

Bean Blossom

Bill Monroe's Bluegrass Hall of Fame & Country Star Museum (& Campground)

Bill Monroe has been dubbed the Father of Bluegrass (not to be confused with Jimmy Martin, the *King* of Bluegrass), and indeed, few folks have done more to preserve this uniquely American musical form. Monroe and his family have hosted the Bean Blossom Bluegrass Festival every spring since the mid-1960s. Performers have included some of the biggest names in country music, and if you step into the Monroes' museum, you can see the outfits they wore: Dolly Parton, Johnny Cash, Loretta Lynn, George Jones, Stringbean, and more. Never heard of Stringbean? You won't forget his costume. If you think kids invented the pants-halfway-down-to-your-knees style, think again.

Back behind the museum is Uncle Pen's Cabin, Monroe's tribute to his Uncle Pendleton Vandiver. Uncle Pen taught Monroe to pick a mandolin and ended up in many of the performer's best-known songs. You're invited to meet Uncle Pen, but he turns out to be a stuffed mannequin, which is a little creepy. If you'd like to set a spell, stay at the adjacent campground or rent a log cabin. The museum hosts many annual music festivals—check its website—so there are plenty of opportunities to listen to banjo-pickin' all night long.

5163 SR 135 N, Bean Blossom, IN 46160
Phone: (800) 414-4677 or (812) 988-6422
Hours: May–October, daily 9 AM–5 PM; November–April, Thursday–Saturday 9 AM–5 PM, Sunday noon–4 PM
Cost: Adults $4, Seniors $3, Kids (12 and under) free
Website: www.billmonroemusicpark.com and www.beanblossom.com
Directions: Five miles north of Nashville on Rte. 135, just north of the Rte. 45 intersection.

Bedford

Bedford Town Crank

In many ways, Sam Shaw is a visionary. Back in 1995, years before everyone started airing their petty personal grievances on the Interwebs, Shaw was taking his issues to the streets. Or at least one street—I Street in Bedford, Indiana, to be exact. And what issues were those? Damned if anyone knows!

It all started when Shaw put up a single hand-painted billboard, which the city unwisely asked him to take down. That was like waving a red flag in front of this cranky bull, as red as the lettering on all his bombastic signs, all liberally filled with quotation marks:

DON'T BE "FOOLED" – GENE MCCRACKEN AND DAN "KIRK" ARE FOR COUNTYWIDE ZONEING

SIMPLE VETERANS "NO" GUTS "NO" GLORY

MAYOR GIRGIS YOU CANNOT DANCE WITH THE "DEVIL" AND GO HOME WITH "JESUS"

FLAG – AMERICAN OR CHINA? NO GUTS NO GLORY – LOOKS GOOD

. . . and on, and on, and on. During the 2016 election he made his political leanings clear:

and suddenly the signs made a little more nonsensical sense.

Shaw's neighbors have recently gotten into the spirit, posting their own signs across the street, all painted in the same red-and-white style. Here's a beaut:

> Honk! If you support Sam for Village Idiot –
> He might actually win!

This uncivil civic debate will likely continue for some time. After all, as another Shaw sign says:

> These signs will "stay" No one pays
> attention anyway

Well, *we're* paying attention!

620 I St., Bedford, IN 47521
Phone: (812) 275-6102
Hours: Daylight
Cost: Free
Directions: One block south of Rte. 58 (Fifth St.).

The debate on I Street.

DOWN UNDER DOWN UNDER

Southern Indiana, with its thick limestone geology, is riddled with caves. For avid spelunkers, there are plenty of undeveloped caverns to explore. But for those tourists who don't want to spend their time crawling through bat guano for the thrill of falling down a bottomless pit, there are safer options. Unfortunately, because of the spread of white-nose syndrome, a fungal infection wiping out North America's bat populations, some familiar attractions like Wyandotte Cave have closed to the public. See the rest while you still can.

Mauckport: Squire Boone Caverns and Village

Squire Boone and his older brother, Daniel, found this southern Indiana cavern in 1787 while exploring the region, and while Daniel went on to bigger and better things, Squire settled down and built a grist mill in 1804. Though he made his living aboveground, Boone spent his free time exploring the hole under his place.

Boone loved his cave so much he requested to be buried there and in 1815 got his final wish. Nobody kept track of where exactly his body was interred, so when human bones were unearthed in 1974, everyone assumed they'd found the cavern's namesake. The remains were placed in a walnut casket along the underground walkway, unburied and chilled to a constant 54°F, which is where you can see them today.

But that's not all. Squire Boone Caverns is more "active" than most caves. Blind, albino crawfish live in an underground river flowing past the cave's stalactites and stalagmites. You can see them, but they can't see you!

100 Squire Boone Rd., Mauckport, IN 47142
Phone: (888) 934-1804 or (812) 732-4381
Hours: June–August, Monday–Friday 10 AM–5 PM, Saturday–Sunday 10 AM–6 PM; September–May, 10 AM–4 PM
Cost: Adults $16, Seniors (60+) $14, Kids (4–11) $8.50

Website: www.squireboonecaverns.com
Directions: Ten miles south of town on Rte. 135, then left on Squire Boone Caverns Rd.

Marengo: Marengo Cave

If you're looking for stalactites and stalagmites, Marengo Cave is your best bet in Indiana. Other caverns have larger "rooms," albino critters, and boat rides, but this is the only place to find formations like Candlestick Park, Crystal Palace, Prison Bars, Indian Bacon, Lion's Cage, Snow White's Castle, Pipe Organ, and the ever-popular Pulpit Rock, where dozens of spelunkers have tied the knot. The cave also has a reverse wishing well where you can toss your loose change *up*—if the coins stick to the clay ceiling, your wish will come true.

Marengo Cave was discovered in 1883 by two siblings and is a National Historic Landmark. Every year the caves host a "marathon" run down the Dripstone Trail. The toughest aspect of the run is dodging stone outcroppings in the near-darkness. The easiest part is jogging along a comfortable 54°F track.

400 E. State Rd. 64, PO Box 217, Marengo, IN 47140
Phone: (888) 702-2837 or (812) 365-2705
Hours: June–August, Monday–Friday 9 AM–6 PM, Saturday–Sunday 9 AM–6:30 PM;
  September–May, daily 9 AM–5 PM
Cost: Adults $16–27, Kids (4–12) $9–16 (Depending on the tour)
Website: www.marengocave.com
Directions: Just north of town off Rte. 64.

Bedford: Bluespring Caverns

White River tributaries have carved an underground wonderland near Bedford where blind, albino fish and crawdads thrive. Visitors to Bluespring Caverns can take a Myst'ry River Voyage in an electric boat through 4,000 feet of flooded passageways, the longest navigable "lost river" in the nation. And this place is cool: 54°F, to be exact.

Bluespring Caverns was discovered in the 1940s by farmer George Colglazier. A pond on his farm drained overnight, and since his livestock didn't seem particularly thirsty, he figured something must be going on below his feet. He was right. Cavers continue to find more passageways; recent discoveries suggest that this hole in the ground is one of the 10 largest in the world.

1459 Bluespring Caverns Rd., Bedford, IN 47421

Phone: (812) 279-9471

Hours: June–August, daily 9 AM–5 PM; March–May, September–October, Monday–Friday 9 AM–4 PM, Saturday–Sunday 9 AM–5 PM

Cost: Adults $16, Kids (3–15) $8

Website: www.bluespringcaverns.com

Directions: Five miles southwest of town on Rte. 50, west on County Road 450S to Bluespring Caverns Rd.

Corydon: Indiana Caverns

If the frigid temperature of the previous three caves concerns you, head over to Indiana Caverns where it's a two full degrees warmer: 56°F. You'll appreciate the extra heat, as this is the state's longest cave at 40 miles. No, you won't be hiking the full length of it—unless you get separated from your tour group—but it's nice to know. Part of your tour will be by boat along the cave's underground river looking for one of the 21 different species of troglobites, a general term for subterranean critters. If you worry that your kids might be claustrophobic or troglobitophobic, have them crawl through the cave's aboveground simulator, the Cavern of the Sabertooth, in search of golden skulls. They're not *real* gold, but they're more valuable than a blind crayfish.

1267 Green Acres Dr. SW, Corydon, IN 47112

Phone: (812) 734-1200

Hours: Daily 9 AM–5 PM

Cost: Adults $19.50, Kids (4–12) $10.50

Website: www.indianacaverns.com

Directions: Head south out of town on State Road 135, then left on Shiloh Rd. to Green Acres Dr.

Foote's Tomb and the Bedford Cemetery

Bedford has long been the epicenter of limestone quarrying operations in southern Indiana. With so many expert stone carvers around, you'd expect the monuments in the local cemeteries to be out of this world. Sadly, the graveyards here look much like everywhere else, with a few notable exceptions.

Something's a Foote.

The best tomb in town isn't in a cemetery at all, but carved into a stone outcropping by "Mr. Toburn" in 1840 for town leader Dr. Winthrop Foote. The doctor wanted a spot to inter his brother, Ziba, who drowned in 1806. When Toburn was done, Ziba was moved into a room in the hollowed-out boulder. Winthrop died in 1856 and was placed there too, though details of the burial were lost. That's why locals were so shocked when vandals broke into the vault in 1957. Apparently, Winthrop had himself placed in a mummy-like coffin with gun and ammo at his feet, along with his doctor's bag. Ziba, as expected, was in another room, but a third chamber contained a horse's corpse. Nobody remembers it being put there. The tomb was resealed as it was discovered, and it remains closed to this day.

Foote's Tomb, E. 16th & D Sts., Bedford, IN 47421
No phone
Hours: Always visible
Cost: Free
Directions: Follow the stone markers down the hill 250 feet, bearing left, from E. 16th St. (Rte. 50) at D St., behind the used car lot.

Nearby, Bedford's Green Hill Cemetery contains a few unique markers. One shows a limestone re-creation of young, unlucky stonemason Louis Baker's sloppy workbench on the day he died in 1917. Another monument, this one for Tom Barton, is a full-sized replica of the man and his set of stone golf clubs, as if Barton has a tee time in Bedrock. World War I soldier Michael Wallner is re-created in his doughboy uniform, and a dead girl's straw hat and shoes, re-created in stone, rest beneath a carved tree over her head.

Green Hill Cemetery, 1202 18th St., Bedford, IN 47421
Phone: (812) 275-5110
Hours: Daylight
Cost: Free
Website: www.facebook.com/pages/Green-Hill-Cemetery/116277988399932
Directions: At L St., one block east and two blocks south of the Rte. 50/450 intersection.

STRANGE HOOSIER HEADSTONES

Winthrop Foote isn't the only dead Hoosier with a weird final resting place. Check out these other markers.

A New Way of Spelling

Union Street Cemetery, Union & Valparaiso Sts., Valparaiso

Universalist minister William Cole Talcott wanted to reform the English language to make spelling simpler—and who can blame him? Think of all the time you'd save if "phone" was "fon," and a "new gnu" was a "nu nu." Talcott called his simplified system phonotypy, which he perfected during the 1840s. He started off on the right track, dropping such useless letters as K, Q, and X, but before he was done he'd added 16 other characters, each with a unique sound. As you probably suspect, unless you're a very poor speller, phonotypy never caught on. In fact, the only place you can still see it used today is on Talcott's century-old tombstone:

In memori uv Wm. C. Tolkut ho woz born Des. 25, 1815, and died Des. 30, 1902. He hopt kooperativ industri wud prov a remedi for poverti. He woz a spelin reformr since 1843 and prepared dis epitaf in sienst spelin in his lif.

Anvil Tombstone

West Lawn Cemetery, Maple & High Sts., Hagerstown, No phone

In 1893 William Jennings Wedekind won a horseshoeing competition at the Columbian Exposition in Chicago, and he's not going to let you forget it. When he died in 1926 he was buried under a tombstone topped with an anvil and a chevron plaque that reads, WORLD'S COLUMBIAN HORSE SHOER AWARDED GOLD MEDAL IN 1893. In his life, Wedekind also amassed a huge collection of historic horseshoes (www .horseshoeingmuseum.com/article2.htm), which you can find today split between the Wayne County Historical Museum in Richmond (1150 N. A St., (765) 962-5756, http://waynecoun tyhistoricalmuseum.org) and the Nettle Creek Valley Museum (906 E. Main St., (765) 489-4005, www.waynet.org/nonprofit /nettlecreek_museum.htm) in Hagerstown.

Kitty Cat Tombstone

Fairview Cemetery, CR W. 300N, Linton

In her twilight years, a black cat was the only friend Pollie Barnett had. She had lost her daughter Sylvia years earlier, in 1858, when the 15-year-old ran away from home. Over the next 30 years Pollie and her other daughter, Angeline, wandered 54,000 miles around the surrounding countryside looking for the daughter who never returned. Angeline passed away before Pollie did, so Pollie adopted a black cat to accompany her on her search. When Pollie died on February 27, 1900, her final words were, "Let my cat go. Let it go look for Sylvia." Locals, probably not those who had accused Barnett of being a witch and of torching their barns, eventually erected a tombstone over Pollie with a cat on top, along with the following:

Here Pollie Barnett is at rest
Fr'm deepest grief and toilsome quest.
Her cat, her only friend,
Remained with her until life's end.

Girl on a Gate

Crown Hill Cemetery, 207 S. Shelby St., Salem, (812) 883-2833

Caddy Naugle is a cute little girl, though she's a little cold . . . cold as a rock. She was made out of limestone by a mysterious traveling stonecutter for Caddy's distraught father in 1901. The carver sculpted the dead four-year-old in her father's favorite pose, standing at the gate waiting for him to return from his job at a monument factory. A rumor later circulated in the community that the carver was actually the spirit of St. Joseph, sent to console the man and his wife. Believe what you want.

Bloomfield
World's Largest Jack

There have been plenty of big Jacks over the years—Jack Nicholson, Jack Johnson, Jack Lemmon, Jack Kevorkian—but when folks in Bloomfield brag about their World's Largest Jack, they're talking about a lowercase-j jack, as in car jack. The Bloomfield Manufacturing Company has been manufacturing the Hi-Lift jack since 1905, and on its 100th birthday they built a 20-foot version of the standard 48-inch model and placed it on a pedestal in front of their headquarters. The jack weighs 2,980 pounds and does not actually work, just in case you were thinking of bringing your 60-foot Hummer to town.

Bloomfield Manufacturing Company, 46 W. Spring St., Bloomfield, IN 47424
Phone: (812) 384-4441
Hours: Always visible
Cost: Free
Website: www.hi-lift.com
Directions: At the corner of Franklin & Spring Sts.

BLOOMINGTON
➡ Rocker David Lee Roth was born in Bloomington on October 10, 1954.

Bloomington
Big Brain

You think you're smart? Do you have a brain the size of the one just outside the Department of Psychological & Brain Sciences at Indiana University? No, you don't, because it just happens to be the largest anatomically correct brain in the world!

Artist Amy Brier carved the colossal noodler from six tons of Indiana limestone in 2014. The brain is illuminated by a circle of colored spotlights. Usually they slowly cycle through a series of rainbow hues, but sometimes the brain is bathed in a single color based on sports victories, the weather, or a holiday like Halloween or Christmas. It's best visited at night.

Psychology Building, 1101 E. Tenth St., Bloomington, IN 47405
Phone: (812) 855-2012
Hours: Always visible
Cost: Free
Website: http://psych.indiana.edu
Directions: Two blocks east of Woodlawn Ave. at Walnut Grove St.

A tremendous thinkafier.

Breaking Away

Ask anyone in Bloomington, "Where's the old quarry from *Breaking Away*?" and you'll always get the same response: "Oh, you can't go down there . . ." followed by a wink and an exact set of directions. The swimming hole plays a pivotal role in the 1980 movie following the lives of four high school friends after graduation. Too bad the thing's now empty.

Argue if you will, *Hoosiers* fans, but *Breaking Away* is the best movie ever shot in Indiana, all filmed in and around Bloomington. Steve Tesich, a hometown boy, wrote the script that earned him an Oscar for Best Original Screenplay. Not bad for a "cutter."

If you can't find anyone to direct you to the **Sanders Quarry** on E. Empire Mill Road, or if you're afraid of getting busted for trespassing, there are plenty of other sites from the film to visit. The **Stoller family home** still stands at 756 S. Lincoln Street. So does the **Chi Delta Delta** sorority at 818 E. Third Street, though it's actually the Delta Delta Delta sorority, where you can still serenade the pledges. If anyone accepts your offer, head over to the **IU Student Union** at 900 E. Seventh Street, but don't throw a bowling ball through the trophy case.

Sadly, other key locations are gone. The **Campus Cars** lot—later Cutter Cars—at 1010 S. Walnut Street has been replaced by the offices of Perry Township trustees. **Moocher's run-down apartment** at 170 E. Seventh Street? Bulldozed, which was probably for the best. You also can't punch the time clock at the **Campus Street Car Wash**, which was actually at 375 S. Walnut Street.

A few other sites do remain, built out of sturdy Indiana limestone: the **Monroe County Courthouse** at Seventh and Walnut Streets, where Moocher and Nancy go stag on a marriage license, and IU's **Herman B. Wells Library** at 1320 E. Tenth Street, where you can have a heart-to-heart with your father about all your unrealized dreams. Sorry to report, the **Little 500 Stadium** on Tenth Street was torn down not long after the movie was wrapped, though the race is still held each spring at a new venue. And you can always bike out through the Brown County countryside, singing in Italian and chasing CinZano trucks. Everyone else does.

Bloomington Visitor's Bureau, 2855 N. Walnut St., Bloomington, IN 47404
Phone: (800) 800-0037 or (812) 334-8900

Hours: Monday–Friday 8:30 AM–5 PM, Saturday 10 AM–3 PM
Cost: Free
Website: www.visitbloomington.com
Little 500 Website: www.iusf.indiana.edu/little500/fans/index.shtml
Directions: North of Rte. 45 (Matlock Rd.) on Walnut St.

Don't jump! Photo by James Lane

George Washington and the Prime Directive

Indiana University's Lilly Library, being both young and well-endowed, has a rare book collection like no other. It has George Washington's acceptance letter for the presidency and the complete scripts of *Star Trek: The Next Generation*. You can find a Gutenberg Bible and Thomas Jefferson's copy of the Bill of Rights next to movie scripts for *Citizen Kane*, *Jaws*, *The Godfather*, and *Gone with the Wind*. It has a copy of the world's first children's book, *The History of Little Goody Two Shoes* (John Newberry, 1768), as well as television scripts from *Hazel*, *The Mary Tyler Moore Show*, *I Love Lucy*, and the complete annotated scripts from *Laugh-In*. A recent donation from Peter Bogdanovich puts Lilly in possession of the *Paper Moon* and *What's Up, Doc?* scripts.

In 2006 the library acquired the Slocum Puzzle Collection, more than 30,000 physical puzzles like the ones your grandparents bought you to keep you occupied and quiet—bent three-penny nails tangled together, deconstructed wooden blocks, Rubik's Cubes, and such. They're not all on display, but you will find 400 or so in cases surrounding the Slocum Puzzle Room.

For obvious reasons, the collection is not open for the general public to thumb through. If they did, there would be a lot of Trekkies violating the Prime Directive. But the Lilly Library does have rotating displays of some of its more interesting artifacts.

The Lilly Library, 1200 E. Seventh St., Bloomington, IN 47405
Phone: (812) 855-2452
Hours: September–April, Monday–Friday 9 AM–6 PM, Saturday 9 AM–1 PM; May–August, Monday–Thursday 9 AM–6 PM, Friday 9 AM–5 PM, Saturday 9 AM–1 PM
Cost: Free
Website: www.indiana.edu/~liblilly/
Directions: East three blocks on Seventh St. from Woodlawn Ave., until it ends.

Kinsey Institute for Research in Sex, Gender, and Reproduction

When university entomologist Alfred Kinsey changed his field of study from the gall wasp to human sexuality in the 1940s, he probably never guessed the impact he would have on society. He founded the Institute for Sex Research in 1947, and in 1948 kicked open the door on this taboo subject with the landmark publication of *Sexual Behavior in the American Male*. He followed it with *Sexual Behavior in the American Female* in 1953. Many believe these two studies, by shining light on issues like female orgasms, homosexuality, and erotica, ushered in the Sexual Revolution.

While in Bloomington, Kinsey lived at 620 S. Fess Street (1921), 615 S. Park Street (1921–27), and 1320 E. First Street (1927–56). He died on August 25, 1956, and was buried in Rose Hill Cemetery. But the Kinsey Institute did not die with him and continues his work today. Though they are often tight-lipped, they are believed to have a collection of erotica that is second only to the Vatican's. No joke.

The institute is *not* interested in walk-in guinea pig volunteers. Your best bet to see what they're working on now is to check out their website, or sign up for one of the bimonthly tours.

Morrison Hall #313, 1165 E. Third St., Bloomington, IN 47405
Phone: (812) 855-7686
Hours: Always visible; Tours, Friday 2:30–3:30 PM
Cost: Free
Website: www.indiana.edu/~kinsey/
Directions: Two blocks west of Jordan Ave., north of Third St.

Rose Hill Cemetery, 1100 W. Fourth St., Bloomington, IN 47403
Phone: (812) 349-3498
Hours: Daylight
Cost: Free
Directions: Follow Third St. east from Rte. 45, and as the road bends left (northeast) the cemetery will be on your right.

So tell me, how many times a week do you . . . well . . . you know . . . . Photo by James Lane

Midwestern Tibet

Bloomington might seem an odd location for the focal point of Tibetan cultural activity in the United States. But the town was the longtime home of the late Thubten Jigme Norbu, the Dalai Lama's older brother and one-time IU professor. He opened the Tibetan Cultural Center here in 1987; the building was consecrated by his Nobel Peace Prize–winning sibling.

The place has a Jangchub Chorten containing hair from the previous 13 Dalai Lamas, and to see their bald heads, that's quite an accomplishment.

As a North American vortex of all things Tibetan, there's also a Tibetan restaurant in town. And if you're thinking of joining a very simple lifestyle, there's always the Dagom Gaden Tensung Ling Monastery in Cascades Park. Do you look good in orange?

Tibetan Cultural Center, 3655 Snoddy Rd., PO Box 2563, Bloomington, IN 47402
Phone: (812) 336-6807
Hours: Grounds, daily 9 AM–6 PM; Cultural Center, check website for programs
Cost: Free
Website: http://tmbcc.org
Directions: Smith Rd. south until it turns into E. Rogers Rd., west three blocks to Snoddy Rd., then south to the center.

Anyetsang's Little Tibet, 415 E. Fourth St., Bloomington, IN 47408
Phone: (812) 331-0122
Hours: Lunch, daily 11 AM–3 PM; Dinner, daily 5–9 PM
Cost: Meals $8–13
Website: www.anyetsangs.com
Directions: One block west of Indiana Ave. at Dunn St.

Dagom Gaden Tensung Ling Tibetan Buddhist Monastery, 102 Clubhouse Dr., Bloomington, IN 47404
Phone: (812) 339-0857
Hours: Daily 9 AM–6 PM
Cost: Free
Website: www.dgtlmonastery.org
Directions: Just west of Business 37, north of Rte. 45, in Cascade Park west of Old Martinsville Rd.

Bruceville
The Blue Flash

When was the last time you went to an amusement park? Expensive tickets, long lines, and all those padded safety bars on the rides—what kind of fun was that?

Well, fret no more. There's a great little park near Bruceville, founded in 2001 by self-taught mechanical whiz John Ivers. And is it small . . . just two rides, both roller coasters. Ivers started with the Blue Flash, a one-hill loop-the-loop that launches from the top of a shed behind his house. He built it using trial and error with leftover junk—parts from old farm equipment and wrecked autos, including the bucket seat you'll ride in. Fasten your seat belt and hold on tight as your one-person car rockets down from the shed's peak through a 360-degree loop and then screeeech, you're done. Ivers does have one safety requirement: nobody over 200 pounds can ride it. Wouldn't want to bend the track.

Ivers later built a second coaster, the Blue Flash II, which has two seats and no loop. It also runs a bit slower, for you wimps out there.

6997 N. Ivers Rd., Bruceville, IN 47516
Phone: (812) 324-9030
Hours: Call ahead; June–September, Saturday–Sunday
Cost: Free
Directions: West of Rte. 150/41 on Ivers Rd.

Giant Peach

In the final pages of Roald Dahl's *James and the Giant Peach*, the enormous fruit tumbles from the skies over New York and is impaled on the antenna of the Empire State Building. The Giant Peach west of Bruceville appears to have missed a similar fate by a mere few feet.

Sitting beside a 40-foot yellow obelisk, the Giant Peach advertises a produce stand on Rte. 41/150. It was designed to look like the famous Trylon and Perisphere at the 1939 World's Fair in Flushing, New York. It makes a perfect photo opportunity if you're traveling with somebody named James . . . or a gigantic, talking grasshopper.

The Big Peach Farm, 7738 N. Old Rte. 41,
   Bruceville, IN 47516
Phone: (812) 324-2548
Hours: Always visible; Farm, daily 10 AM–6 PM
Cost: Free
Website: www.facebook.com/thebigpeach14/
Directions: West of Bruceville, five miles
   north of Vincennes on the west side of the
   highway.

Where's James?

Buckskin

Henager's Memories & Nostalgia Museum

Once called the "Loneliest Museum in America," James Henager's bizarre and ramshackle collection of anything and everything is only slightly less lonely these days. Part of the problem might be curb appeal, or lack of it. When you pull into the small gravel parking lot you're not entirely sure you're in the right spot. Is this somebody's home? Garage? Workshop?

Yes, all three . . . and the museum is upstairs! Henager personally leads the tour, which he says takes four hours minimum to fully appreciate, but six is better. Every square inch of this place is covered in autographed photos of B-list actors, faded comic books, old commercial advertisements, antique lithographs, and LP record covers. The aisles are crammed with old radios and phonographs and eight-track players, displays of Smokey Bear and the Boy Scouts and Christmas ornaments, shrines to Roy Rogers and Dale Evans, and cast-off props from *A League of Their Own*. All throughout the tour, Heneger peppers you with questions, usually, "Do you know what this is?" And of course you don't, so he flips on a five-minute educational video about Abraham Lincoln or Wells Fargo or the Civil War . . .

On and on it goes—it's all very charming and informative until it isn't, at which point you should have a readymade excuse. Perhaps you're due for an MRI, or you need to get home to feed your diabetic cat. *Anything*, but have an escape plan. Don't say you weren't warned.

8837 S. Hwy. 57, Buckskin, IN 47613
Phone: (812) 795-2230
Hours: September–May, Monday–Friday 8 AM–5 PM, Saturday 8 AM–4 PM; June–August, Monday–
   Thursday 8 AM–7 PM, Friday 8 AM–5 PM, Saturday 8 AM–4 PM
Cost: Adults $6, Kids $3
Website: www.henagermuseum.com
Directions: South of Main St. on Rte. 57.

Clarksville

Crazy Mary Kay Driver

Madison Avenue executives take note: if you want to create an eye-catching advertisement on a limited budget, consider buying an old

Cadillac, some pink paint, and a department store mannequin. That's what the owner of Couch's Body Shop did, and he's been drawing customers like flies ever since.

Couch's painted the Caddy hot pink, buried it nose-down along Blackiston Mill Road, and perched a female mannequin atop the back bumper. It's as if a drunken Mary Kay Lady had ditched her vehicle and was sitting around, waiting for a tow truck. Depending on the season, she is clad in a different seasonal outfit. Mrs. Claus at Christmastime. A leggy leprechaun at St. Patrick's Day. Red, white, and blue for the Fourth of July. Elvira at Halloween.

Don't call the cops.

And what does this have to do with what they're selling? Well, what other body shops do you see getting free publicity in a travel guide?

Couch's Body & Frame Shop, 2803 Blackiston Mill Rd., Clarksville, IN 47129
Phone: (812) 944-4044
Hours: Always visible; Store, Monday–Friday 8:30 AM–5 PM
Cost: Free
Website: www.couchsbodyshop.com
Directions: Exit Charlestown Rd. southbound from I-265, after three blocks turn left (east) on Blackiston Mill Rd., five blocks ahead on the right.

World's Second Largest Clock

Clarksville has long played third fiddle to neighboring Jeffersonville, Indiana, and Louisville, Kentucky, just across the river. Louisville has a baseball bat named after it; Jeffersonville has its famous steamboats. But neither of those towns has the World's Second Largest Clock. That's in Clarksville.

The Colgate Clock, shaped like a gigantic stop sign to resemble Colgate Octagon Soap, is 40 feet in diameter and outlined in red neon. For the record, that's larger than London's Big Ben. Its hour hand is 16 feet long, its minute hand measures 20.5 feet, and its pendulum weighs 330 pounds. The clock looms over the old Colgate-Palmolive plant, housed in the former Indiana Reformatory for Men. It was moved here in 1924 from another Colgate facility in New Jersey where (presumably) workers had a better on-time performance. Rather than have it face north, toward Clarksville, the clock faces south, toward Kentucky. During the summer the states don't share the same time zone, so it becomes less useful for its southern neighbors.

1410 S. Clark Blvd., Clarksville, IN 47129
No phone
Hours: Always visible
Cost: Free
Directions: Just northwest of the I-65 bridge to Louisville, at the Ohio River.

Columbus

Birthplace of Corn Flakes

Columbus is mighty proud of its architectural legacy, and with good reason; few towns outside Chicago and New York have as many examples of modern architecture. But one building on the city's "significant building" tour stands out above all others, at least to breakfast lovers: the former "Mill A" at Fifth and Jackson Streets. It was here, in the late 1870s, that James Vanoy invented corn flakes . . . by accident. Originally sold wholesale in 1880 for beer preparation, somebody realized the crunchy creation tasted good all by itself. So in 1884 the nation got its first taste of corn flakes, Cerealine, sold by the newly formed American Hominy Company.

The mill was later converted into the headquarters of the Cummins Engine Company. This manufacturer foots the bill for most of the innovative architecture in Columbus, widely known as the "Athens of the Midwest." (There are plenty of tour guides available to show these stunning buildings, if you're interested.)

Cummins Engine Company, Cerealine Building, 500 Jackson St., Columbus, IN 47201
Phone: (812) 377-5000

Hours: Always visible
Cost: Free
Website: www.columbus.in.us/columbus/cummins-corporate-office-building
Directions: Two blocks east of Rte. 11 (Lindsey St.), three blocks north of Rte. 7 (Third St.).

World's Largest Toilet

Have the kiddies been little turds on your family vacation? Or maybe *big* turds? Well then, stop by Kids Commons and flush your problems away! On the top floor of this charming children's museum is the World Largest Toilet, ready for doody. Have the stinkers climb on in to swirl on down to the floor below, like Augustus Gloop in reverse. That'll give you only a moment's peace before they climb back up the stairs to take the ride again (and again, and again), but you'll probably find the whole exercise strangely therapeutic.

Author as excrement.

Of course, that's not all Kids Commons has to offer. They've got an interactive bubble-making area, a laser-activated harp, a hands-on mini grocery, a controllable robotic arm, and much more to play with. But most Number 2 kids will find this crap chute the Number 1 attraction.

Kids Commons, 309 Washington St., Columbus, IN 47201
Phone: (812) 378-3046
Hours: Tuesday–Saturday 10 AM–5 PM, Sunday 1–5 PM
Cost: Adults $7, Kids (18 months+) $7
Website: www.kidscommons.org
Directions: Just north of Rte. 46 (Third St.), four blocks east of the river.

HAVE A SEAT

Maybe you're too classy to be photographed sitting on a giant toilet, or are afraid you might fall in and become clogged. Fair enough. Here are a few oversized chairs for photo shoots where you're in no such danger.

Big John

Long's Furniture World, 4108 S. US Hwy. 31, Franklin, (317) 738-3302, www.longsfurnitureworld.com

Long's Furniture World, a nondescript outlet store south of the city of Franklin, claims that the 18-foot-tall rocking chair outside is the World's Largest Rocking Chair, but that's not true anymore—others are larger. Still, it is impressive at 6,000 pounds and is too tall for you to climb onto the seat . . . so don't even try! And the thing actually rocks, which was made quite clear when a windstorm blew it over in 2007.

Big Rocking Chair

Rte. 31 N, Bunker Hill, (765) 564-2898

Just west of the small community of Bunker Hill sits a 15-foot-tall yellow rocking chair. At one time it was an advertisement for McCoy's Furniture Junction, a refinishing business, but now it's all alone in a grassy field.

Big Highback Chair

Richmond Furniture Gallery, 180 Fort Wayne Ave., Richmond, (765) 939-3325, http://richmondfurnituregallery.com

An enormous high-back chair upholstered in white-and-blue striped fabric guards the entrance to a furniture store in Richmond's historic district. In fact, it *is* the entrance—you have to walk beneath its seat to get to the front door.

Enormous Adirondack

Do It Best, 1091 W. Broadway St., Monticello, (574) 583-7181, www.doitbest.com

The only chair in this foursome that you're encouraged to climb onto is an Adirondack lawn chair in the parking lot of a chain hardware store on the southwest side of Monticello. It's brick red and sturdy enough to hold the whole family, so jump on up!

Dale

Dr. Ted's Musical Marvels

Somewhere between humankind's first animal-skin drum and today's digital audio devices was a short-lived era of mechanical instruments. These music makers were not playback machines, like phonographs, but were constructed of recognizable instruments. Player pianos, music boxes, and calliopes are the most common "musical marvels," but hold on to your ears when you step into Ted Waflart's place—they can be much, much larger.

Dr. Ted's museum contains some of the most elaborate mechanical instruments around, and what's more, he'll play them all for you on the 90-minute tour. The largest device, the Decap Belgian Dance Organ, was used in a small European town that couldn't afford an orchestra for its parties. The 24-foot-long contraption contains a 535-pipe organ, two saxophones, cymbals, tempo blocks, two accordions, drums, and more. Plug it in and get ready to boogie! Other machines, beautifully restored by Dr. Ted, bang out tunes controlled with air-driven valves, copper-coated rotating disks, and punched paper rolls. Who needs digital-quality sound when you can have the real thing?

11896 S. US Hwy. 231, Dale, IN 47523
Phone: (812) 937-4250
Hours: Groups only, by appointment
Cost: Depends on the tour
Website: www.drteds.com
Directions: Half mile north of I-64, Exit 57, on Rte. 231, turn right on County Line Rd., then left (north) at the access road.

Elberfeld

Big Model Airplanes

Some may have outgrown their childhood hobby of model airplane building, but not Lloyd "Tud" Kohn. For years this Vietnam veteran has been constructing models of American warplanes—without kits, mind you— and mounting them on poles in his backyard near Elberfeld. If he lived somewhere else, few might see them, but his property backs up to I-64, so travelers on the interstate can watch them spin in the wind. Most days Tud sits out in the yard with his trusty dog and warplane whirligigs, waving at truckers and bikers. Not a bad retirement.

If you stop for a visit, you'll likely see his next creation being built in his garage workshop. Then take the artist's tour—every plane has a story.

11133 Dassel Dr., Elberfeld, IN 47613

Phone: (812) 983-2608

Hours: Call ahead

Cost: Free

Directions: Head east on Rte. 68 from I-69, the first exit north of the I-64/I-69 interchange; turn south on N Rd. until just before the I-64 overpass, turning right on Dassel Dr.

Two of Tud's treasures.

Evansville
Braiiiiiiins!

The Hilltop Inn first opened in 1839 as a stagecoach stop and has operated under a variety of names over the years. Yet as historic as it is, the place today is best known for a menu item that is relatively new: the Jumbo Pork Brain Sandwich. The pig brains they use are about the size of cantaloupes but are squished down into two-inch-thick patties, batter-fried, and plopped on buns too small to cover them; customers have to hold the brains in their hands to get their jaws around them.

And what do they taste like? Sort of like chicken McNuggets, only fluffier and much, much larger. They don't so much have a brain *flavor*—does anyone really know what that would be?—as they do have a brain *texture*. Getting one down is less of a challenge for the tongue than for the brain, YOUR brain. It's not for the faint of heart. Any wonder that *Asylum Magazine* crowned the Hilltop Inn the "Manliest Restaurant in America" in 2009? And of course, by "manly" they meant "stupid enough to eat anything as long as it's deep-fried."

Hilltop Inn, 1100 Harmony Way, Evansville, IN 47112
Phone: (812) 422-1757
Hours: Monday–Thursday 11 AM–9 PM, Friday–Saturday 11 AM–10 PM
Cost: Free; Brain sandwich, $7.45
Website: http://hilltopinnrestaurant.com
Directions: Two blocks north of Upper Mt. Vernon Rd. at Maryland St.

Chow down, zombies!

The Lady in Gray

Tales of ghosts in old buildings are not uncommon, but photographic "evidence" of these spirits is rare, and ghost-hunting webcams are almost unheard of. But not in Evansville.

The Lady in Gray has haunted this town's main library since 1937. Most believe her to be an old librarian. Others claim she's the spirit of Louise Carpenter, daughter of the collection's founder, Willard Carpenter, since ghosts often hang out where their living bodies experienced pain and suffering. Carpenter had every reason to be bitter toward the library for, as she saw it, her inheritance was gobbled up by this elaborate building and all its fancy books.

Luckily, the Lady in Gray is not a vengeful ghost. She likes to hang out near the Children's Room and the restrooms on the lower level. She's always dressed in a gray Victorian outfit. If patrons don't see her, they often experience "cold spots" or smell her perfume, which reminds many of patchouli. Could the Lady in Gray be a Dead Head, sneaking a little doobie between the racks? Some folks aim to find out.

A security camera once caught a glimpse of her wispy figure near the restrooms. Realizing she could be photographed, the *Evansville Courier & Press* set up a pair of ghost-cams, one in the main library and the other in the Children's Room. They snap a shot every 10 minutes during the day; at night the image refreshes every 30 seconds. Visitors to the website are encouraged to save and report anything suspicious, and you're welcome to view their findings, under "Proof!" Some of the obvious hoaxes are found under "Spoof!", such as the spooky appearances of Colonel Sanders, Kathy Lee Gifford, Pokémon, the Three Stooges, and numerous Teletubbies. According to the *Courier*, the Willard Library ghost-cam is one of the most visited webcams on the Internet.

Willard Library, 21 First Ave., Evansville, IN 47710
Phone: (812) 425-4309
Hours: Monday–Tuesday 9 AM–8 PM, Wednesday–Friday 9 AM–5:30 PM, Saturday 9 AM–5 PM, Sunday 1–5 PM
Cost: Free
Website: www.willardghost.com; *Courier & Press*, www.courierpressblogs.com/libraryghost
Directions: At the corner of First Ave. and Division St., just north of the Lloyd Expressway (Rte. 62).

Roseanne Town

Every fan of the sitcom *Roseanne* (1988–97) knows that the Conner family lived at 914 Delaware Street in Lanford, Illinois, about halfway between Chicago and Rockford. Only there is no Lanford, Illinois. The 1925 bungalow seen throughout the series wasn't located in Hollywood either, but is a real home that still stands on a quiet street in Evansville, Indiana. It was originally photographed by Matt Williams, the show's first producer, in the town where he attended college. Once *Roseanne* took off, the place became a landmark.

But that's not all! The Lobo Lounge, Roseanne and Dan's favorite local dive, is also located in Evansville. It's really the Talk of the Town Pizza Bar, and it's nowhere near the Conner's house. Chalk it up to the magic of Hollywood.

619 S. Runnymeade St., Evansville, IN 47714
Private phone
Hours: Always visible
Cost: Free
Website: www.roseanneworld.com
Directions: One block south of Lincoln Ave., seven blocks east of Rte. 41.

Talk of the Town Pizza Bar, 1200 Edgar St., Evansville, IN 47710
Phone: (812) 402-8696
Hours: Always visible; Restaurant, Sunday–Monday 11 AM–9 PM, Tuesday–Saturday 11 AM–11 PM
Cost: Free
Website: www.facebook.com/pages/Talk-of-The-Town-Pizza/108031905949571
Directions: Four blocks north of Columbia St., five blocks west of Main St., at Louisiana St.

Hello, Lanford!

Wilson's General Store & Café

Any fan of classic roadside signage, ephemera, or BBQ ribs needs to make a trip to Wilson's General Store and Café, a southern-style roadhouse on the southwest side of Evansville. It's like an ancient burial ground for greasy spoons. In fact, there are so many old signs that you'd be forgiven for mistaking whether you're at the right place. Is this the Rebel Truck Stop Pit BBQ? The Flamingo Motel? A Chevrolet dealership? The Happy Hopper Rabbitry? Because these establishments' advertisements are all prominently displayed on the walls outside, though not present inside.

Wilson's has a particular passion for any sign that features an old cartoon character on it, such as Popeye or Peter Pan or Scooby Doo, but also has big cutout figures of Lippy the Lion, Morocco Mole, and other cartoons your grandparents might remember. The food's pretty good, too.

11120 Broadway Ave., Evansville, IN 47712
Phone: (812) 985-0202
Hours: Tuesday–Thursday 11 AM–7 PM, Friday–Saturday 11 AM–8 PM, Sunday 10 AM–2 PM
Cost: Meals $7–25
Website: www.wilsonsribs.biz
Directions: On Rte. 62 (Broadway Ave.) west of the University of Southern Indiana.

French Lick
Wild Hair Museum

"My life revolves around hair," admits hair stylist Tony Kendall, and he's not joking. It's been that way since he was born; his parents named him after Toni, the once-popular do-it-yourself hair permanent. He eventually grew up to be a cosmetologist with his own salon *and* hair-themed museum.

This small museum has tools of the trade, both antique and modern—curling irons, clippers, brushes, combs, razors, hair tonics, relaxers, and things you'd never think of letting touch your scalp today. He also has rare art, like a creepy Victorian wreath where each flower is made from a different family member's hair. (One of the reasons it's so rare is that many hair wreaths were burned after a rumor circulated that they transmitted the plague.) But Kendall's most treasured artifact is a few wisps of Elvis's locks, plucked from a brush years ago and framed for your viewing enjoyment. It's hairstoric!

Body Reflections, 448 S. Maple St., French Lick, IN 47432
Phone: (812) 936-4064
Hours: Tuesday–Friday 9 AM–7 PM, Saturday 9 AM–2 PM
Cost: Free
Website: www.hairshow.biz/museum.htm
Directions: Just south of Main St., across the street from the French Lick Springs Hotel.

World's Largest Teeny Tiny Circus

The French Lick West Baden Museum has plenty of interesting exhibits, but by far the most popular is the elaborate Hagenbeck-Wallace Circus Diorama, which includes more than 6,000 human and animal figures—the world's largest collection! It covers more than 1,100 square feet in three main scenes: the Circus Train, the Circus Parade, and the Circus Tents. Marvel at the sideshow freaks and exotic menageries, trapeze artists and clown acts, carnival barkers and elephant handlers, as well as the behind-the-scenes operations of this historically accurate reproduction.

It took more than 40 years for craftsman Peter Gorman to create this enormous work of folk art, and when it was moved to the museum it took dozens of volunteers three months to arrange the 150,000 pieces just so. Please don't jiggle the display cases.

French Lick West Baden Museum, 469 S. Maple St. #103, French Lick, IN 47432
Phone: (812) 936-3592
Hours: Monday–Saturday 10 AM–4 PM
Cost: Adults $8, Seniors $7, Kids $2
Website: www.flwbmuseum.com
Directions: At the intersection of College Ave. and Maple St., just east of Rte. 56 (Wells Ave.).

Gosport
The Chivalry Trough

Long before American bachelor parties became opportunities to embarrass and blackmail new grooms with stripper videos, pre-wedding customs were a bit more down to earth. In the town of Gosport, it was a tradition for friends to toss a soon-to-be hubby into an 8-by-4-foot concrete ditch filled with cold water. The dunking place was dubbed the Chivalry Trough, and the whole process was a symbolic welcome into the cold, hard reality of matrimony.

As fun as it was, the practice eventually faded away. Today, the Chivalry Trough can be found among the weeds near the railroad trestle by the ruins of the old Brewer Flour Mill. Be advised that if you want to resurrect a dunking for old time's sake, there are serious risks. First, the trough is empty, but worse, it is surrounded by poison ivy, and all the groomsmen could end up with a nasty rash. How do you explain *that* on your wedding night?

North St., Gosport, IN 47433
No phone
Hours: Always visible
Cost: Free
Directions: Follow North St., which runs parallel to Main St. (one block north), eastward until it goes down the hill; on the left, at the bend, are four pillars, and on the right, in the weeds, is the trough.

One reason bachelor parties hire strippers today.

Haubstadt

Hillbilly Rick's Campground

Though officially known as the Weather Rock Campground, those who return year after year affectionately call it Hillbilly Rick's. That's no surprise, because this place looks like it's been duct-taped together from leftover junk—it's Country with a capital C. A menagerie of fiberglass animals make the cement pond look extra purty: a giraffe, a lion, an elephant, and a gorilla wearing bright yellow board shorts. An even larger critter, a 10-foot trout on a jumbo fishing line, stands by the office and is great for gag photos. Junked cars, rusty farm equipment, chainsaw sculptures, and knee-high weeds make for a unique putt-putt course with a nasty rough.

And are you wondering about the place's official name? The campground has in its possession a special rock, hanging on a chain, that can predict the weather with 100 percent accuracy. A sign explains how to use it for nonmeteorologists. Is it wet? Rain is in the forecast. Does it swing? Must be windy. Does it swing in a circle? A tornado's approaching. Apparently it can even predict Nuclear Armageddon (Is it vaporized?) and acts of God (Has it turned into a loaf of bread?).

Weather Rock Campground, 12848 S. Weather Rock Dr., Haubstadt, IN 47639
Phone: (812) 867-3401
Hours: Always visible
Cost: Free; Campsites, $40–50/night
Website: www.weatherrockcampground.com
Directions: East of Rte. 200 E, just north of I-64.

Hindustan
Don't Sit in the Witch's Throne!

Most people can recall an urban legend from their high school days about a local cemetery and a curse associated with it. The story of the Witch's Throne is one of those tales.

The dead buried in Stepp Cemetery were from a religious sect called the Crabbites. They were snake-handling fundamentalists and practitioners of Free Love—not your typical congregation. While the sex might have attracted converts, the poisonous vipers kept the believers to a manageable number.

One follower, a young woman named Anna Something-or-Other, had a baby who was tragically killed by a hit-and-run driver on old Route 37. The mother buried her daughter in this rural graveyard but returned every night to exhume the girl's body and cradle it in her arms. Not long after she began her nocturnal activities, a tree near the grave was struck by lightning. The smoking stump made a fine chair for the grieving, slightly nutty mom. She always dressed in black and could be seen most nights, rocking back and forth, on what became known as the Witch's Throne.

This "witch" didn't live forever, but the curse that claimed her child lingers on. According to legend, anyone who sits in her chair during a full moon will die one year to the day after the brazen act. Not much is left of the old cemetery but a few tombstones and a lot of empty beer cans. Several old stumps *could* be chairs, but none look very comfortable. That alone should be reason enough not to test fate.

Stepp Cemetery, Morgan-Monroe State Forest, Old State Highway 37, Hindustan, IN 47401
Phone: (765) 342-4026
Hours: Daylight
Cost: Free
Website: http://www.in.gov/dnr/forestry/4816.htm
Directions: In the park, follow the trail leading away from the curved stone wall along old Rte. 37, just west of the Shady Pines Picnic Area.

Jasper
Big Popcorn Box

As any dietician will tell you, American portion sizes have gotten out of control. Example: the 17-foot-tall popcorn box on the north side of Jasper. It is filled with buckets of delicious puffs . . . delicious if you like the taste of fiberglass. If you have a taste for more traditional flavors, step inside. Here you'll find 90 different varieties, from traditional butter, caramel, and cheddar to more exotic concoctions: dill pickle, cinnamon roll, barbeque, and tutti fruiti.

Jasper's started out as Eckert's Pool Supply, but given the vagaries of Indiana weather, they added a popcorn and chocolate business to keep the cash flowing in the winter months. Perhaps one day they will sell miniature pools filled with Coca-Cola, but not yet.

Jasper Gift Basket and Popcorn Company, 1522 Newton St., Jasper, IN 47546
Phone: (855) 634-2700 or (812) 634-2700
Hours: Always visible; Store, Monday–Friday 8 AM–5:30 PM, Saturday 8 AM–2 PM
Cost: Free
Website: www.jaspergiftbasketandpopcornco.com
Directions: One block north of 15th St. on Rte. 231 (Newton St.), at the north end of town.

Providence Home Geode Garden

It's easy to find a simple grotto built alongside an old Catholic church in the Midwest. But the Geode Garden in Jasper? When did the builders, Fr.

Thad Sztucko and (later) Phillip Ottavi of the nearby Providence Home, decide enough was enough?

The garden stretches for two city blocks and contains dozens of statue-filled niches lumped together in several areas. Most of the pedestals, fences, fountains, pillars, light posts, and benches are encrusted with unsplit geodes, making the whole structure look like a collection of carefully arranged popcorn balls.

520 W. Ninth St., Jasper, IN 47546
No phone
Hours: Always visible
Cost: Free
Directions: Two blocks due west of the St. Joseph's Catholic Church, between Ninth and Eleventh Sts. along Bartley St.

Just the tip of the geode-berg.

JASONVILLE
➡ The town of Jasonville was once headed by a professional Elvis impersonator, Bruce Borders. His motto was "By day the Mayor, by night . . . THE KING!"

Jeffersonville

Candy Museum

Ever wonder why grandma and grandpa needed dentures? Drop on by Shimpff's Confectionery, one of the oldest candy store/soda fountains in the nation, for all the sugary details. Gustav Schimpff and son opened the business in 1891, and it has been in the Schimpff family ever since. Today's owners, Warren and Jill Schimpff, took over from Warren's deceased aunt in 1990, but don't expect them to be making any "upgrades." How can you improve on confection perfection?

That's not to say they haven't *expanded*, however. The store purchased an adjoining storefront for a candy demonstration area, chocolate dipping room, and museum of old-timey candy packaging, manufacturing equipment, and sweet, sweet ephemera. They've also got a soda fountain from the 1950s for nostalgic bobby-soxers. Schimpff's specialty is cinnamon Red Hots—they sell several tons a year—but there are hundreds of other candies to satisfy your sweet tooth . . . assuming it hasn't already rotted out.

Schimpff's Confectionery, 347 Spring St., Jeffersonville, IN 47130
Phone: (812) 283-8367
Hours: Monday–Saturday 10 AM–5 PM
Cost: Free
Website: www.schimpffs.com
Directions: Three blocks east of I-65, one block south of Court Ave.

Howard Steamboat Museum

The paddlewheel steamboat was a powerful force in American history, yet it is all but extinct today, save for riverboat casinos that rarely venture a foot from shore. At the Howard Steamboat Museum you can explore the legacy of these floating hotels where many of them first touched the water.

James Howard launched his Jeffersonville operations in 1834 at the dawn of the steamboat age. He was 19 years old at the time. The operation grew at a breakneck pace, to the point where half the flat-bottom side-wheelers in the then-western rivers had been built in the Howard Shipyard. James Howard died here in 1876; the 62-year-old underestimated a jump onto a departing steamboat, fell into the Ohio River, and drowned.

But the Howard family carried on his work until 1941 when the yards were sold to the US Navy at the outset of World War II. Workers then built LSTs, sub chasers, and other oceangoing craft to aid in the war effort. Today, the shipyards operate under the name of Jeffboat.

You'll learn all the details, and much more, at a museum housed in the 1894 Howard Mansion. The ornate 22-room structure was built by the shipyard's craftsmen, and if it had a couple paddlewheels and was painted white, might be mistaken for a ship run aground. The first floor has been restored to its original turn-of-the-century appearance following a fire in the 1970s. The second floor contains dozens of steamboat models and items salvaged from the *Robert E. Lee*, the *Natchez*, and others. These beautiful boats could float in only 18 inches of water and achieve speeds of 40 knots. On the museum's top floor is an exhibit of the WWII boats built here, focusing on the LST landing craft used during the D-day invasion. Look around the museum and you'll find a few odd items, including a wooden typewriter and the original 22-ton paddlewheel shaft from the *Delta Queen*.

1101 E. Market St., Jeffersonville, IN 47130
Phone: (812) 283-3728
Hours: Tuesday–Saturday 10 AM–4 PM, Sunday 1–4 PM
Cost: Adults $7, Seniors (65+) $6, Teens (6–18) $5
Website: www.howardsteamboatmuseum.org
Directions: Thirteen blocks northeast of the I-65 bridge, along the Ohio River.

Lawrenceburg
Peggy the Flying Red Horse

Peggy the Flying Red Horse is today confined to a glass gazebo adjacent to the American Legion post in Lawrenceburg. For years you could see her in Ohio River–area parades, spinning in circles on her hindquarters to the delight of the crowds. But don't fret—Peggy is not a real horse, nor does she fly. She's a car.

Back in the 1930s Frank Taylor and his buddies took an old Model T and mounted a red flying horse on its hood. They then modified the car's frame and seats so that when the whole crew sat in the back, holding her reigns, Peggy would pop a wheelie and spin around like a clown car. The vehicle was a rolling advertisement for Mobil Oil with its Pegasus mascot, hence the name Peggy.

Though today she is tamed and caged, at least she hasn't been sent to a junkyard or glue factory. Come see her while she's still around.

American Legion Post 239, 201 Second St., Lawrenceburg, IN 47025
Phone: (812) 537-0349
Hours: Always visible
Cost: Free
Website: www.facebook.com/LawrenceburgAmericanLegionRiders/
Directions: One block south of the Eads Pkwy., three blocks east of the river, at Front St.

Leopold
Thou Shalt Not Steal

By all accounts, the Civil War's Andersonville Prison Camp in Georgia was no picnic. Disease. Starvation. Packs of man-eating bloodhounds. It was in this "maniac's nightmare" that three Union prisoners from Indiana—Lambert Rogier, Henry Devillez, and Isidore Naviaux—pledged to honor the Virgin Mary if they survived the ordeal, even if it meant *stealing*.

The trio made it home, and in 1867 Rogier set sail for Luxembourg, his eyes on Our Lady of Consolation. The statue he sought was carved in 1628 for Father Broquart, a priest who, having made a similar pact with the Mother of God, miraculously survived a bubonic plague outbreak in Europe. Rogier made a copy of the centuries-old statue, then swapped it with the original.

Many in Indiana today deny Rogier did anything but make a copy of the statue, but the original statue's owners asked King Leopold to intercede on their behalf. When the king learned the statue had ended up in a town that shared his name, he calmed the nerves of the finger-pointers and the whole issue was swept under the rug.

The statue remains in Leopold today. Depending on the season, Our Lady of Consolation is dressed in a variety of liturgical outerwear. The baby Jesus sits in her outstretched hand. A larger marble replica of the statue stands outside the church, but the original is locked up at night . . . for good reason.

Shrine of Our Lady of Consolation, St. Augustine Church, 18020 Lafayette St., Leopold, IN 47551
Phone: (812) 843-5143
Hours: Daily 9 AM–6 PM
Cost: Free
Directions: On the south side of town, at the corner of St. Augustine and Lafayette Sts.

Lincoln City
Don't Drink the Milk!

Mother always told you, "Drink your milk!" Well, mom wasn't always right. Take Abe Lincoln's mother, Nancy Hanks Lincoln; she perished on the family farm on October 5, 1818, the victim of "milk sickness."

While not understood at the time, "milk sickness" should have been called "milk poisoning." It was sometimes called "puking sickness" or "the trembles." During times of drought, cattle would eat plants they would normally avoid, one of them being the white snakeroot. Toxins from this plant accumulated in the tissues of the animals and passed through their milk. If a person drank too much of that milk, it wasn't pretty: vomiting, muscle pain, constipation, coma, and then death.

The Lincolns had moved to Indiana in December 1816 to escape land title disputes in Kentucky, and now, two years later, Abe's mother was dead. He was only nine years old. His father Thomas remarried, to a woman Abe would come to regard as his mother, Sarah Bush Johnston.

The Lincoln family abandoned their Hoosier farm for Illinois in 1830. Today you'll find a reconstructed homestead. The locations of the cabin and Nancy's grave are approximate. There is a bronzed sill and hearthstone believed to be part of the original cabin, and an elaborate tombstone rests atop a hill where Nancy was buried. Adjoining the farm is a visitors' center and museum.

Lincoln Boyhood National Memorial, Rte. 162, PO Box 1816, Lincoln City, IN 47552
Phone: (812) 937-4541
Hours: October–March, Monday–Tuesday 7 AM–3 PM, Wednesday–Sunday 8 AM–4 PM; April–
September, daily 8 AM–5 PM
Cost: Adults (17+) $5, Families $10
Website: www.nps.gov/libo
Directions: Four miles west of Santa Claus on Rte. 162.

MORE FOR LINCOLN LOVERS

The good folks of southern Indiana want you to remember that even though Illinois calls itself the Land of Lincoln, the Hoosier state was his home during Abe's formative years. And if you enjoyed visiting his childhood home, there are three other Lincoln attractions nearby and an infamous artifact a little farther north.

Lincoln Pioneer Village

928 Fairground Dr., Rockport, (812) 649-9147, www.lincolnpioneervillage.com

Though this "historic" town did not exist during Lincoln's lifetime, several of its 14 buildings did, and some were even visited by the future president during his Indiana days: Little Pigeon Baptist Church, Brown's Tavern, and John Pitcher's Law Office. The Works Progress Administration built the village in 1935, and in 1954 *The Kentuckian*, with Burt Lancaster and Walter Matthau, was filmed here. The attraction also has some Lincolnobelia in its museum, including a split fence rail from the 1860 Railsplitter Campaign, a clipboard made by Abe's father, and a block of wood from the last Indiana cabin in which the not-yet-president stayed.

Lincoln Landing

First St., Rockport, www.iupui.edu/~linctech/locations/lincoln-landing/index.php

In 1828, 19-year-old Abraham Lincoln and his friend Allen Gentry pushed off the banks of the Ohio River in Rockport on a flatboat bound for New Orleans. The slavery Lincoln witnessed on his trip to the Gulf forever changed his views on the "peculiar institution." Today a simple monument marks the pair's departure point.

Young Abe Lincoln

Lincoln Amphitheatre, 15032 N. CR 300 E, PO Box 7-21, Lincoln City, (812) 937-9730, www.lincolnamphitheatre.com

Though the Lincoln Amphitheatre has an extensive lineup of musical acts, Lincoln fans will want to see the venue's signature play, *Young Abe Lincoln*, which has been wowing crowds since 1987. Performed outdoors (though covered for rain), the show focuses on the Railsplitter's formative years along nearby Pigeon Creek.

Lincoln's Blood

Johnson County Historical Museum, 135 N. Main St., Franklin, (317) 346-4500, www.johnsoncountymuseum.org

On April 14, 1865, Maj. Henry Rathbone escorted his fiancée, Clara Harris, to a performance of *Our American Cousin* at Ford's Theatre. The pair shared the presidential box with President and Mrs. Lincoln that evening. When John Wilkes Booth shot the president, Harris's decorative fan was spattered with Lincoln's blood, and it can now be seen in its grisly glory at this small museum in Franklin. Or the fan could just be dirty.

Loogootee
Bill's Yard

The sign outside Bill "The Nut" Larkin's place near Loogootee is the first indication you're someplace special:

FREE SHOW

3,900 BIRD HOUSES

GREAT VIEWS FROM THE DECK

NO STEPS—NO CHARGE

NOT SELLING ANYTHING

1,900 BIRD HOUSES IN THE DOME

Just Laugh and Have Fun
Free—No Money

Stand on the deck that wraps around Larkin's geodesic dome and just try to absorb it all: thousands of brightly painted birdhouses on poles run along both sides of a wide, tree-lined ravine. Covering the hillsides are dozens of themed pebble beds filled with concrete gnomes and woodland critters, all separated by species and surrounded by tens of thousands of concentric painted-rock mandalas. It's easy to be gobsmacked.

If you're lucky, you'll get to meet the artist himself, who loves having visitors. Ask to see inside the dome, where thousands of smaller birdhouses and a gazillion Christmas lights dangle overhead like a gaudy galaxy. He'll even give you a free birdhouse to take home with you to remember the visit . . . not that you're likely to forget it.

5024 N. 1215 E, Loogootee, IN 47553
Phone: (812) 709-9944
Hours: Daylight
Cost: Free, but "if you want to show your gratitude to Bill, just bring him a 6-pack of the cheapest beer you can find"
Website: www.billsyard.com
Directions: Head north from town on Rte. 1200 E, turn right on Rte. 500 N; just ahead on Rte. 1215 E.

Bill "The Nut" Larkin and his birdhouse wonderland.

Martinsville
The Touchables Sculpture Garden

Touuuuuuuuuch them! Photo by author, courtesy of C. R. Schiefer

Go ahead, touuuuuuuch them! Stroke ... caress ... explore ... that's why these works of art are here. To listen to sculptor C. R. Schiefer describe his art, there is no way to fully appreciate the pieces until you put your hands all over them. There are more than 180 figures scattered over a 10-acre outdoor gallery, so it'll take you a while to grope them all. Quite a few are anatomically correct—enjoy yourself!

Schiefer spent a quarter century working as a speech pathologist before he discovered, just by chance, his talent for stone carving. As the years rolled by, he developed his own unique style, focusing heavily on the human form and images from native cultures around the world. He also enjoys carving animals, many of which can be seen along the shores of a holding pond on his land.

The entrance to the Touchables Sculpture Garden is marked by a large piece called *Population 999*: three stacked blocks covered with 999 faces. Respectful guests are welcome during daylight hours to wander the property, but be forewarned—there are 1,998 eyes trained on your every move.

5270 Low Gap Rd., Martinsville, IN 46151
Phone: (765) 342-6211
Hours: Always visible
Cost: Free
Directions: Southeast of town on Mahalasville Rd. for three miles, turn right (south) onto Low Gap Rd. for three miles, on the right, south of Downey Rd. (County Road 525).

Milan, Indianapolis
The Real *Hoosiers*

There are few things in Indiana more important than basketball. Mom and her apple pie can just wait in the bleachers when Hoosier Hysteria, the spring tournament, rolls around. Not until 1997 did Indiana rank its high schools by size divisions, so until very recently, every school's team had a shot at the state title. And one team, known as the "Milan Miracle," pulled off just such an upset in 1954.

In 1953 the Milan Indians made it to the state semifinals, so it was not like this was a complete fluke. They had talent, but it was remarkable that they could field a team of 12 from only 75 boys in the student body. To make a verrrry long story short, the Milan David slew the Muncie Central Goliath 32–30 with a last-second, 18-foot jump shot by Bobby Plump. If you want the full story, ask anyone around Milan and reserve several hours in your day.

The 1987 movie *Hoosiers*, with Gene Hackman and Dennis Hopper, is loosely based on Milan's championship season. The fictitious town is named Hickory, and the exterior locations were shot in New Richmond. The Knightstown Hoosier Gym (355 N. Washington St.) in Knightstown was used for the Hickory High School gym. And the championship game was filmed at the Hinkle Fieldhouse (510 W. 49th St.) at Butler University in Indianapolis, where the original championship game was held.

The old Milan High School has been traded in for a new model, though the school brought along part of the original gym floor, the scoreboard (with the 32–30 score still showing), and the Championship Trophy, which is in a display case just inside the entrance. More Milan Miracle mementos can be seen at a museum downtown.

(Old) Milan High School, Carr St. & Lakeside Dr., Milan, IN 47031
No phone
Hours: Never visible; torn down
Cost: Free
Directions: East one block on Carr St. from Rte. 101, turn north on Lakeside Dr.

1954 Milan Museum, 201 W. Carr St., PO Box 54, Milan, IN 47031
Phone: (812) 654-2772
Hours: Wednesday–Saturday 10 AM–4 PM, Sunday noon–4 PM
Cost: Free
Website: http://milan54.org
Directions: Two blocks east of Rte. 101 on Carr St., one block south of the railroad tracks.

(New) Milan High School, 609 N. Warpath Dr., Milan, IN 47031
Phone: (812) 654-3096

Hours: Call for an appointment
Cost: Free
Website: http://hs.milan.k12.in.us
Directions: Two blocks south of Rte. 350, on the east side of Rte. 101.

You also have one more option to relive this 60-year-old story: visit Plump's Last Shot restaurant in Indianapolis, owned by none other than Bobby Plump. The place is filled with Milan basketball memorabilia, and a grainy video of the game runs on a constant loop. Plump is almost always around, too, and is more than willing to tell his story . . . one . . . more . . . time.

Plump's Last Shot, 6416 Cornell Ave., Indianapolis, IN 46220
Phone: (317) 257-5867
Hours: Monday–Friday 11 AM–3 AM, Saturday–Sunday 11 AM–3 AM
Cost: Free; Meals, $9–12
Website: www.plumpslastshotbroadripple.com
Directions: Three blocks east of College Ave., north of 64th St.

Milltown
Shoe Tree

Do you have an old pair of sneakers in your laundry room but don't have the heart to throw them *out*? Well, bring them to Milltown and throw them *up* . . . into a tree!

Nobody is sure who started it, but 25 years ago, shoes were spotted hanging from the branches of a white oak at the intersection of two gravel roads south of town. Soon it became the most exciting thing to do in Milltown—take off your footwear and toss them in the air! (If you've been to Milltown, you know this is still the case.) When a bolt of lightning hit the tree a few years back, kill-

Fun times in Milltown.

ing some of the branches, visitors started tossing their shoes into nearby empty trees.

Here's the trick to successful shoe tossing: tie the laces together with some length, heave the pair in a pinwheel motion, and pray like hell they tangle with any of the thousand or so pairs already dangling above.

Though Milltowners would never toss their sneakers anywhere else, there are other shoe trees in the state: along Edgewater Road in Albany, Franklin Street in Troy, and 109th Street and Calumet Avenue in St. John, which is not a Shoe Tree but a Shoe Corner—just toss them out your car window. Then, every Monday, a crew picks up, cleans, and distributes the shoes to local families.

County Roads 23 & 30, Milltown, IN 47145
No phone
Hours: Always visible
Cost: Free
Directions: Five miles south of town on County Road 23, at the intersection with County Road 30.

Mitchell
Virgil I. Grissom State Memorial

Can a kid from a small town in Indiana grow up to be an astronaut? You bet! And not just any astronaut but the second American to break the gravitational bonds of Earth. Virgil "Gus" Grissom would also go on to command the first manned Gemini mission and die in a tragic launch pad fire on *Apollo I*.

Grissom was born here on April 3, 1926, and attended Riley Elementary. That school later burned to the ground, but bricks from the structure were saved and later used to build a low wall around a 44-foot limestone rocket erected on the site. Nearby is the Gus Grissom Boyhood Home, open for occasional tours.

As a pilot in the Korean War, Grissom earned a Distinguished Flying Cross and the chance to be an astronaut in the upstart space program. Piloting the *Liberty Bell 7* on July 21, 1961, his career almost sank with the capsule at splashdown. Evidence later proved him to be not at fault, but the near disaster plagued him long after the event. It is no coincidence that the craft he piloted on his second space flight, *Gemini III*, was nicknamed the

"Unsinkable Molly Brown." The former pilot was chosen to command the first Apollo mission and died with the rest of his crew in a freak fire on January 27, 1967. Much of the world's Grissom-obelia is located in a memorial museum just outside Mitchell. You'll see the space suit and helmet he wore on the ill-fated Mercury mission, the nearly whole *Gemini III* capsule he piloted on March 23, 1965, Norman Rockwell's painting of Gus in his Apollo flight suit, and personal items from his Indiana childhood.

Redstone Rocket Memorial, Sixth & Vine
    Sts., Mitchell, IN 47446
No phone
Hours: Always visible
Cost: Free
Directions: Next to the Mitchell Municipal Building, three blocks north of Rte. 60, one block west of the railroad tracks.

World's Largest Condom Model.

Virgil I. Grissom Memorial, Spring Mill State Park, 3333 State Rd. 60 E, Mitchell, IN 47446
Phone: (812) 849-3534
Hours: Daily 8 AM–5 PM
Cost: In-state $7, Out-of-state $9
Website: www.in.gov/dnr/parklake/2968.htm
Directions: Three miles east of town on Rte. 60 to the park entrance, just to the right of the main gate.

Gus Grissom Boyhood Home, 715 W. Grissom Ave., PO Box 431, Mitchell, IN 47446
Phone: (812) 849-4940
Hours: Call ahead
Cost: Call ahead
Website: www.facebook.com/GusGrissomBoyhoodMuseum/info/
Directions: Three blocks south of the railroad tracks, between Seventh and Eighth Sts.

Morgantown
Rock House

When James "Smith" Knight dreamed of a home for his new family in 1894, he did what today is called "thinking outside the box." He built the outer walls of the 10-room home with concrete blocks in which he embedded anything he could get his hands on, mostly small stones. But if you look long enough, you can also find broken dishes, marbles, geodes, shells, chains, dolls' heads, a boar's skull, and more sticking out of the siding. Knight fashioned his name out of lumps of coal placed over the front door and included his wife Isabelle on another panel. She died 23 years after they moved in, and Knight remarried. He fathered 20 children between both marriages and died in 1934.

The building is in remarkable shape for being more than a century old. The Rock House was later made into a bed-and-breakfast but today is a private residence.

380 W. Washington St., Morgantown, IN 46160
Private phone
Hours: Always visible; view from street
Cost: Free
Directions: Just east of the intersection of Rtes. 135 and 252 (Washington St.).

Needmore
Cursed Pyramid and Crumbling Wall of China

The limestone used to build the Empire State Building was excavated from the Empire Quarry near Bedford, the "Limestone Capital of the World." Stone from the region was also used to construct the Pentagon, Jefferson Memorial, Lincoln Memorial, and Washington National Cathedral; New York's Cathedral of St. John the Divine, Rockefeller Center, Yankee Stadium, and Radio City Music Hall; Chicago's Tribune Tower and Merchandise Mart; and the University of Moscow. That's quite a rocky résumé.

But then, like the prideful folk of Babel, the quarries of Bedford overreached. In the 1970s the town planned to build a 1/5 scale, 8-story model of the Pyramid of Cheops, and a 650-foot segment of the Great Wall of China. The promoters intended to demonstrate the skills of local stonecutters, to inject a little life into the local economy, and perhaps touch the face of God.

Who was paying for it? You! After the project received $700,000 in federal funds, construction began. Soon legislators bowed to pressure to cut off the pork barrel project, and the bankroll vanished like a mirage in the desert. Two pyramid-topped columns mark the entrance to this now-abandoned boondoggle. Follow the road for a half mile and you'll find the remains of the pyramid's base among the weeds.

Limestone Tourist Park, Needmore, IN 47421
No phone
Hours: Always visible
Cost: Free
Directions: Take Trogden Rd. east off Rte. 37, keep bearing right as you pass through town, take a right at the "T" and follow the road until it ends with boulders in the road.

The pharaohs didn't give up so easily.

New Albany
Yenawine Exhibit

After retiring from his job on the railroad at the age of 60, Merle Yenawine vowed to keep busy. Drawing from his childhood experiences and his skill with tools, Yenawine began creating dioramas of rural life in southern Indiana. What made his 60 miniature scenes unique was that his figures *moved*, controlled from beneath by small motors and machinery. Yenawine would bring his creations to local schools for the kids to enjoy, and when he grew too old to do that, he sold most of the collection to the NA-FC School Corporation for $800. Today they are on permanent display in the basement of the city library. The enormous body of work has 475 different moving figures, all of which can be activated by buttons on their display cases.

Yenawine's scenes are humorous and action-packed. Two men fight near an outhouse in the Shotgun Wedding diorama. Kids misbehave in the One Room Schoolhouse. Ducks dance on the Family Farm. Reluctant pigs battle with farmers in the bloody Community Butchering—and who can blame them? The Town Carnival has a woman waltzing with bears, geese on a teeter-totter, ax throwers, and acrobats atop high poles. If you'd like to see how these contraptions function, the Main Street exhibit has a foot-level mirror to reflect the mechanics beneath the diorama.

New Albany–Floyd County Public Library, 180 W. Spring St., New Albany, IN 47150
Phone: (812) 944-8464
Hours: Monday–Thursday 9 AM–8:30 PM, Friday–Saturday 9 AM–5:30 PM, Sunday 1–5 PM
Cost: Free
Website: http://nafclibrary.org
Directions: Along Scribner Dr. between Elm and Spring Sts., two blocks east of I-64.

New Harmony

The Angel Gabriel's Footprints

A long, long time ago, the Archangel Gabriel stood on a flat stone to blow his holy horn, and when he stepped off, his footprints were indelibly etched into the rock. Hard to believe, yes, unless you are the type of person who would willingly follow Lutheran visionary George Rapp into the malaria-ridden swamps of southern Indiana.

That's what the folks of the Harmony Society did in 1814, so tales of a rock-stomping angel made as much sense as anything. A biblical Grauman's Theater? Sure—why not? Rapp told them the rock was from the Holy Land, but in actuality, his son purchased the carved limestone in St. Louis.

The true story, when it got out, didn't sit too well with the folks who remained in New Harmony, yet it didn't bother them so much that they tossed out the fake. Instead, it ended up in the backyard of the Rapp-Maclure House. Today, the home is privately owned and the footprints are protected by a high wall and fence. Historic New Harmony claims the site will one day be open to the public. But when will that be? The Second Coming? Why all the security? Could those tootsie tracks be real?

Rapp-Maclure Home, c/o Historic New Harmony, PO Box 579, New Harmony, IN 47631
Phone: (800) 231-2168 or (812) 682-4488
Hours: Daylight; view from street

Cost: Free
Website: www.newharmony.org
Directions: At the corner of Main (Rte. 69) and Church (Rte. 66) Sts.

New Harmony Labyrinth

Lutheran separatist George Rapp had his own ideas about how the world worked, and he convinced 1,000 "Harmonists" (sometimes called Rappites) to leave rural Pennsylvania and follow him to Indiana in 1814. Their experiment became known as Harmonie, "That Wonder in the Wilderness." Rapp and his followers used their time constructively while waiting for Christ's return: clearing land, building homes, brewing beer, and distilling whiskey. But after 10 years and no Jesus, they packed their bags and headed back to Pennsylvania. The whole operation was sold to utopian Robert Owen for $150,000 in 1825.

Christening the failing enterprise "New Harmony," Owen revamped the commune with a socialist philosophy, and the place thrived as a cultural center of the Midwest prior to the Civil War. New Harmony slowly faded over the next century until an influx of cash in the 1980s helped spruce it up into a modern tourist trap.

Part of restoring this community was rebuilding the New Harmony Labyrinth, originally laid out by Rapp. This single-path hedge maze was intended to represent the path of life: twisted and difficult. But because it has no dead ends or alternative paths, you're bound to end up in the center if you walk long enough. And, apparently, at the end of our lives we'll end up at a dinky shack.

New Harmony, 520 Church St., New Harmony, IN 47631
Phone: (812) 682-4846
Hours: Always visible
Cost: Free
Website: www.newharmony-in.gov
Directions: Labyrinth at the south end of town on Main St. (Rte. 69).

NEWBURGH

➡ On July 18, 1862, Newburgh was the first town north of the Mason-Dixon Line to be captured by the Confederate Army during the Civil War.

LETHER LABYRINTHETHS

Yeth, there are other labyrintheths in thith thtate, though they're not ath thofithticated ath New Harmony'th ith. Thtill, they're thirtenly worth a thtop.

Kenneth E. Smith Memorial Labyrinth

Hawthorn Park, 6067 E. Old Maple Ave., Terre Haute, (812) 462-3225, www .vigocounty.in.gov/eGov/apps/services/index.egov?view=detail;id=20

The outdoor labyrinth in Terre Haute's Hawthorn Park is based on an indoor labyrinth—the one found on the floor of France's Chartres Cathedral. This one's larger, 80 feet in diameter, and fully wheelchair accessible. It sits in the middle of a meditation garden, just in case the 34-turn path leaves you aggravated.

Golf Course Labyrinth

7453 County Rd. 400 S, Marion, (765) 998-7651, http://walnutcreekgolf.com

The labyrinth at the Walnut Creek golf course is also a reproduction, but it is based on a turf pathway in Hannover, Germany, known as Das Rad ("The Wheel"), built around 1500. It is 105 feet in diameter, and its path is 1,400 feet long . . . and it's not even the coolest thing here. The course was built in a former Abolitionist settlement that was a stopover station on the Underground Railroad, the Israel Jenkins House.

Oolitic
A Big Palooka

Boxer Joe Palooka represented many American values—honesty, integrity, and punching an opponent's light out—so it was only appropriate that he be honored on the face of Mt. Rushmore. And, if you've followed his comic strip since the 1940s, you know he was right up there with the presidents, for a while. But then the federal government got involved, and Joe's square-jawed mug was blasted off the mountain, leaving only Washington, Jefferson, Lincoln, and Roosevelt. No Palooka.

It hardly seemed fair to the folks in limestone country who had it in their power to re-carve the character's image, albeit on a smaller scale. George Hitchcock Sr. created a new monument in 1947, a full figure, right down to Joe's boxing trunks. It was erected in a ceremony attended by "Ham" Fisher, the comic strip's creator, in June 1948. Due to vandalism from some good-fer-nothin' kids, the statue was bounced to various locations

Ya big Palooka!

around the area until it ended up outside the Oolitic Town Hall, where it stands today. Palooka still has six-pack abs, but his rib cage sticks out like a runway model's. Hey Joe, put some meat on those bones!

Town Hall, 109 Main St., Oolitic, IN 47451
Phone: (812) 275-6813
Hours: Always visible
Cost: Free
Directions: On Main St. between Lafayette St. and Hoosier Ave.

Orangeville
The Lost River and the Orangeville Rise

Somewhere near Route 337, eight miles due east of Orangeville, the Lost River lives up to its name and disappears into the earth. After meandering through 22 miles of subterranean caverns and passing beneath the village of Lost River, it pops back to the surface at a large natural spring called the Orangeville Rise.

To geologists, this below-ground activity is known as the Karst Region, and because it's so unique, there's a group dedicated to its preservation: the Indiana Karst Conservancy. It successfully lobbied to have the Orangeville Rise designated a National Natural Landmark in 1975, which is one reason you can still see it bubbling to the surface in Orangeville today.

Center of town, Orangeville, IN 47452
No phone
Hours: Always visible
Cost: Free
Website: http://ikc.caves.org
Directions: Head north of Rte. 150 on the first road east of the Rte. 145 intersection to Orangeville and follow the signs.

Santa Claus
Holiday World

If you think Walt Disney came up with the concept of the theme park, think again. More than a decade before the Magic Kingdom opened its doors, Santa Claus Land welcomed Christmas-loving tourists. The year was 1946, and the park was more of a kiddie land than anything else. Over time it expanded, forming four "worlds"—Christmas, for the tykes; Fourth of July, with carnival rides; Halloween, with two roller coasters and a few other thrill rides; and Thanksgiving, with all the most recent additions. The Raven roller coaster, which roars through the wooded hillside, is consistently voted by enthusiasts as the best wooden roller coaster in the nation.

Purists needn't worry the place has "taken the Christ out of Christmas," for there's a concrete nativity scene just inside the gate where you can pose as a Wise Man with your I'M WITH STUPID T-shirt. The Hoosier Celebration Theater offers daily gospel performances of "Hallelujah!" And don't forget the park's mascot, Holidog—he's in the Bible *somewhere*, isn't he?

The newest addition to Holiday World is the Splashin' Safari water park. The slides have jungle names, not reindeer names. Perhaps the park was worried that a North Pole theme might freeze out potential guests.

Holiday World, 452 E. Christmas Blvd., Santa Claus, IN 47579
Phone: (877) 463-2645 or (812) 937-4401
Hours: May–October, hours vary, check website
Cost: Prices vary by day, time of entry, and season—check website
Website: www.holidayworld.com
Directions: Exit 63 from I-64, at the junction on Rtes. 162 & 245.

Santa Claus Town

There's no need to drive to the North Pole to hang out with Santa—come to southern Indiana! This small town was named (according to legend) by a confused child on Christmas Eve 1852. Citizens were meeting in a local church to discuss what to call their town. Their first choice, Santa Fe, was already taken by another Indiana burg. Outside, a snowstorm blanketed the countryside and a sleigh approached the church. Hearing the jingle bells, a young girl shouted out, "Santa Claus!" and the town got its name. (Other reports of the meeting claim the adults had been drinking heavily during the long meeting and were "ready for anything.")

This town's enthusiasm for all things Christmassy hasn't waned. In fact, many otherwise normal homes and businesses have been modified to look like castles and elf huts. They sit along cutely named streets like Candy Cane Lane, Sled Run, Noël Street, Ornament Lane, Chestnut by the Fire, Prancer Drive, Silver Bell Street, and Three Kings. New developments have branched out into other holidays, like Good Friday Boulevard, Easter Circle, Ides of March, Pro Super Bowl, and New Year's Eve Road. The town's fire truck is named Rudolph and has a red light on its hood's "nose."

For the best Santa photo, check out the 22-foot, 40-ton concrete Kris Kringle on the outskirts of town. This statue was erected in 1935, mounted on a Star of Bethlehem–shaped slab of concrete pointing toward the original manger in Israel. It is dedicated to all the children of the world, even those who don't believe in the jolly fellow. (If you don't want to climb the hill for a photo, there are other Santa statues all over town.)

Santa Claus Statue, Santa Claus, IN 47579
No phone
Hours: Always visible
Cost: Free
Website: http://santaclausind.org
Directions: Just southwest of the intersection of Rtes. 245 & 162, on the east side of town.

Don't make me get the lumps of coal!

Each December since 1914 the Santa Claus post office (the only one in the nation!) will postmark your cards with a special verse and Christmas image designed by a local high school student. If you're going to all the trouble of sending out cards, ship them all—stamped, of course—to the post office and "elves" do all the rest.

Postmaster, Santa Claus Station, 45 N. Kringle Cir., Santa Claus, IN 47579
Phone: (812) 937-4469
Hours: Monday–Friday 9 AM–12:30 PM, 1:30–4 PM; Saturday 9:30–11:30 AM
Cost: Free
Website: http://santaclausind.org/listings/santa-claus-post-office/
Directions: Northwest of the Rte. 162/245 intersection on the northwest side of town.

It was longtime Santa Claus postmaster James Martin who began the tradition of answering kids' letters to Santa. You can see the typewriter he used for 30 years to answer kids' letters to Santa at the Santa Claus Museum & Village. It also contains the archives of Holiday World, which is the museum's primary funder.

SALEM
➡ The beverage known as 2 percent milk was invented by Roy Robertson of the Salem Creamery in 1936.

Santa Claus Museum & Village, 69 State Rd. 245, PO Box 1, Santa Claus, IN 47579
Phone: (812) 544-2434
Hours: June–September and December, daily 10 AM–6 PM
Cost: Free
Website: www.santaclausmuseum.org
Directions: Just south of the Rte. 162/245 interchange on the east side of town.

If you want to make your yuletide visit to Santa Claus spectacular, spend a night at Santa's Lodge, just southwest of Holiday World. This lakeside hotel is decorated in green and red and has a year-round Christmas tree. Have a meal at St. Nick's Restaurant, or get blitzed in Blitzen's Bar. Pose with the statue of Kris Kringle on the lawn. It's a yuletidal wave of possibilities! The hotel's only shortcoming is that it isn't staffed with elves, just regular folk.

Santa's Lodge & St. Nick's Restaurant, 91 W. Christmas Blvd., Santa Claus, IN 47579
Phone: (812) 937-1902
Hours: Always open
Cost: $99–175/night
Website: www.santaslodge.com
Directions: On Rte. 162 (Christmas Blvd.), just west of the Rte. 162/245 interchange on the west side of town.

Just across the road from Santa's Lodge is a minigolf attraction with a North Pole theme. The holes surround a large snowman fountain that rains down water from his top hat, almost as if he's melting before your eyes . . . yet he doesn't melt. A Festivus miracle! The place also serves ice cream and pizza and has a video arcade.

Frosty's Fun Center, 15 S. Cedar Ln., Santa Claus, IN 47579
Phone: (812) 544-3338
Hours: Sunday–Thursday 6 AM–8 PM, Friday–Saturday 6 AM–9 PM
Cost: Golf, free
Website: www.facebook.com/frostysfun
Directions: West of the Rte. 162/245 interchange, next to Santa's Lodge.

SEYMOUR

⇒ John [Cougar] Mellencamp was born in Seymour on October 7, 1951.

⇒ Fish rained down in Seymour on August 8, 1891.

Want some sweets for your stocking? Head over to Santa's Candy Castle. The structure was built in 1935 by Milton Harris, who added an eight-building Toy Village and Santa's Workshop a year later. However, Harris's roadside attraction was eclipsed by the much larger Santa Claus Land just down the road, and it never took off.

After Harris died in 1950, the castle sat vacant until 2006. Its new owner, Kevin Klosowski, refurbished the structure and stuffed it with old-timey confections. (There are also several abandoned North Pole structures in the field north of the castle, if you're interested.)

Santa's Candy Castle, 15499 N. State Rd. 245, Santa Claus, IN 47579
Phone: (812) 544-3900
Hours: June–August, daily 9 AM–8 PM; September–November, Saturday–Sunday 9 AM–5 PM; December, daily 9 AM–5 PM
Cost: Free
Website: www.santascandycastle.com
Directions: One mile south of Holiday World on Rte. 245, at Candy Castle Rd. (Rte. 700).

And if you're the Grinchy type, you might want to visit a special location on the northwest end of town: the Santa Claus Cemetery, burial place of elves and congregants of the nearby United Methodist Church.

Santa Claus Cemetery, Rte. 245, Santa Claus, IN 47579
No phone
Hours: Always visible
Cost: Free
Directions: Northwest of the Rte. 162/245 intersection, just past the United Methodist Church.

SHOALS
➡ The team name at Shoals High School (7900 US Hwy. 50, (812) 247-2090, www.shoals.k12.in.us) is the Jug Rox, named for a 60-foot, jug-shaped limestone formation at Albright Lane, northwest of town.

TELL CITY
➡ A statue of William Tell and his trusting son Walther stands in front of city hall (700 Main St., (812) 547-5511, www.tellcityindiana.com) in Tell City. Swiss settlers colonized the area in 1856 under the guidance of Casper Gloor.

Seymour
America's First Train Robbery

The Reno family was filled with bad 'uns. Ask the folks of Rockford, just north of Seymour. During the 1850s the town was plagued by a series of mysterious fires, leveling Rockford one building at a time. Each time property was torched, another Reno clan member appeared and bought the charred land to build something new. This continued until five of every six properties in town were Reno-owned. Later, some of the more ambitious male family members formed the Reno Gang and terrorized southern Indiana.

It came as no surprise to locals when three members of gang (John and Simeon Reno and Franklin Sparks) launched a new innovation in thievery: train robbery. On October 6, 1866, the trio jumped on the eastbound Ohio & Mississippi train as it pulled out of the Seymour station, knocked out a guard, and tossed two safes from the moving boxcar a half mile east of the depot (100 feet east of the Burkart Boulevard railroad overpass). It was the nation's first train robbery. The Reno Gang got more than $10,000 from the Adams Express courier.

Emboldened by their success, they hit another train on September 28, 1867, and another on May 22, 1868, about 14 miles south of town by the Marshfield station, netting another $96,000 from Adams Express. Up to four Reno brothers, along with other Hoosier lowlifes, participated in these heists.

But you can only abuse a populace so long. A posse calling themselves the Seymour Regulators, sometimes called the Scarlet Mask Society, eventually caught up with several gang members on July 20, 1868. Val Elliott, Charles Roseberry, and Fred Clifton were pulled from a train and hanged from a beech tree beside the tracks near where Second Street crosses the B&O tracks today. On July 24, another three gang members—Frank Sparks, John Moore, and Henry Jerrell—were swinging from the same tree. Though the tree is long gone, locals still affectionately call the intersection "Hangman's Crossing."

Later that year, on December 12, Frank Reno, William Reno, Simeon Reno, and Charles Anderson were yanked by an angry mob from their New Albany jail cells. The vigilantes didn't bother taking the brothers back to the Regulators' favorite hanging tree but lynched the robbers on the spot. The Regulators were not much for ceremony, so the three brothers were dumped in a common pine box and buried in Seymour. Years later, individual tombstones were erected over their grave.

Old City Cemetery, Ninth & Ewing Sts., Seymour, IN 47274
No phone
Hours: Always visible
Cost: Free
Directions: Inside the iron fence just north of Ninth St., halfway down the block, west of Rte. 11.

Solsberry
Tulip Trestle

Though officially known as the Greene County Viaduct, most locals call it the Tulip Trestle because the Illinois Central Railroad bridge runs between Solsberry and the town of Tulip. And what makes it so special? Numbers! Erected in 1906, it proudly holds the title of the Longest Railroad Trestle in the United States and the third longest in the *world*—2,295 feet from end to end. That's almost a half mile. The 18-tower structure soars as high as 180 feet above the valley below. And no, you may not walk across it, because it is still in use. But you can look at it from below. That's almost as impressive, and much safer.

County Road 480 E, Solsberry, IN 47459
No phone
Hours: Always visible
Cost: Free
Directions: West out of Solsberry following the railroad tracks on County Rd. 375 N, five miles ahead turn south on County Rd. 480 E.

Stone Head
Stone Head

You don't have to have a stone head to live in Stone Head, but it helps. In fact, little is left of this community but the stone head after which it was named. The roadside bust was carved in 1851 by Henry Cross as part of his obligation to the local government. At the time, able-bodied men were required to put in six days' labor on public works projects around Brown

County (in addition to paying taxes). Cross proposed to work off his obligation by carving three busts to place on roadside markers along New Bellsville Pike, and since one was going to be of the venerable George Summa, the road's supervisor, officials agreed.

Two of the busts on the old road are long gone, but one remains: the stone head of Stone Head. Today it is painted white with black features, the stern face of a humorless mime. It has seen happier times, but then so has the town of Stone Head.

Route 135, Stone Head, IN 47448
No phone
Hours: Always visible
Cost: Free
Directions: South of Rte. 46 on Rte. 135.

Top rock head in Stone Head.

Tell City and Cannelton
Finding Out the Hard Way

As originally designed, the Lockheed Electra turbojet had one major flaw, but nobody realized it until St. Patrick's Day in 1960. Northwest Airlines Flight 710 was flying from Minneapolis to Miami when an engine vibration created a sympathetic vibration in its wings, causing both to snap off at 18,000 feet. Without wings, the fuselage rocketed toward the earth, plowing into a soybean field at 600 mph. All 63 aboard the plane perished when it buried itself on impact.

Only eight of the victims were able to be identified. Remains of the 55 others were interred in 16 coffins in Tell City's Greenwood Cemetery beneath a monument donated by Northwest Airlines. The Cannelton Kiwanis Club erected a similar monument at the crash site along the Ohio River.

Crash Memorial, Millstone Rd., Cannelton, IN 47520
No phone
Hours: Always visible
Cost: Free
Directions: Southeast from Cannelton on Rte. 66, turn south on Rte. 166 to County Rd. 4 (Millstone Rd.), follow the signs east one mile, on the north side of the road.

Greenwood Cemetery, Payne St. & Cemetery Rd., Tell City, IN 47586
Phone: (812) 547-6872
Hours: Always visible
Cost: Free
Directions: On Rte. 37 (Payne St.), east of the Rte. 66 intersection.

Vevay

Big Rubber Ducky

Ernie might be awfully fond of his rubbery ducky on *Sesame Street*, but the one outside this Vevay childcare facility is a little creepy. For one, it stands about five feet tall, hardly able to make bath time lots of fun—you're more likely to be crushed or pinned underwater. But even more disturbing are its zombielike bug eyes. Scary indeed, but at least its spooky stare keeps the little ones from darting past it, out into the street.

Little Lambs Childcare Ministry, 723 Main St., Vevay, IN 47043
Phone: (812) 427-9002
Hours: Always visible
Cost: Free
Directions: Seven blocks east of Ferry St. (Rte. 56) on Rte. 156 (Main St.), at the river.

Mary Wright's Creepy Piano

Mary Wright was a weird woman, though she didn't start out that way. Wright was the child of English immigrants who came to the new frontier

---

TREVLAC
➡ The town of Trevlac was named by founder Colonel Calvert, who simply wrote *Calvert* backward.

VEVAY
➡ The preserved Switzerland County Courthouse (212 W. Main St., (812) 427-3237, www.switzerland-county.com) in Vevay still has its original six-sided privy.

---

in 1817 with a pile of money and a Muzio Clementi piano, the first set of ivories ever seen in the yet-to-be state of Indiana. But before long, the family was broke and had nothing left but the piano, and no way to return to their homeland. Mary did not take this well, for her true love was back in London. In her depression, she retreated to the second floor of her parents' home, coming downstairs once a week, in formal dress, to give a morose recital for anyone who would listen ... not that she cared if anyone showed up. This Dickinson-wannabe never acknowledged those who'd come to hear her play, and performed until her death.

Today, Wright's Muzio Clementi is part of the collection of the Switzerland County Historical Museum. If you visit, don't miss the second floor where you'll see Vevay's retired Electrostatic Shock Machine. A certain "Mr. Henry" used this device for many years at the local high school for "rejuvenating" the pupils. Perhaps Mary could have benefited from a few volts.

Switzerland County Historical Museum, 208 E. Market St., Vevay, IN 47043
Phone: (812) 427-3560
Hours: April–October, daily noon–4 PM
Cost: Free
Website: www.switzcomuseums.org/files/County-History.html
Directions: Two blocks north on Rte. 156 (Ohio River Scenic Byway) from the Rte. 56 (Ferry St.) intersection.

West Baden Springs
The New West Baden Springs Hotel

Back when Las Vegas was a few shacks more than a desert, French Lick and West Baden Springs were popular vacation destinations for the rich and famous. In 1902 the West Baden Springs Hotel set a new standard for elegance and over-the-top architecture. Its central dome had a 200-foot diameter, larger than St. Peter's Basilica in Rome, and was the largest unsupported dome in the world until the Astrodome opened in 1965. Below, it took more than 12 million 1-inch Italian marble tiles to cover the hotel's main floor. Outside, on the grounds, the resort had a double-decker riding track, the top level for bicyclists and the bottom for horse-drawn carriages, both circling around a baseball diamond. Visitors such as Helen Keller, Al Capone, and Gen. John J. Pershing could stroll through the elaborate gardens, relax in the Roman baths, or drink the spring's "Sprudel Water," which was said to cure almost anything.

With the stock market collapse of 1929, the hotel closed its doors and started on a downhill slide. At one time it was used as the winter home of the Hagenbeck-Wallace Circus. Then, in 1934, it was sold to the Jesuits for one dollar. They proceeded to tear out anything they felt was too opulent, which was a lot. From 1966 to 1983, it was home to the Northwoods Institute, a private college. As it fell further into disrepair, it was rescued by the Historic Landmark Foundation of Indiana and given a $32 million restoration. A developer finally finished the job, and today the place is open for guests. Rich guests. But you're still welcome to come inside and take a look.

French Lick Resort & West Baden Springs Hotel, 8670 W. State Rd. 56, West Baden Springs, IN 47432
Phone: (888) 936-9360 or (812) 936-2100
Hours: Always open
Cost: Free; Rooms, $200+
Website: www.frenchlick.com/hotels/westbaden
Directions: Just southwest of the intersection of Indiana Ave. (Rte. 56) and Rte. 145.

Worthington
Remnants of the World's Largest Deciduous Tree

Look out Kokomo! Sure, that town might lay claim to the World's Largest Stump, but proud Worthingtonians are quick to point out that just because you have the largest *stump*, that doesn't mean you have the largest *tree*. In fact, the 150-foot-high sycamore, which once grew a mile and a half west of town, at its peak had a circumference of 45'3" at a foot above the ground. Its largest branch was 27'8" around, and another measured 23'3".

As powerful as it was, the tree toppled during a violent windstorm in 1925. Both the stump and largest branch were too large to save or move, so a smaller branch was transported to a city park. A roof was built to protect the blunt end from rain and snow, and the town bought a piece of surplus army artillery to guard it from jealous Kokomoans.

If you wonder whether the Pacific Northwest's redwoods dwarf this stupendous sycamore, you're engaging in technical hair-splitting which proud Worthingtonians will not entertain. They said *deciduous*, and redwoods are *evergreens*.

City Park, Dayton & Worthington Sts., Worthington, IN 47471
No phone
Hours: Always visible
Cost: Free
Directions: Two blocks west of Rte. 157 (Jefferson St.) on Worthington St., at the north end of town.

Just try and take their branch, you Kokomoans!

ZOAR
➡ The town of Zoar celebrates Mosquito Fest each August.

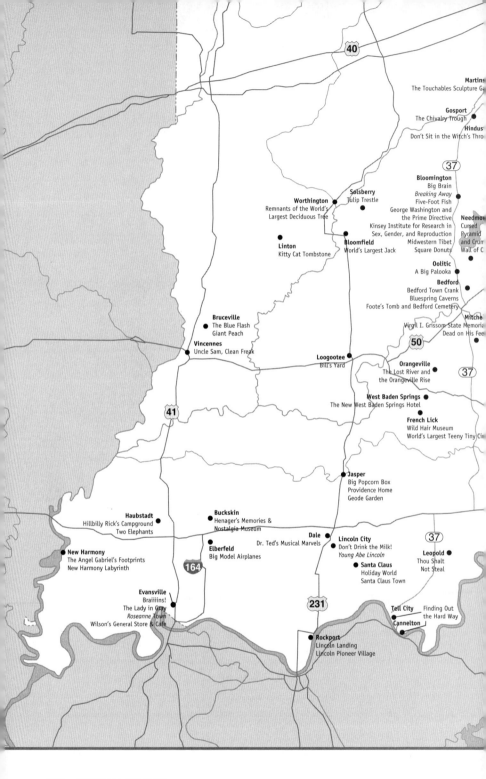

Martins
The Touchables Sculpture G

Gosport
The Chivalry Trough

Hindus
Don't Sit in the Witch's Thro

Bloomington
Big Brain
Breaking Away
Five-Foot Fish
George Washington and
the Prime Directive
Kinsey Institute for Research in
Sex, Gender, and Reproduction
Midwestern Tibet
Square Donuts

Needmo
Cursed
Pyramid
and Crum
Wall of C

Worthington
Remnants of the World's
Largest Deciduous Tree

Solsberry
Tulip Trestle

Bloomfield
World's Largest Jack

Linton
Kitty Cat Tombstone

Oolitic
A Big Palooka

Bedford
Bedford Town Crank
Bluespring Caverns
Foote's Tomb and Bedford Cemetery

Bruceville
The Blue Flash
Giant Peach

Mitche
Virgil I. Grissom State Memoria
Dead on His Fee

Vincennes
Uncle Sam, Clean Freak

Loogootee
Bill's Yard

Orangeville
The Lost River and
the Orangeville Rise

West Baden Springs
The New West Baden Springs Hotel

French Lick
Wild Hair Museum
World's Largest Teeny Tiny Cir

Jasper
Big Popcorn Box
Providence Home
Geode Garden

Haubstadt
Hillbilly Rick's Campground
Two Elephants

Buckskin
Henager's Memories &
Nostalgia Museum

Dale
Dr. Ted's Musical Marvels

Lincoln City
Don't Drink the Milk!
Young Abe Lincoln

Leopold
Thou Shalt
Not Steal

New Harmony
The Angel Gabriel's Footprints
New Harmony Labyrinth

Elberfeld
Big Model Airplanes

Santa Claus
Holiday World
Santa Claus Town

Evansville
Braiiiins!
The Lady in Gray
Roseanne Town
Wilson's General Store & Cafe

Tell City Finding Out
the Hard Way

Cannelton

Rockport
Lincoln Landing
Lincoln Pioneer Village

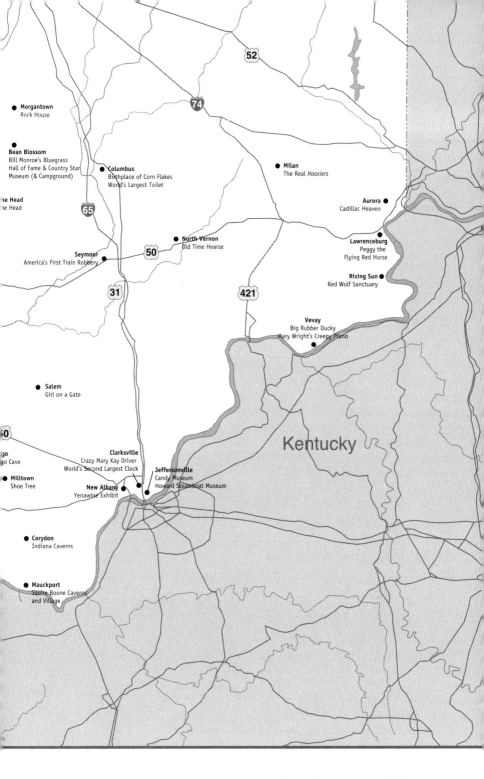

Morgantown
Rock House

Bean Blossom
Bill Monroe's Bluegrass
Hall of Fame & Country Star
Museum (& Campground)

ne Head
ne Head

Columbus
Birthplace of Corn Flakes
World's Largest Toilet

Milan
The Real *Hoosiers*

Aurora
Cadillac Heaven

Lawrenceburg
Peggy the
Flying Red Horse

North Vernon
Old Time Hearse

Seymour
America's First Train Robbery

Rising Sun
Red Wolf Sanctuary

Vevay
Big Rubber Ducky
Mary Wright's Creepy Piano

Salem
Girl on a Gate

Kentucky

go
go Cave

Clarksville
Crazy Mary Kay Driver
World's Second Largest Clock

Jeffersonville
Candy Museum
Howard Steamboat Museum

Milltown
Shoe Tree

New Albany
Yenawine Exhibit

Corydon
Indiana Caverns

Mauckport
Squire Boone Caverns
and Village

INDIANAPOLIS AND SUBURBS

*I*ndianapolis sometimes has an undeserved reputation as being a Nowheresville, dismissed as Indiana-no-place. Yet it's everything but. It's got the world's largest children's museum, sports and recreation facilities that rival most big cities, art, theater, fine dining, and more.

Yeah, yeah, yeah. Go read about that stuff somewhere else. You didn't purchase this guide looking for *culture*. You want to know about century-old ghosts and fiberglass monstrosities. You wonder what Jim Jones was doing selling South American monkeys door-to-door to the residents of this fair city. And what happened to the upstanding local citizens who tossed a former American president into a mud puddle? All good questions—read on!

Indianapolis

Birthplace of Wonder Bread

Don't act so surprised! If Wonder Bread wasn't invented in Indianapolis, where do you think it might have been? This shockingly white bread was developed at the Taggart Baking Company in 1921. Vice president Elmer Cline came up with the bread's name after seeing a balloon race at the Indianapolis Speedway; he claimed to be "filled with wonder," much the same way Wonder Bread seems to be filled with air. Four years later, Taggart and its Wonder Bread were sold to the Continental Baking Company, and it's been baking the loaves ever since.

If you're one of those folks who don't quite understand how every loaf of Wonder Bread can look *exactly* the same or who think the uniformity is achieved by some sort of nefarious process, you're invited to take the factory tour. The secret? "It's Slo-Baked."

Wonder and Hostess Bakery, 2929 N. Shadeland Ave., Indianapolis, IN 46219
Phone: (866) 245-8921
Hours: Call ahead for tour hours
Cost: Free
Website: www.wonderbread.com
Directions: South of E. 30th St. on Shadeland Ave.

Bread doesn't get much whiter than this.

Daniel Boone, Tree Vandal

Though the truth of its origin is questionable at best, a graffiti scar on a tree in Indianapolis is attributed to Daniel Boone, who was a surveyor in the Northwest Territory around 1800. The carving on the beech's trunk gives Boone's name and trademark bear paw insignia. Some historians believe its location, high up the trunk, was probably the result of Boone being on horseback when he carved it. Visitors to Eagle Creek are strongly discouraged from adding their own Boone-like insignias anywhere else in this park. Today it's called vandalism and can get you in real trouble.

Eagle Creek Park, 7840 W. 56th St., Indianapolis, IN 46254
Phone: (317) 327-7110
Hours: Dawn–dusk
Cost: $5/car ($6 for noncounty residents)
Website: http://eaglecreekpark.org
Directions: Just west of I-465 on 56th St.; the Boone Tree is approximately one block north of the Nature Center.

David Letterman, Bag Boy

David Letterman was born in Indianapolis on April 12, 1947. His family lived in the Broad Ripple neighborhood, and his father owned the first FTD Florist in the city. Dave attended Public School 55 (today Eliza A. Blaker School 55, 1349 E. 54th St., (317) 226-4000, www.myips.org/elizablaker55) and seemed to be living the life of typical baby boomer . . . until he got a job as a bag boy.

Why the Atlas Supermarket was so instrumental in Letterman's comic development is no mystery; kindhearted owner Sidney Maurer not only tolerated Letterman's pranks but also would cover for the teenager when customers failed to appreciate the humor. Other bosses might have fired the smart-ass. Letterman held raffles for sports cars that didn't exist. More than once he announced that a mah-jongg tournament would be held on Sunday, and players showed up with their tiles to find an empty parking lot and a locked store. Other times he conducted fire drills and marched confused customers out into the parking lot.

Letterman attended Broad Ripple High School (1115 Broad Ripple Ave., (317) 693-5700, www.myips.org/brmhs) from 1961 to 1965 where he served as a hall monitor. Marilyn Quayle also attended Broad Ripple but was two years younger than Dave (and remembered not liking him very much).

After college and a short stint at a radio station in Muncie, Dave returned to Indy in 1970 with his wife, Michelle, where he secured a five-year "temporary" job at WLWI-TV (channel 13, now WTHR). His first job was to read the station's call letters and public service announcements, but he was later given a few shows. He hosted the 2 AM *Freeze-Dried Movie*, a Saturday morning 4-H show called *Clover Power*, and the weekend weather. As a meteorologist, he took liberties with the forecasts, making up tropical storms and town names. In 1975 he left for California to become a stand-up comedian.

The Atlas Supermarket was torn down and replaced with an upscale grocery a few years ago.

The Fresh Market, 5415 N. College Ave., Indianapolis, IN 46220
Phone: (317) 259-9270
Hours: Daily 8 AM–9 PM
Cost: Free
Website: www.thefreshmarket.com
Directions: Seven blocks east of Meridian (Rte. 31) at 54th St.

Hannah House

According to legend, a basement fire ignited by an overturned lamp in this 1858 mansion killed several escaped slaves, and rather than have this station on the Underground Railroad exposed, the runaway's bodies were buried secretly beneath the house.

Things haven't been the same since. Moaning, phantom footsteps, and mysterious scratching noises are as common as the creaky floorboards. There's also the smell of rotting flesh in the upstairs bedrooms, but that could just be a dead rat in the walls. Some have seen the ghost of a stillborn baby. Far from being still, it tends to run around on the second floor. And when *PM Magazine* was filming a segment on the hauntings, a chandelier swung unassisted and a picture leapt from its nail on the wall. What more proof do you need?

3801 Madison Ave., Indianapolis, IN 46227
Phone: (317) 787-8486

Hours: Check website; only open for occasional open houses
Cost: Free
Website: http://thehannahmansion.org
Directions: At the southeast corner of National and Madison Aves.

Indiana Medical History Museum

The Indiana Medical History Museum is one of the hidden gems of Indianapolis, tucked away on the grounds of the old Central State Hospital for
the Insane. It is housed in the nation's oldest pathology building, built in
1898 under the direction of Dr. George Edenharter. The facility had three
cutting-edge laboratories, a library, a photography studio, an anatomical
museum, a morgue, and an amphitheater used for its teaching program.
Edenharter's facility was a leader in the study of syphilis (particularly as it
affected the brain), mental illness, and brain injuries.

The current museum has 15,000+ artifacts in its collection, but remarkably few of them are on display. Instead, the building has been restored to
the way it looked shortly after it opened a century ago, to give visitors a
sense of what it might have looked like. But in one room on the ground
floor, dozens of jars filled with brains and parts of brains fill cabinets along
two walls. The curators admit this is the room school kids enjoy the most.

Old Pathology Building, 3045 W. Vermont St., Indianapolis, IN 46222
Phone: (317) 635-7329
Hours: Thursday–Saturday 10 AM–4 PM
Cost: Adults $10, Seniors (65+) $9, College students (with valid ID) $5, Kids (under 18) $3
Website: www.imhm.org
Directions: Two blocks south of Michigan St., three blocks east of Tibbs Ave.

Indiana Walk of Legends

Laugh if you will, but Hoosiers are proud of their native sons and daugh-
ters: Orville Redenbacher, John Mellencamp, Eli Lilly, Earl Butz . . . and
they're all here on the Indiana Walk of Legends! Sadly, most are commemorated with signatures in cement, not footprints à la Grauman's Chinese
Theatre, so you can't see if your shoes match those of the Popcorn King.

The best time to view the Walk of Legends is the off-season, since it's
free to enter the State Fairgrounds when the fair isn't in progress. You also
won't have to fight the throngs of Earl Butz groupies who attend each year.

State Fairgrounds, 1202 E. 38th St., Indianapolis, IN 46205
Phone: (317) 927-7500
Hours: Always visible
Cost: Free
Website: www.indianastatefair.com
Directions: Enter from Parkway Dr. (Rte. 37) entrance, drive forward past the Coliseum, turn
   right at the end of the lot; Walk is in front of the buildings at the northwest corner.

Popcorn landmark.

King Tut and the Scots

Two Indianapolis buildings look distinctly out of place in this Midwestern city, and both were built by Masons: the Murat Temple and the Scottish Rite Cathedral. And if you think these so-called "secret societies" are shrouded in mystery, you haven't spoken with the chatty guides at the Scottish Rite Cathedral. Just try to escape without a fistful of literature about their hush-hush organization.

As you'll learn on the tour, the Gothic Cathedral was built from 1927 to 1929 using the number 33 (the number of Degrees in the Masonic Rite) as a reference: 33 windows, 33 feet between pillars, 33 foot-square tiles between pillars, and so on. You'll see all the main rooms in the elaborate structure, including the grand hall where the costumed induction ceremonies are performed. Believe it or not, a new member can move through the first 32 Rites on two successive Saturdays.

If you obtain the Mason's 33rd Rite, you become a Shriner and move down the street to the Murat Temple, headquarters of the Mystic Shrine. This Middle Eastern structure was built in 1910 and contains one of the largest theaters in town. The interior is designed with a King Tut motif, complete with murals, tile work, and stained glass. Its lounge is open to non-Shriners at lunchtime.

The Shriners are much more formal than the Scots, who don't wear fezzes or drive around in tiny cars. They also raise an incredible amount of money for children's hospitals and volunteer as clowns, which makes it easy to forgive them for the silly, pseudomystical antics.

Murat Temple (Oasis of Indianapolis, Desert of Indiana), 510 N. New Jersey St., Indianapolis, IN 46204
Phone: (317) 635-2433
Hours: Always visible; Lobby, Monday–Friday 8:30 AM–4:30 PM
Cost: Free
Website: www.muratshrine.org
Directions: At the intersection of Massachusetts Ave. and New Jersey St.

Scottish Rite Cathedral, 650 N. Meridian St., Indianapolis, IN 46204
Phone: (800) 489-3579 or (317) 262-3100
Hours: Always visible; Tours, Tuesday–Friday & third Saturday of month 10 AM–2 PM
Cost: Free
Website: www.aasr-indy.org/scottish-rite/tour-cathedral
Directions: At North St. on Rte. 31 (Meridian St.), four blocks west of the Murat Temple.

Koorsen Fire Museum

Imagine being the insurance broker trying to draw up a quote for this unique, singular-subject museum. "Lemme see . . . 700 different historic fire extinguishers . . . housed *inside* a fire safety business . . . how about we pay *you*?"

This museum is the collection of Randy Koorsen, owner of Koorsen Fire and Security. As you'll see from the collection, Koorsen's industry has a long and varied history dating back to 1789. There have been many approaches to dousing flames over the years, including glass grenades—saltwater-filled glass orbs—which acted as reverse Molotov cocktails that you would throw at flames to kill them. The museum also has Antifyre Pistols, smoke helmets, sprinklers, hoses, and chemical-filled canisters.

When you visit, please obey the No SMOKING signs. Or else.

Koorsen Fire and Security, 2719 N. Arlington Ave., Indianapolis, IN 46218
Phone: (317) 252-0654
Hours: Monday–Friday 8 AM–4 PM, by appointment only
Cost: Free
Website: https://koorsen.com/about-koorsen/koorsen-museum/
Directions: North of I-70 (no exit) at Arlington Ave.

Kurt Vonnegut Memorial Library

"Peculiar travel suggestions are dancing lessons from God." So says the narrator in Kurt Vonnegut's novel *Cat's Cradle*, but it could just as easily be the motto of this book. And though this particular suggestion might not be *peculiar*, the Kurt Vonnegut Memorial Library certainly is worth a stop.

Vonnegut was born in Indianapolis on November 11, 1922, the son of a prominent local architect, Kurt Sr., and socialite mother, Edith (Lieber) Vonnegut. He attended Shortridge High School (3401 N. Meridian St., (317) 226-2810, www.myips.org/shs) from which he graduated in 1940. He left for Cornell in the fall, but after the United States entered World War II he enlisted in the army. Captured during the Battle of the Bulge, he ended up a POW in Dresden just before the Allied firebombing of the city in February 1945. What he witnessed would later influence his writing about the horrors of war.

Much of the author's life is chronicled on a time line mural that wraps around the walls of this small museum. You will also see a re-creation of his personal library and writing space, complete with his rooster reading lamp. You are encouraged to sit down at the desk and type out a message to the late author on a Smith Corona typewriter, just like the one he used. The *actual* Smith Corona is also here, on display, but under glass. For you struggling writers, you can also gain strength from seeing some of his many rejection letters that he received in his early career. You're in good company!

340 N. Senate Ave., Indianapolis, IN 46204
Phone: (317) 652-1954
Hours: Monday–Tuesday & Thursday–Friday 11 AM–6 PM, Saturday–Sunday noon–5 PM
Cost: Free; donations welcome
Website: www.vonnegutlibrary.org
Directions: On the southwest corner of the intersection of Vermont St., Indiana Ave., and Senate
   Ave., two blocks north of the State Capitol Building.

Kids, this is what old people call a "typewriter."

Legends Museum

One of the strange realities of today's celebrity culture is that you don't
have to be alive to make a pretty decent living. Look at Elvis—dying was a
brilliant career move! Of course, when you're not around you need somebody to look after your affairs, such as the Curtis Management Group.
CMG specializes in protecting the legal rights of famous (and usually
deceased) clients, including Marilyn Monroe, Michael Jackson, Princess
Di, James Dean, Babe Ruth, Jackie Robinson, and Garfield the Cat.

Because CMG is so closely tied with celebrity estates, it often has access to their personal effects, or knows the people who do. Many stars' personal items can be seen in the lobby "museum" at the company's northeast Indianapolis headquarters. Though the artifacts change, on a recent visit you could see a dress worn by Bettie Page, Marilyn Monroe's wig from *The Misfits*, Bette Davis's blue hat and shawl, Hugh Hefner's pajamas, Liberace's fur cape, and O. J. Simpson's golf bag. Who knows what you might find on your visit?

10500 Crosspoint Blvd., Indianapolis, IN 46256
Phone: (317) 570-5000
Hours: Monday–Friday 9 AM–5 PM
Cost: Free
Website: www.cmgworldwide.com/about/museum.html
Directions: Off 106th St., just west of Rte. 37.

Mega-Popcorn Blast

It is more than a little bizarre that only steps from the Indiana Walk of Legends' tribute to Orville Redenbacher (see page 189) is the site of the world's most deadly popcorn-related tragedy. It happened on Halloween night in 1963. Thousands were watching a "Holiday on Ice" show at the State Fairgrounds Arena, unaware of a liquid propane gas leak beneath the grandstands. The gas was used to fuel an industrial popcorn popper in a concession stand and had been accumulating for hours. Finally, a spark from an improperly wired machine ignited the flammable gas. The explosion blew a section of the first-class seats onto the rink and into the cheaper folding chairs on the opposite side of the arena. In all, 73 were killed and 340 more were injured.

Oddly enough, this wasn't the first time that a crowd perished at the state fairgrounds due to an explosion. On October 1, 1869, the blast from an overheated boiler caused a stampede that left 27 dead fairgoers in its wake.

Indiana Farmers Coliseum, Indiana State Fairgrounds, 1202 E. 38th St., Indianapolis, IN 46205
Phone: (317) 927-7500
Hours: Always visible
Cost: Free
Website: www.indianastatefair.com/coliseum
Directions: Enter from Coliseum Ave. entrance on 38th St.; the Coliseum is ahead on the right.

Mike Tyson Gets Busted

In retrospect, perhaps it wasn't a great idea to have Mike Tyson judge the Miss Black America Pageant at the 1991 Black Expo in Indianapolis. Before and during the show he was said to have taken a hands-on approach to the contestants; 11 of the 23 contestant filed a joint $21 million lawsuit against what they labeled a "serial buttocks fondler."

But his groping troubles were just the start. At 2 AM on July 19, 1991, he invited Miss Rhode Island, 18-year-old Desiree Washington, to his hotel room. Exactly what happened in Suite 606 is up for debate. Tyson claimed Washington wanted revenge after they had consensual sex, and he told her, "The limousine is downstairs. If you don't want to use the limousine, you can walk." Washington claimed Tyson raped her.

The jury believed Washington, and Tyson was convicted on one count of rape and two counts of criminal deviant sexual behavior. He was sentenced to six years at the Indiana Youth Center in Plainfield (727 Moon Rd., (317) 839-2513, www.in.gov/idoc/2405.htm). He served about three years and was released on May 9, 1995. While there, he claimed to have read a lot: "When I was in prison, I was wrapped up in all those deep books. That Tolstoy crap. People shouldn't read that stuff."

Le Meridian Hotel (formerly the Canterbury Hotel), Suite 606, 123 S. Illinois St., Indianapolis, IN 46225
Phone: (317) 737-1600
Hours: Always visible
Cost: Free; Rooms, $239 and up
Website: www.lemeridienindianapolis.com
Directions: One block west of Meridian St. (Rte. 37), two blocks south of Washington St.

Mr. Bendo

As you pull up to Ralph's Muffler Shop you'll be greeted by a man in a red polo shirt and white slacks, his right arm upraised in a Black Power salute. He's not really that radical; he's more of the silent type and stands guard over this northwest side business. Oh, and he's 20 feet tall.

Yes, Mr. Bendo is a Muffler Man, a fiberglass giant that first appeared in 1962 outside the PB Cafe in Flagstaff, Arizona. He looked like Paul Bunyan—the PB in PB Cafe—and he was great for business. Soon the International Fiberglass Company of Venice, California, was cranking out these statues for other eateries as well as filling stations, amusement parks, and most popularly, muffler shops, which liked to install a complete exhaust system in its hands (hence the nickname). Oddly enough, Indianapolis's Mr. Bendo isn't holding anything. Probably doesn't want to get his white pants dirty.

The mechanics are regular sized.

Ralph's Muffler Shop, 1250 W. 16th St., Indianapolis, IN 46202
Phone: (317) 632-9565
Hours: Always visible
Cost: Free
Website: www.ralphsmufflerandbrakesshops.com
Directions: Just east of the intersection of Indiana Ave. and 16th St.

HEY, BIG FELLAS!

Mr. Bendo isn't the only monstrous mega-man gracing Indiana's roadways. In addition to the state's giant Indians (see page 101), here are a few more:

Big Mac

MacAllister Rentals, 3400 N. Lee Pit Rd., Yorktown, (765) 759-2228, www.macallisterrentals.com

For years Big Mac, a classic muffler man, stood outside Jack Smith's RV dealership on I-69 outside Yorktown, holding a miniature Winnebago in his outstretched hand. (He also graced the cover of the first edition of this book.) But that business has since closed and been replaced. Big Jack is now

Big *Mac*, for MacAllister Rentals. The small RV in his palm is gone, leaving just a black, rectangular platform that looks like a smartphone. Why should he look any different than everybody else today?

Big Boy

Frisch's Big Boy, 500 Broadway St., Anderson, (765) 644-1223, www. frischs.com

Most people are familiar with the traditional Big Boy statue, who stands upright in checkered bib overalls, hoisting a burger aloft like a culinary Statue of Liberty. But in Anderson, the Big Boy holds a burger in his outstretched hands, rushing it to a table in a dead sprint. He seems to have forgotten the plate in his enthusiasm.

Uncle Sam, Clean Freak

Ducky's Express Wash, 1629 Hart St., Vincennes, (812) 304-0265

Uncle Sam wants YOU to wash your car! In fact, he'll stand over you until you finish the job. The 20-foot statue of the iconic patriot looms over the business's central island of high-powered vacuums. Some say that if looked at from the side at sunset, his hand looks like an erect penis. Juvenile people would say that, not me . . . except maybe just this once.

Ice House Man

Ice House Tavern, 1550 Walnut St., New Castle, (765) 529-9990, www. facebook.com/Ice-House-Tavern-157541627420/

Look closely at the pose of the large figure outside New Castle's Ice House Tavern, and you'll realize that he's the same fiberglass model as the Uncle Sam statue in Vincennes. His top hat has been replaced with a golfing cap, and he wears sensible blue slacks instead of red-and-white striped pants, but other than that, they're brothers.

Huge Hobo

Ruben's Restaurant, 2230 Ripley St., Lake Station, (219) 962-3212

Since the late 1950s, a fiberglass statue of a hobo has decorated this googie-style burger stand in Lake Station. In one hand he holds a bunch of balloons and in the other a mean-looking stick, poised to strike any dog that might go for the string of sausages dangling out of his jacket pocket. The statue blew over in a November 2015 storm but has since been restored.

Baloony Burger Man

315 S. Railroad St., Shirley

The attention-getting figure atop this old, closed diner doesn't hold any balloons but looks like he might have swallowed a few. He's very round, wears a baker's hat, and carries a lunch pail (which looks like a dollhouse) in his right hand. He once held a burger in his left hand, but the sandwich is long gone.

Timbers Lounge Lumberjack

Timbers Lounge, 2770 W. Kilgore Ave., Muncie, (765) 282-8461, www.timberslounge.com

The 30-foot lumberjack statue between two trees outside the Timbers Lounge in Muncie is made of fiberglass and carries a large ax, so wisecracks about his mangy facial hair are best kept to yourself. He first appeared outside the Kirby Wood Lumber Company in the 1960s but retired to spend his twilight years at this bar.

Muncie Tin Man

Delbert M. Dawson & Son, 1405 W. Kilgore Ave., Muncie, (765) 284-9711

An oversized tin man guards the entrance to a metal fabrication business on the west side of Muncie. Like its *Wizard of Oz* prototype, this metallic man appears frozen in a pose, though he does have a smile on his face.

Museum of Psychophonics

It hovers in a small, dimly lit back room at the Joyful Noise recording studio in Fountain Square: Parliament-Funkadelic's original Mothership, the centerpiece of this weird minimuseum. Like Spinal Tap's original Stonehenge, it too is small enough to be crushed by a dwarf. This Baby Mothership was later eclipsed by a larger version that George Clinton would emerge from during his shows.

The museum has other oddball artifacts, too. It has the "Soundtrack to Infinity" on a cassette tape under a bell jar. A golden tin ashtray from the Burger King in Kalamazoo, Michigan, where Elvis was spotted in 1988. The front page from a Roswell newspaper reporting on the 1945 UFO crash. A bone from a black cat, a bottle of Victorian Bed-Bug Killer, and an orange-and-clove pomander to fight off the plague and keep things smelling nice.

What is this collection all about? A nearby sign explains it all: "We live in a world where all things not strange are propped up as a fiction of normalcy. We aim to correct this charade with a new normal—a psycho-

The coolest thing in Indianapolis.

phonic disruption, a shared consciousness built upon outlawed narratives and talismans. It is a temple, a secret mechanical garden, an extraterrestrial portal, a museum of the post-internet age."

Any questions?

Joyful Noise, 1043 Virginia Ave. #208, Indianapolis, IN 46203
Phone: (317) 632-3220
Hours: Monday–Friday 11 AM–7 PM
Cost: Free
Website: www.joyfulnoiserecordings.com
Directions: One block north of Prospect St., one block east of Shelby St.

The Original People's Temple

Jim Jones and his wife Marceline made a big impression on Indianapolis during the 1950s and '60s. Arriving in the summer of 1951, the couple brought along their pet chimpanzee, very little money, and a burning desire to minister to (and fleece) the poor. Jones started as a student pastor at the south side's Somerset Methodist Church (S. Keystone Ave.) but didn't enjoy playing second or third fiddle to anyone.

Jones left Somerset to start his own ministry, Community Unity, and lived in a bungalow on nearby Villa Street. To raise funds to fix the place up, he sold South American monkeys door-to-door at $29 a pop, grossing $50,000. That's more than 1,700 monkeys! He was also invited to guest minister at the nearby Laurel Street Tabernacle (Fountain Square), where he became well known for healings that included yanking cancerous blobs from (supposedly) sick parishioners. Marceline helped with the act.

The Laurel Street Tabernacle never brought Jones on full-time, so in 1956 Jones headed north to found a new, larger church. He christened it Wings of Deliverance, a name he soon changed to the People's Temple Full Gospel Church. His message attracted many poor and liberal followers. He set up food and clothing banks, opened soup kitchens, took poor kids to the zoo, and delivered free coal to shut-ins. He also helped to integrate at least one Indianapolis hospital. His message was so successful, Jones moved the congregation a year later to a former synagogue at 10th St. and Delaware (destroyed by fire in 1975) and moved his family's home to a duplex at 2327 N. Broadway Street.

But Jim had his dark side. When he felt his congregation wasn't attentive enough, he threw his Bible on the ground, spit on it, and screamed, "Too many people are looking at this and not ME!" He devised an elaborate scheme where People's Temple members ran local businesses that

Go ahead—take a sip!

channeled money back into the church, a plan that would eventually force him to move westward.

In 1961 Jones was appointed director of the Indianapolis Human Rights Commission by the mayor. He used the position to draw more attention to himself, including creditors and IRS investigators. Paranoid that he would soon be found out (and rightly so), he announced in 1965 that the congregation would move to Ukiah, California, to escape the coming Armageddon. According to an article he'd read, Ukiah was naturally protected from radioactive fallout. Jones led a westward-bound caravan of 100 or so faithful in his black Cadillac. He carried with him a $100,000 check but still owed Indiana creditors $40,000.

Community Unity (today abandoned), 720 S. Randolph St., Indianapolis, IN 46203
No phone
Hours: Always visible
Cost: Free
Directions: Six blocks west of S. Keystone Ave., three blocks north of Prospect St.

People's Temple (today Restoration Baptist Church; no affiliation), 1502 N. New Jersey St., Indianapolis, IN 46202
Phone: (317) 602-7360
Hours: Always visible; Services, Sunday 11 AM; Bible study, Wednesday 12:30 PM and 7 PM
Cost: Free
Website: http://restorationbc.org
Directions: Seven blocks east of Meridian (Rte. 31), one block south of 16th St.

Robert Kennedy Saves the Day

On April 4, 1968, when Sen. Robert Kennedy was running for president, he was preparing for an evening campaign stop in Indianapolis when reports came that Martin Luther King Jr. had been assassinated in Memphis. When Kennedy arrived at the rally he realized many had not yet heard the tragic news, and it was up to him to tell them that King had died.

Standing in the back of a flatbed truck at the corner of 17th and Broadway, Kennedy made a brief, unprepared speech to the crowd. It was less than five minutes long, yet contained one of his most memorable statements, a plea that today marks his grave at Arlington National Cemetery: "What we need in the United States is not division; what we need in the United States is not hatred; what we need in the United States is not violence or lawlessness, but love and wisdom, and compassion toward one another, and a feeling of justice towards those who still suffer within our country, whether they be white or whether they be black." That night, and in the days to follow, riots erupted across America, but not in Indianapolis. Two months later Kennedy would also be felled by an assassin's bullet.

Kennedy's speech in Indianapolis is today commemorated in a park at the site of the speech. A sculpture, *Landmark for Peace* (1995) by Greg Perry, depicts RFK reaching out to MLK over a sidewalk. The metal used to make it is from guns collected by police from amnesty buy-back programs around the city.

Martin Luther King Jr. Memorial Park, 1701 N. Broadway St., Indianapolis, IN 46202
Phone: (317) 327-7418
Hours: Dawn–dusk
Cost: Free
Website: http://funfinder.indy.gov/#/details/45
Directions: Just north of 17th St., one block west of College Ave.

Sleep in a Train

If you want to sleep in a train today you have two options: sneak into a rail yard and find an open boxcar, or head to Indianapolis and the Crowne Plaza Hotel. The first is inexpensive, but you run the risk of having your skull split open by a company goon. But there's no danger of that at the Crowne Plaza. Parked within the city's old Union Station train shed,

26 nonmoving Pullman cars have been converted into Victorian guest rooms. These cars are sealed off from the rest of the hotel, so the only way to see them up close is to book one for the night.

If they're out of your price range and you just want to stroll through, the Crowne Plaza's lobby and hallways are filled with creepy white statues of passengers frozen in time, forever waiting for the train that never arrives. Not unlike Amtrak.

Crowne Plaza Union Station, 123 W. Louisiana St., Indianapolis, IN 46225
Phone: (317) 631-2221
Hours: Always open
Cost: $285 and up
Website: www.downtownindianapolishotel.com
Directions: Just west of Meridian St., four blocks south of Monument Circle.

Suzanne Walking in a Leather Skirt

You can find Suzanne most days at the corner of Alabama Street and Massachusetts Avenue, in a short skirt, swinging her hips to attract the attention of drivers and passersby. Actually, she's there more than just most days—she's there *every* day, 24 hours a day, rain or sun or snow, unless there's a power outage, because Suzanne isn't really a person. Artist Julian Opie created her animated image using a four-sided array of computerized lights. Just an outline of a woman with a circle for a head, swaying back and forth, like a 1960s go-go dancer rocking to a beat nobody else hears. Can you dig it?

Alabama St. & Massachusetts Ave., Indianapolis, IN 46204
No phone
Hours: Best after dark
Cost: Free
Directions: On the northeast corner of the intersection.

USS *Indianapolis* Memorial

In the final days of World War II, the USS *Indianapolis* delivered a shipment of uranium to Tinian Island in the Pacific. This material would later be used for the bombs dropped on Hiroshima and Nagasaki. The heavy cruiser was 600 miles west of Guam, heading home, when it was torpedoed by a Japanese submarine on the night of July 29–30, 1945. The ship

No longer lost at sea.

sank so quickly that other vessels did not know where it had gone down, and because the navy didn't want to reveal by its actions that it had broken the Japanese Navy's submarine codes, no rescue party was launched.

Of the *Indianapolis*'s 1,197 crew, about 900 made it into the water that night, but only 317 were pulled alive from the water five days later. The survivors were saved only by a chance sighting of their oil slick by a passing aircraft. Most sailors died of injuries or dehydration, but many were eaten by sharks. The character Quint (Robert Shaw) would recount the story in the movie *Jaws*.

Captain Charles Butler McVay III was court-martialed for failing to zigzag his ship to avoid being torpedoed, though the navy had clearly told him he would encounter no submarines on his journey, a statement they knew to be untrue. McVay was the only commander of the 700 vessels sunk in the war to be court-martialed. Blamed by victims' families in a constant stream of hate letters, McVay committed suicide in 1968.

But then in 1996, an 11-year-old boy named Hunter Scott began asking questions after seeing *Jaws*. Remarkably, he uncovered new evidence pointing to the incompetence of navy brass, errors that led to the ship's sinking. This information led to a Congressional inquiry, which posthumously exonerated McVay. A monument to all the crew now stands in Indianapolis, the city that gave the ship its name. In 2007 the state opened a gallery dedicated to the *Indianapolis* within the Indiana War Memorial Museum, including a seven-foot replica of the doomed ship. (The War Memorial is interesting in its own right, built to resemble the Tomb of King Mausolus at Halicarnassus, present day Bodrum, Turkey.)

Ellsworth & Walnut Sts., Indianapolis, IN 46202
No phone
Hours: Always visible
Cost: Free
Website: www.in.gov/iwm/2328.htm
Directions: Five blocks south of 10th St., take Walnut St. west seven blocks to Ellsworth St.

USS *Indianapolis* Museum, Indiana War Memorial, 51 E. Michigan St., Indianapolis, IN 46204
Phone: (317) 232-7615
Hours: Wednesday–Sunday 9 AM–5 PM
Cost: Free
Website: www.ussindianapolis.us
Directions: Between Meridian and Pennsylvania Sts., four blocks north of Monument Circle.

World's Largest Trowel

Have you ever had one of those ambitious gardening weekends where, by the time the sun went down on Sunday, only about half of your annuals were in the ground? Well, perhaps you weren't using the right tool. If you used one of those teeny tiny trowels, perhaps that was your problem. You needed something a bit more industrial—like the trowel at Habig's gardening center.

This T-rex trowel could dig out your entire flower bed with one scoop. Properly mounted on the front of a small tractor, it could also

Paul Bunyan's gardening tool.

be used by undertakers to plant dead gardeners who want to return to the earth, compost style.

5201 N. College Ave., Indianapolis, IN 46220
Phone: (317) 283-5412
Hours: Always visible
Cost: Free
Website: http://habiggardenshop.weebly.com
Directions: Eight blocks east of Meridian St. (Rte. 31) at 52nd St.

SUBURBS

Acton

Ice Tree

Back in 1961, Vierl G. Veal wanted to make an ice slide for his children, so in the freezing cold he pulled out a hose and set it up to spray a hill on his property. But that night a stiff breeze blew the mist onto a nearby honeysuckle bush, and by morning he had an ice-covered shrub instead. Veal liked it, so he decided to make it a regular wintertime feature. More than a half century later, the family keeps the tradition alive.

The Veals have learned a lot over the years and have made improvements to the ever-changing organic sculpture. Each fall they build a skeleton out of lumber—a new shape every year—for the tree to "grow" on. However, they have no idea how each one will turn out—that's Mother Nature's job. And rather than waste fresh water, they pump it out of a nearby pond and even add coloring to cover the Ice Tree with brilliant hues of blue and red and violet.

Visitors are asked to view it from a safe distance during daylight hours, but the Veals do illuminate it after sundown until 10 PM. You can see it if you look south from I-74 near Exit 99.

11333 Southeastern Ave., Acton, IN 46259
Private phone
Hours: Winter, daytime
Cost: Free
Website: http://vealsicetree.wix.com/vealsicetree
Directions: Exit Acton Rd. southbound from I-74, then immediately turn east onto Southeastern Ave.

Avon

Dead Dad Jones

Dad Jones was a worker on the Inter-Urban Railroad project west of Indianapolis when he was tragically entombed in cement after the platform on which he was standing collapsed, plunging him into a concrete grave. The quick-drying cement below had been poured for a bridge piling. Rather than fish the poor guy out (and slow down the work), his body was left inside, where it remains to this day . . . or so the story goes.

After trains began running on the line, folks started noticing weird things. When a train crossed the trestle, some could hear the screams of Dad's ghost, trapped in the foundation, squished by the weight of the passenger cars. After the train passed, he would thump on the cement with his fists until he could pound no more. Other witnesses claim that water condenses on the piling and oozes red, like blood. While particularly visible on the night of a full moon, you can clearly see from the photo below that something's seeping out in broad daylight.

Urban legend or OSHA violation? Stop on by on a moonlit night and decide for yourself.

Here's Dad Jones.

White Lick Creek Bridge, Dad Jones Rd., Avon, IN 46123
No phone
Hours: Always visible
Cost: Free
Directions: Turn north off Rte. 40 onto Dad Jones Rd., three blocks west of the Rte. 267
  intersection.

Carmel
The Healing Waters of Carmel

Back in 1903 a few local men were drilling for natural gas and instead hit an underground aquifer that burst forth to the surface. Their immediate disappointment soon gave way to excitement when somebody drank the mineral water and discovered it healed one of their maladies. Or all of their maladies—people claimed a sip of this artesian brew cures headaches, sore throats, arthritis, and lumbago, just to name a few. Mind you, this was years before antibiotics and other modern therapies.

That makes it all the more fascinating that today, nine decades after the discovery of penicillin and pain killers, people still swear by it. The spring is protected by a gazebo in a park where you'll bump into locals filling up jugs of the stuff. Ask how it makes them feel better—it's essential to the psychosomatic process.

Flowing Well Park, 5100 E. 116th St., Carmel, IN 46033
Phone: (317) 848-7275
Hours: Daylight
Cost: Free
Website: http://carmelclayparks.com/parks/park-features/
Directions: Two blocks east of Gray Rd. on the north side of 116th St.

Museum of Miniature Houses and Other Collections

Dollhouses are more than just elaborate toys for little children; they're windows to the past, as you'll see at this small museum filled with even smaller buildings. An antique dollhouse might reflect decorating styles at the time it was built, as well as the sorts of objects found in a typical home, much the same way a pink Barbie Dreamhouse reflects our current plastic lifestyle.

OK, so maybe using dollhouses for historical research is a bit of a stretch, but they're cool nonetheless. The oldest dollhouse in this museum's collection has a short message hidden beneath the wallpaper on a back wall, written by Thomas Russell to his young daughter in 1861. Other pieces in the constantly rotating collection could more accurately be called scenes, like a princess running through a forest blanketed in snow, followed by her Prince Charming, past unicorns and trees draped in jewels. You know . . . *history*.

111 E. Main St., Carmel, IN 46032
Phone: (317) 575-9466
Hours: Wednesday–Saturday 11 AM–4 PM, Sunday 1–4 PM
Cost: Adults $5, Kids (under 10) $3
Website: www.museumofminiatures.org
Directions: One block east of Rangeline Rd. on Main St. (131st St.).

World's First Automatic Traffic Light

Local electrician Leslie Haines had a great idea to help auto drivers avoid accidents in Carmel's main intersection: a stoplight! However, his 1923 invention had one major flaw: it had no yellow. Without a warning that the lights would turn, motorists received an excessive number of tickets for running red lights. Long after it was clear that the well-intentioned device was inadequate, it was removed in 1934.

Today you'll find a standard, three-color stoplight at the same intersection of Main Street and Rangeline Road, and Haines's contraption is in the possession of the Carmel-Clay Historical Society, where it can't hurt anyone.

Interestingly enough, today Carmel is leading a new revolution in traffic technology: the roundabout. There are more than 70 roundabout intersections around town, more than any other city of its size. But out of respect to its place in history, the original traffic light location remains unchanged.

Main St. & Rangeline Rd., Carmel, IN 46032
No phone
Hours: Always visible
Cost: Free
Directions: On 131st St. (Main St.) in the center of town.

Carmel-Clay Historical Society, 211 First St. SW, Carmel, IN 46032
Phone: (317) 846-7117
Hours: Saturday–Sunday 1–4 PM
Cost: Free
Website: www.carmelclayhistory.org
Directions: Two blocks west and one block south of the intersection.

World's Smallest Children's Art Gallery

Just a couple of blocks from Carmel's museum of small houses is a museum of small art, or rather, a small museum of smaller artists. Curated by Doreen Squire Ficara, this tiny gallery features works by local children, as well as by kids from Kawachinagano, Japan, Carmel's sister city. It is housed in a building that measures 9 feet 5 inches by 15 feet 4 inches, which the *Guinness Book of World Records* has certified as the World's Smallest Children's Art Gallery.

The kids whose works are shown here receive certificates documenting their accomplishments, which come in handy when trying to gain admittance to elite private elementaries or when applying for finger-painting fellowships.

40 W. Main St., Carmel, IN 46032
Phone: (317) 844-4989
Hours: Check website; shows vary
Cost: Free
Website: www.carmelartscouncil.org/category/childrens-art-gallery/
Directions: One block west of Rangeline Rd. on Main St., at First Ave.

Fishers

Balloon Ride to the Past

On August 17, 1859, aeronaut John Wise took off from Lafayette in a balloon, the *Jupiter*, with 123 stamped letters bound for New York City. Unfortunately, strong winds forced him to crash-land in Crawfordsville about 30 miles away. Wise then took the letters to a train station where they completed the journey by rail. Because the mail went at least part of the way by balloon, through the sky, this postal innovation is considered the world's first airmail flight.

Today the eastbound journey is re-created, minus the crash landing of course, by a ride at Conner Prairie near Indianapolis. Weather permitting, you can ride this helium-filled contraption 370 feet into the sky over Fishers. The attraction can lift up to 20 people and is securely tethered to Mother Earth. It's part of the 850-acre Conner Prairie historic pioneer village, where you can learn even more about the way things used to be done—butter churnin', dandle-dippin', yarn-spinnin', and, when the chores are done, stick-whittlin'.

Conner Prairie, 13400 Allisonville Rd., Fishers, IN 46038
Phone: (800) 966-1836 or (317) 776-6000
Hours: May–October, Tuesday–Sunday 10 AM–5 PM; Balloon, April–October, weather permitting
Cost: Balloon $15, +Park admission, Adults $17, Seniors (65+) $16, Kids (2–12) $12
Website: www.connerprairie.org/Places-To-Explore/1859-Balloon-Voyage
Directions: South of 146th St. on Allisonville Rd.

Jolietville
Homemade Lawn Ornaments

You know the expression: give someone a welded animal, they have a lawn decoration, but teach someone to weld, they'll make a menagerie. Whoever taught Ernie Taylor to weld did the world a great service, for today Taylor has more than 40 weird animals made from car parts and tools and scrap metal, with plenty of room for more. They're all lined up along

Forty and counting.

a ditch—dinosaurs, flowers, oversized insects, barnyard animals, crabs, whirligigs, peacocks, troll people—framed by a fence of brightly painted antique farm equipment.

10985 Base Line Rd., Jolietville, IN 46077
Private phone
Hours: Always visible
Cost: Free
Directions: West of the Indianapolis Executive Airport on Rte. 32 (Base Line Rd.), just west of Rte. 1100 E, on the south side of the road.

Plainfield
Dump the President!

There was a time when the American public took a more active role in national politics. The case of the Van Buren Elm is a prime example.

As president, Martin Van Buren vetoed an appropriation bill for improvements to the National Road. This enraged voters along the essential east–west artery, an anger that didn't subside until 1842. Van Buren was then an ex-president, traveling through Plainfield by carriage. Earlier, locals had coached his driver to aim for a particularly large pothole along their still-unimproved road. The carriage tipped, and old Martin was dumped out into a mud puddle. For his successful effort, the driver received a silk hat. The tree at the site became known as the Van Buren Elm. And no other president blocked funding; the National Road was completed by 1851.

The original Van Buren Elm fell victim to Dutch elm disease, but it has been replaced by a new sapling—so watch out, all you present and future office holders!

Friends' Meetinghouse, 205 S. East St., Plainfield, IN
    46168
No phone
Hours: Always visible
Cost: Free
Website: http://plainfieldfriends.com
Directions: One block west of the Rte. 267 Intersection
    with Rte. 40 (East St.).

Hands-on democracy.

Speedway

The Speedway and Hall of Fame Museum

The Speedway and Hall of Fame Museum is both the state's most visited attraction and one of the coolest. You don't have to be a rabid fan of the sport to get goose bumps as you drive onto the grounds through a tunnel beneath the grandstands and track—the museum is on the infield!

There are about 75 autos on display, from the first racers in 1911 (including the winner, No. 32, the yellow Marmon Wasp) to the most recent winners of the Borg-Warner Trophy, as well as the trophy itself. You'll also see the fastest Indy winner (Arie Luyendyk's Lola Chevy at 185.981 mph average) and Eddie Rickenbacker's 1914 Duesenberg. The World War I flying ace owned the speedway from 1927 to 1945 and is fondly remembered . . . though perhaps not by the Germans. And it's educational. You'll learn plenty about the Memorial Day race, like how (reportedly) 70 percent of auto improvements have originated here, from the rearview mirror to balloon tires. One vehicle is available for photo ops, though think twice about whether you want to squeeze in for a picture—this car isn't exactly roomy.

Don't pass on the Track Tour just to save the extra $8; it's the best part of the visit. Guides take you on one lap around the track in a rental-car shuttle van, after announcing "Gentlemen, start your engines!" Along your journey, you'll hear many interesting facts: the 2.5-mile track has curves that bank at 9°12'; the track began as a testing facility in 1909; and most of the Brickyard's original 3.2 million bricks are still just below the concrete surface. You'll stop in front of the green, pagoda-shaped viewing tower to take photos of the only bricks still exposed (including a gold-plated one), the Finish Line. In the time it takes you to putt around the track just once, a typical racecar would have lapped you 15 or 16 times.

Indianapolis Motor Speedway, 4790 W. 16th St., Speedway, IN 46222
Phone: (317) 492-8500
Hours: March–October, daily 9 AM–5 PM; November–February, daily 10 AM–4 PM
Cost: Adults $8, Kids (6–15) $5, Track Tour, Adults $8, Kids (6–15) $5
Website: www.indianapolismotorspeedway.com/at-the-track/museum
Directions: Crawfordsville Rd. Exit from I-465; head southeast until you reach 16th St.

Zionsville

Antique Fan Museum

This place blows. A lot. Which is not to say that it isn't cool. In fact, it's all about cooling yourself down . . . with fans! Hosted by the Fanimation company, a manufacturer of ceiling and standing fans, the Antique Fan Museum has more than 450 different air circulating devices on display, some going back to the 1880s. They've got electric-, steam-, battery-, belt-, alcohol-, and water-powered models, and lots of handheld, cool-yourself fans. Many have been rescued from old factories, churches, businesses, and even railroad cars. The museum is the repository of the Antique Fan Collectors Association, which holds conventions and swap meets for those interested in this unique appliance. Hey, everybody needs a hobby.

Fanimation, 10983 Bennett Pky., Zionsville, IN 46077
Phone: (317) 733-4113
Hours: Monday–Friday 10 AM–4 PM
Cost: Free
Website: www.fanimation.com/museum/
Directions: Exit on 106th St. from Rte. 421, west three blocks to Bennett Pky., then north one block.

INDIANAPOLIS

➡ A four-foot alligator was caught by fisherman Jack Herring in the White River near Indianapolis on August 14, 1999.

➡ Dr. Richard Gatling invented the machine gun in Indianapolis in 1862. The first model shot 250 rounds per minute, but later models soon got up to 500. His stated goal, after witnessing the Civil War, was to invent a weapon so horrible that nobody would dare use it. Nice theory.

➡ Jane Pauley was born in Indianapolis on October 31, 1950. She attended Warren Central High School (9500 E. 16th St., (317) 532-6200, http://wchs.warren.k12.in.us), graduating in 1968, and was a member of the prom court.

NOBLESVILLE

➡ A fist-sized meteorite almost hit a Noblesville youth on August 31, 1991.

JOHN DILLINGER
Diapers to Death Tour

J ohn Dillinger was front-page news in 1934—bold, fearless, and one hundred percent Hoosier. His deadly crime spree began in the summer of 1933, but he wasn't a superstar until he made daring escapes from jails in Lima, Ohio, and Crown Point, Indiana, and foiled FBI dragnets in St. Paul, Minnesota, and the Little Bohemia Lodge in Manitowish Waters, Wisconsin.

Dillinger seldom operated alone. He and his fellow thugs were nicknamed the Terror Gang. At one point, the Indiana governor and National Guard proposed using tanks and poison gas to fight them. In retrospect, it might have made the fight more balanced, for it was later learned the gang had once planned to raid the Fort Harrison Arsenal in Indianapolis for mortars and even more powerful weapons.

The American Legion offered to deputize 30,000 of its members for roadblocks and posses to stop him. Though the plan was never implemented, vigilante groups did set up roadblocks around the state in a haphazard way. Locals were warned in 1933 to *not* dress up as gangsters for Halloween.

Still, as deadly as his spree became—some believe as many as 16 died by his hand alone—Dillinger won the hearts of many citizens. At the height of the Depression, he took on the persona of Robin Hood, sticking it to the fat-cat bankers while acting with courtesy toward bystanders . . . just as long as they behaved.

His brief, violent life still fascinates the public almost 80 years after his death outside Chicago's Biograph Theater at the age of 31. If you're intrigued by this native prodigal son, come along on a tour of Dillinger sites in the state he called home. But take the back roads, and watch out for the coppers; they're everywhere, I tell ya'—everywhere!

Indianapolis
John Dillinger's Birthplace

John Herbert Dillinger was born on June 22, 1903, in the Oak Hill neighborhood of Indianapolis. He was a normal baby and did not emerge from the birth canal with guns a-blazing. At the time, Dillinger's father ran a grocery store (2210 Bloyd Ave., torn down) and was a deacon at Hillside Christian Church (1737 Ingram St., (317) 632-4988), which still holds services to this day. John's mother, Mollie, died when he was only three years old, and his father remarried in 1912, to a woman named Elizabeth "Lizzie" Fields.

There is little left of the Dillinger birthplace. A new home sits on the lot, but the curbside retaining wall is original. It's not hard to imagine little Johnnie playing marbles on the sidewalk along this wall.

Dillinger attended Public School No. 38 just a block away, and later Public School No. 55 (17th & Sheldon Sts.). Only the first of these buildings still stands. Today it is the Greater Love Temple Apostolic Church (2050 Winter Ave., (317) 926-9224). At 16, just before high school, Dillinger dropped out and eventually went to work in a plywood mill.

Dillinger Birthplace, 2053 Caroline Ave. (formerly Cooper St.), Indianapolis, IN 46218
No phone
Hours: Torn down; a new home stands on the site
Cost: Free
Directions: Exit I-70 at Keystone Ave./Rural St., south to Bloyd Ave., then west seven blocks to Caroline Ave.

Mooresville
John Dillinger's First Crime

The Dillinger family moved to Mooresville in March 1920, shortly before John turned 17. He joined the US Navy in 1923 but turned up back in Mooresville five months later, absent without leave from the USS *Utah*, then docked in Boston.

Still AWOL in 1924, Dillinger married 16-year-old Beryl Hovious. He didn't seem as interested in spending time with her as he did hanging out in a Mooresville poolroom with the guys. There, he met up with Edgar Singleton, the town's resident hoodlum. Singleton enlisted Dillinger to help him mug a local grocer, Frank Morgan, on the night of September 6,

1924. The pair drank and waited near the side entrance to the Mooresville Christian Church. When Morgan passed by heading south, walking home after closing, Singleton hit him over the head with a large bolt wrapped in a handkerchief. After being struck twice, the grocer got back up and smacked the gun out of Dillinger's hand, causing it to discharge. The muggers got $150, but not for long.

Morgan gave the Masonic distress signal, which, along with the gunshot, woke the neighbors. Singleton drove off without Dillinger, who then fled to the local pool hall covered in blood. Soon both were apprehended. Morgan could not positively identify Dillinger, though the cops tricked him into confessing on an empty promise of leniency. The judge sentencing Dillinger reneged on the offer and packed him off to jail for 10 to 20 years. Singleton pleaded not guilty, his case went to trial, and he drew only 2 to 14 years.

Heritage Christian Church (former Mooresville Christian Church), 61 W. Harrison St., Mooresville, IN 46158
Phone: (317) 831-3860
Hours: Always visible
Cost: Free
Directions: Two blocks north of High St. (Rte. 42) and two blocks east of Monroe St. (Rte. 267), on the southeast corner of S. Jefferson and W. Harrison Sts.

The start of something big.

Pendleton, Michigan City
John Dillinger Learns the Trade

Dillinger's first prison home was the Indiana State Reformatory at Pendleton, northeast of Indianapolis. Shortly after arriving, the new con tried to escape by hiding in a pile of excelsior but was flushed out after the quick-thinking guards set fire to it.

After Dillinger's fifth year in prison, Beryl filed for divorce. Not long after that, on July 25, 1929, he asked to be transferred to Indiana State Prison in Michigan City. It was not to mend his broken heart; it was because Michigan City had a baseball team.

As Inmate #13225, he started hanging with a much rougher crowd. During his nine years of incarceration he joined a plot to break out. According to the plan, the first conspirator released would launch weapons over the wall, into the prison yard, and they would be retrieved by gang members who were still locked up. Those on the inside would then shoot their way out.

Meanwhile, back in Mooresville, folks were trying to get Dillinger's harsh sentence reduced. Johnnie was eventually paroled on May 22, 1933, on an order signed by the governor. The governor had been persuaded by a petition signed by victim Frank Morgan and trial judge Joseph Williams (among others), and compassion for the imminent death of Dillinger's stepmother. As bad luck would have it, the Dillingers' car broke down on the way back from Michigan City, and the ex-con arrived home a few hours after she died of a stroke.

Though there is no conclusive proof, many believe Dillinger later had weapons smuggled into the Michigan City prison that were eventually used by 10 inmates to escape on September 26, 1933. Their actions immediately following the jailbreak make that theory all the more convincing: they headed to Lima, Ohio, to spring Dillinger where *he* was then being held.

And how did Johnnie end up behind bars in Lima? That's the next part of the tour.

Indiana State Reformatory, 4490 W. Reformatory Rd., Pendleton, IN 46064
Phone: (765) 778-2107
Hours: Always visible, view from street
Cost: Free
Website: www.in.gov/idoc/2411.htm
Directions: Just northwest of Rte. 36 at Pendleton Ave. (Rte. 9).

Indiana State Prison, 1 Park Row, Michigan City, IN 46360
Phone: (219) 874-7258
Hours: Always visible, view from street
Cost: Free
Website: www.in.gov/idoc/2413.htm
Directions: Where southwest-bound Chicago St. ends at Woodlawn Ave.

Daleville, Rockville, Montpelier, Indianapolis
Dillinger's First Crime Spree

When he wasn't working to spring his Big House buddies, Dillinger was robbing banks all over the Hoosier state. The first hit was less than a month after his release from Michigan City, and in less than four months he would be back behind bars.

The events listed below reflect only major *Indiana* crimes. Dillinger and his cohorts robbed many establishments around the Midwest, as well as groceries and filling stations here and there. There are certainly more crimes attributed to Dillinger than he committed. Some could argue for additions or deletions to this list, but for the most part, these are definite Dillinger jobs.

July 17, 1933

Assisted by "Handsome Harry" Copeland and Hilton Crouch, the trio was able to walk away with $3,500 and a pile of jewelry from the Commercial Bank of Daleville. The former bank has a carved split log over the old vault proclaiming DILLINGER WAS HERE.

The Closet Thrift Store, 7850 Walnut St., Daleville, IN 47334
No phone
Hours: Always visible; open occasionally
Cost: Free
Directions: At the intersection of Main St. (Rte. 32) and Walnut St., two blocks north of Daleville Rd.

July 19, 1933

Two days after the Daleville holdup, Dillinger and Copeland robbed the National Bank in Rockville. A son of the bank's president was in another room when the commotion started, and fired a shot that just missed Copeland. Dillinger rushed the shooter and tried to fire his gun point-blank into the man's stomach, but his weapon misfired. The pair fled with only $140.

For Dillinger tourists, this is one of the few holdup sites that still operates as a bank, today known as the Old National Bank. If you're hungry, stop on by the nearby Jailhouse Café.

Old National Bank, 128 W. Ohio St., Rockville, IN 47872
Phone: (765) 569-4270
Hours: Always visible; Lobby, Monday–Friday 9 AM–5 PM, Saturday 9 AM–Noon
Cost: Free
Website: www.oldnational.com
Directions: At the northwest corner of town square.

Jailhouse Café, 123 S. Jefferson St., Rockville, IN 47872
Phone: (765) 569-2233
Hours: Daily 8 AM–8 PM
Cost: Free; Meals $7–10
Website: www.jailhouse-cafe.com
Directions: One block south of Ohio St., one block east of Market St., on Courthouse Square.

Today your deposits in Montpelier are insured.

August 4, 1933

Copeland and Crouch were again involved in a Dillinger heist that netted $10,110 and a .45-caliber gun from the First National Bank of Montpelier. The gang then headed to Bluffton, Ohio, for another bank job before returning to the Hoosier state.

As with Dillinger's previous bank robbery, this location still operates as a bank.

Citizens State Bank, 110 S. Main St., Montpelier, IN 47359
Phone: (765) 728-2411
Hours: Always visible; Lobby, Monday–Thursday 10 AM–4:30 PM, Friday 9 AM–5 PM, Saturday 9 AM–Noon
Cost: Free
Website: https://citizensstatebankindiana.com
Directions: One block north of Huntington St. (Rte. 18) on Main St.

September 6, 1933

Dillinger, Copeland, and Crouch robbed the Massachusetts Avenue State Bank in Indianapolis of $24,000. The bank was located near the then headquarters of the Indiana State Police, and because of this false sense of untouchability, security was lax. Some believe the gang buried the loot in Oak Hills, just west of town, and that it is still there for the finding.

The old bank building is still around and open to visitors, though these days it's an art gallery. Some of the bank fixtures, including the vault, are still intact.

Art Bank Gallery, 811 Massachusetts Ave., Indianapolis, IN 46204
Phone: (317) 624-1010
Hours: Always visible; Gallery, Wednesday–Friday 1–8 PM, Saturday 1–9 PM, Sunday Noon–4 PM
Cost: Free
Website: www.artbankgallery.com
Directions: Just north of St. Clair St. on Massachusetts Ave., southwest of the I-65/I-70 interchange.

Auburn, Peru, Greencastle, East Chicago
Dillinger's Second Crime Spree

Dillinger was captured in Dayton, Ohio, on September 22, 1933, at the apartment of Mary Jenkins Longnacker, sister of jailhouse buddy Joseph Jenkins. At the time, he was carrying a map of the Michigan City prison. The significance of the map became more apparent five days later when 10 armed inmates broke out of the facility. Officials didn't realize it at the time, but the gang was headed for the Allen County Jail in Lima, Ohio, to spring their helpful pal.

Meanwhile, Dillinger had confessed to robbing the Bluffton bank on August 14. His statement was never used in court since he was liberated by the outlaws on October 12. In the jailhouse shootout, Allen County Sheriff Jesse Sarber was killed.

Back in business, the Terror Gang's crime spree resumed operations two days later.

October 14, 1933

Fresh out of prison and needing arms and ammunition, Harry Pierpoint, Walter Dietrich, and Dillinger marched into the Auburn Police Station Arsenal, guns drawn, and asked, "Have you got any guns?" The police did. The Terror Gang walked out with two Thompson submachine guns, eight other firearms, three bulletproof vests, and plenty of ammo.

Ninth & Cedar Sts., Auburn, IN 46706
No phone
Hours: Always visible
Cost: Free
Directions: One block east of Main St., two blocks south of Seventh St. (Rte. 8).

October 21, 1933

A week later, the same trio walked away with two Thompsons, eight other guns, a tear-gas launcher, and six bulletproof vests from the Peru Police Station Arsenal. One of the machine guns was later recovered and today is in a display case at the town's new police station. (You have to ask the on-duty clerk to see it, and there's no guarantee somebody will be able to escort you inside, but it's worth a try.)

21 E. Third St., Peru, IN 46970
No phone
Hours: Always visible
Cost: Free
Directions: Across the street, to the south, from the new police station.

Peru Police Station, 35 S. Broadway, Peru, IN 46970
Phone: (765) 473-5522
Hours: Monday–Friday 8 AM–4 PM
Cost: Free
Website: www.cityofperu.org/peru_police_department.html
Directions: One block southeast of Main St. (Rte. 24 Business) on Broadway.

The old Peru Police Station Arsenal.

October 23, 1933

Unable to eat bullets, the Terror Gang next planned an armed withdrawal from the Greencastle Central National Bank and Trust on the southeast corner of Washington and Jackson Streets in Greencastle. Dillinger and seven others got $75,346, enough to keep them fed for a while. The gang headed for Daytona Beach and spent the New Year's holiday in the Florida sun.

Putnam County Family Support, 20–24 W. Washington St., Greencastle, IN 46135
Phone: (765) 653-4820
Hours: Always visible
Cost: Free
Website: www.pcfss.net
Directions: Where Rte. 231 turns from westbound Washington St. to northbound Jackson St.

January 15, 1934

The first Hoosier holdup of 1934 took place at the First National Bank of East Chicago, netting $20,376. During their getaway, Dillinger shot and killed patrolman William Patrick O'Malley with a machine gun. The gangster was also hit by gunfire—four slugs to the chest—but he was wearing a bulletproof vest. John "Three Fingers" Hamilton and Harry Pierpont assisted Dillinger on the job. Hamilton was shot seven times but escaped with Dillinger and was patched up in Chicago.

Indianapolis Blvd. & W. Chicago Ave., East Chicago, IN 46312
No phone
Hours: Always visible
Cost: Free
Directions: Where Indianapolis Blvd. (Rte. 20) intersects with Chicago Ave. (Rte. 312).

Crown Point
John Dillinger and the Wooden Gun

John Dillinger's bold exit from the Crown Point Jail on March 3, 1934, established his reputation as a cool-headed, confident hoodlum. However, the tales surrounding the event are often fuzzy and inaccurate, from how he got there to how he escaped.

Here's what happened. Following the East Chicago job, Dillinger and company headed to the Southwest, ending up in Tucson, Arizona. The gang had just checked in to the Congress Hotel on January 22, 1934, when the building caught fire. Flush with cash, they tipped the firemen who rescued their luggage a little too generously, raising suspicions. They were captured three days later. Though many states wanted him, Dillinger was extradited to Indiana on January 30 to face murder charges on the killing in East Chicago. (Gang members Harry Pierpont, Charles Makley, and Russell Clark were sent back to Lima, Ohio, to faces charges in the murder of Sheriff Sarber.)

Dillinger was housed in the Crown Point Jail where he entertained a parade of private investigators, shifty lawyers, fawning press, and then-girlfriend Billie Frechette. According to legend, he used his spare time to carve a wooden gun out of an old washboard, then coated it with shoe polish to make it look like a real pistol. Not true. More likely, the weapon was carved in Chicago and slipped to him by a guard, Frechette, or private investigator Arthur O'Leary. Dillinger then dumped wood shavings in his cell to throw suspicion off his accomplice.

On Saturday morning, March 3, Dillinger pulled the fake firearm on a guard in the second-floor exercise bullpen and, one by one, captured and incapacitated the jail's remaining officers and a civilian visitor, fingerprint expert Ernest Blunk. Assisted by murder suspect Herbert Youngblood, Dillinger stole two machine guns and a .45 automatic not made of wood, ducked out the rear kitchen entrance with "hostage" Blunk, and drove off in Sheriff Lillian Holley's car. He found her vehicle in the Main Street Garage, two buildings north up East Street, and ordered the all-too-willing Blunk to act as getaway driver. The pair also took a mechanic from the garage, Edwin Saager.

The four headed west but ran off the road at Lilley Corners, just east of Peotone, Illinois. It took half an hour to put chains on the tires and get the vehicle out of the ditch, yet Dillinger reportedly was calm through it all. He dumped Blunk and Saager near Peotone and gave them four dollars each for carfare back to Indiana. "It's not much, but it's all I can spare," Dillinger told them. "Maybe I can remember you at Christmas." (Blunk would regret ever returning; he was eventually thrown in prison for being a little too helpful to the bank robber.) Youngblood and Dillinger then parted ways. (Youngblood parted with the living two weeks later in a shootout in Port Huron, Michigan.)

By crossing state lines to avoid capture, Dillinger committed a federal offense. The FBI became involved, and within months he earned the moniker of Public Enemy #1. While Dillinger's reputation grew, Crown Point's image fell. The press dubbed the town Clown Point—some even suggested changing its name to Dillinger, Indiana—and Republican politicos gleefully passed out souvenir wooden guns to mock Sheriff Holley, a Democrat.

Today, the jail from which Dillinger escaped is a restored landmark open for guided tours, including spooky night tours. Check the building's website for more details.

Old Sheriff's House, 226 S. Main St., Crown Point, IN 46307
No phone
Hours: Always visible; Tours, April–September, Thursday 5:30–7:30 PM, Saturday 9 AM–1 PM
Cost: Adults $5, Kids (6–12) $2
Website: www.oldsheriffshouse.org
Directions: Two blocks south of the Lake County Courthouse on Rte. 55 (Main St.).

Mooresville
Dillinger Family Reunion

Amazing as it sounds, John Dillinger returned to Mooresville for a family reunion on April 8, 1934, hiding out for a couple days in plain sight of authorities. The whole clan got together for a Sunday picnic with fried chicken and coconut cream pie, Johnnie's favorites, and the gangster was spotted walking around town. Dillinger posed with his infamous wooden gun by the side of the house, then left the fake weapon with his father.

Johnnie must have done some lobbying around town, because residents soon began circulating *another* petition for the governor to pardon Dillinger if the criminal promised to walk the straight and narrow. The once-bitten governor didn't bite a second time, and the locals were widely criticized for even suggesting such a plea bargain.

The FBI believes Dillinger buried $600,000 in stolen cash on his father's farm during the visit, but others put the loot's sum closer to $1 million. It would be rather difficult to locate the cache today, for the farmhouse was eventually torn down and the land turned into a housing development.

Some people claim the ghosts of those who attended the picnic can still be heard, laughing, on the get-together's April 8 anniversary each year. Others have smelled the faint odor of fried chicken.

Dillinger Farm, 535 Rte. 267, Mooresville, IN 46158
No phone
Hours: No longer there
Cost: Free
Directions: On the east side of Monroe St. (Rte. 267) at Carlisle St., where the housing development now stands.

Warsaw, South Bend
Dillinger's Final Crime Spree

John Dillinger didn't spend too much time in his home state following his Crown Point escape, though he did return for two more heists.

April 13, 1934

Homer Van Meter helped Dillinger bump off his third Indiana police station. In Warsaw the pair got two handguns and three bulletproof vests, despite an officer's attempt to stall the holdup. Today the building houses the Kosciusko County Jail Museum.

Kosciusko County Jail Museum, 121 N. Indiana St., Warsaw, IN 46581
Phone: (574) 269-1078
Hours: Always visible; Museum, March–December, Wednesday–Saturday 10 AM–4 PM
Cost: Free
Website: http://kosciuskohistory.com
Directions: One block north of Center St., two blocks west of Detroit St. (Rte. 15).

June 30, 1934

In what would be his last Hoosier holdup, Dillinger, Van Meter, John Paul Chase, and "Baby Face" Nelson hit the Merchants National Bank in South Bend for $29,890 and murdered policeman Howard Wagner in the process. Wagner had been directing traffic near the bank when he heard gunshots and went to investigate; Van Meter killed him before he even got inside. Nelson was shot by a jeweler who came out of a storefront, but was wearing a bulletproof vest and survived. The bullet-riddled bank was later torn down and replaced with a nondescript commercial office building called Center City Place.

Center City Place, 229 Michigan St., South Bend, IN 46601
No phone
Hours: Always visible
Cost: Free
Directions: Downtown, one block north of Wayne St., one block east of Main St. (Rte. 31 Business).

Indianapolis
John Dillinger's Grave

John Dillinger was gunned down outside Chicago's Biograph Theater on July 22, 1934, and two days later his body was returned to his Indiana family (minus its brain, which was removed "for study"). It first rested at the E. F. Harvey Funeral Home in Mooresville (Harrison & Indiana Sts., since torn down), then was taken to the home of his sister, Audrey Hancock, in Maywood, just outside Indianapolis. The public viewing was halted after an hour when a drunken admirer tried to give Johnnie a swig from his flask.

Dillinger's father was offered $10,000 by a traveling sideshow for his son's body, but he didn't accept the offer. The hucksters insisted the fee was just to *rent* the corpse and that the Dillingers would eventually get it back.

The gangster's grave was lined with a three-foot-thick concrete vault and rebar to discourage grave robbers. Headstone thieves would find things a little easier; his gravestone has been stolen four times (to date), and its popularity shows no sign of waning.

Crown Hill Cemetery, 700 W. 38th St., Indianapolis, IN 46208
Phone: (317) 925-3800 or (317) 920-2644 (Tours)
Hours: April–September, daily 8 AM–6 PM; October–March, daily 8 AM–5 PM
Cost: Free; Heritage Tours, Adults $5, Seniors (55+) $4, Kids (18 and under) $3
Website: www.crownhill.org
Directions: Bound by 32nd St., Boulevard Pl., 38th St., and Dr. MLK Jr. St.; enter from 3402 Boulevard Pl.

PARTNERS IN CRIME

What happened to the other members of the Terror Gang? Most ended up like Dillinger: dead. Charles "Fat Charley" Makley and "Handsome Harry" Pierpont were sentenced to the Ohio electric chair for the murder of Lima's Sheriff Sarber. Makley was reported to have claimed, "I'd rather take the hot squat than see Johnnie caught." He never had to make the choice; he died in a botched prison escape on March 27, 1934. On that day, Makley and Pierpont tried Dillinger's fake gun trick, carving a replica from a bar of soap, but with less success. Guards shot both men. Makley died, but Pierpont survived, then was executed on October 17, 1934. He was buried in Indianapolis's **Holy Cross Cemetery** (435 W. Troy Ave., (317) 784-4439, http://catholiccemeteries.cc). Homer Van Meter was gunned down by police officers in St. Paul, Minnesota, on August 23, 1934. He is planted in Ft. Wayne's **Lindenwood Cemetery** (2324 W. Main St., (260) 432-4542, www.dignitymemorial.com/lindenwood-cemetery/en-us/index.page).

Indianapolis
John Dillinger's Guns

Many of the guns Dillinger used in his crime sprees were stolen from Hoosier law enforcement officials. It seems only appropriate that the main police museum in the state might get some of them back. But the Indiana State Police Historical Museum spends less time on its greatest foe than you might think—perhaps there's still a little bad blood. They do have one display with a few firearms, a bulletproof vest, a replica of the wooden pistol, Johnnie's death mask, a mannequin handing over some ill-gotten (fake) money, one of the gangster's many stolen headstones, and other Dillinger-obelia.

But that's not all—this museum also has a large stash of bongs and crack pipes, uniforms and squad cars, confiscated jailhouse weaponry, radar guns, smashed slot machines and stills, and Drunkometers. Be sure to bring a camera to get a gag "head-cutout" photo of yourself as a jewel thief, nabbed by the ever-vigilant Indiana State Police. Crime does not pay! At least not forever . . .

Indiana State Police Historical Museum, 8660 E. 21st St., Indianapolis, IN 46219
Phone: (317) 899-8293
Hours: Monday–Friday 9–3 PM, third Saturday of each month, noon–4 PM
Cost: Free
Website: www.in.gov/isp/museum.htm
Directions: Exit I-70 southbound at Post Rd., then west three blocks on 21st St.

Crown Point
John Dillinger Museum

So you say you don't have the time to run around the state looking at crumbling banks, jails, and police stations. That's where the John Dillinger Museum comes in handy. Sponsored by the South Shore Convention and Visitors Association, this fascinating hands-on collection (purchased from the estate of Dillingerphile Joe Pinkston) is probably the most entertaining museum in the state. Surprisingly, the curators are not shy about their town's association with the most embarrassing tale in the Dillinger saga, the Crown Point jailbreak, but give accurate and complete information, even if it hurts.

The museum is arranged chronologically according to Dillinger's short life. You start by visiting John's early years on the farm, then BAM! you're in prison. The small cell and looped recording of an angry guard have a distinctly *Oz*-like feel. Judge for yourself whether Dillinger's sentence fit the Mooresville crime with an interactive game. Once in prison, see the faces of the Terror Gang formed in Michigan City.

Next, follow the gang's crime spree as a witness to the East Chicago holdup—see how many details you can remember after staring down the barrel of a gun. Check out the 1933 Hudson Essex Terraplane, Dillinger's getaway car of choice. And see a replica of the wooden gun that fooled Crown Point officials. (The original gun is part of the museum's collection but is too valuable to put on display.)

Do you think a life of crime might be a glamorous career option? Think again—the next exhibit is an FBI lab where you are fingerprinted and booked. View the aftermath of the Little Bohemia shootout and the bloody end for Dillinger. The final, shocking displays include Johnnie's "pants of death," a bleeding wax dummy of Johnnie on the autopsy slab at the Cook County Morgue, and the undertaker's basket used to transport his body.

Scattered throughout the museum are dummies of other Depression-era hoodlums, like Pretty Boy Floyd, Baby Face Nelson, Ma Barker, and Bonnie and Clyde, all of whom would die of acute lead poisoning. As a bonus, they've also got the Lindbergh baby kidnapper Bruno Richard Hauptmann strapped down in an electric chair, just seconds from death.

1 Courthouse Square, Crown Point, IN 46307
Phone: (219) 989-7979
Hours: Tuesday–Saturday 10 AM–4 PM, Sunday Noon–4 PM
Cost: Adults $4, Seniors (50+) $3, Kids (6–12) $2
Website: www.southshorecva.com/dillinger-museum/
Directions: At the intersection of Rte. 55 (Main St.) and Rte. 231 (Joliet St.).

Goshen

Bankrobbers Beware!

In a move akin to shutting the barn door after the cows got out, the city of Goshen erected a bulletproof police booth along the transcontinental Lincoln Highway, five years *after* Dillinger was laid to rest in an India-

QUICKIE MARRIAGES OF CHICAGOLAND

The Dillinger Museum is housed in the Lake County Courthouse, the "Grand Old Lady of Lake County," which was long used as a place to get a quick hitch, for the county didn't require blood tests or have a waiting period. Couples visiting Chicago would drive over the border to tie the knot. Ronald Reagan married his first wife Jane Wyman there in 1923. Rudolph Valentino, Joe DiMaggio, Red Grange, Tom Mix, and Muhammad Ali were also married at the courthouse, as were Michael Jackson's parents. You can learn about all of it at the **Lake County Historical Museum** (1 Courthouse Square, (219) 662-3975, www.cpcourthouse.com) in the same building, which also contains a collection of 5,000+ pencils.

napolis cemetery. The octagonal limestone watch post was built by the WPA at a busy intersection in sight of three banks, one on each of the adjoining corners, and had gun portholes and impenetrable glass.

The booth was in 24-hour use until 1969. Though some laughed at the over-the-top effort while it was in operation, no bank robberies occurred at any nearby Goshen institutions.

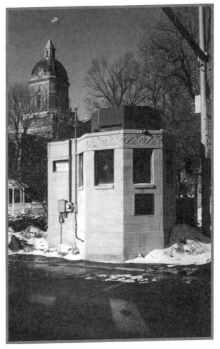

Main St. & Lincoln Ave., Goshen, IN 46528
No phone
Hours: Always visible
Cost: Free
Directions: On Rte. 33 (Main St.) at Rte. 4 (Lincoln Ave.), on the southeast corner of the courthouse square.

Ready for anything.

EPILOGUE

When the first edition of this book was released 15 years ago, it included a bizarre costume shop on a lonely country road southeast of Martinsville: Clown Heaven, a destination either charming or terrifying depending on your opinion of clowns. Today, Clown Heaven is in clown heaven, and you have to go somewhere else for your oversized shoes and squirting flowers.

Carried away in a tiny little hearse.

Gone, too, is Chesterton's Oz Museum, carried off by a tornado of poor attendance; Lafayette's Rain Forest Car Wash, clear-cut by mall "progress"; Vandalia's wacky Barn House, burned down by vandalias;

Carmel's magic-themed Illusions restaurant; and Pumpkin Center's aptly named Museum of All Sorts of Stuff.

This has been an ongoing problem. Indianapolis was once home to some interesting architecture, like the ship-shaped Barge Fish 'N' Chips that stood at Washington and Denny Streets, the Polk Sanitary Milk Building with its two white bottle towers on 15th Street, and the TeePee Restaurant on Fall Creek Boulevard. All are history. Austin's two-story Coffee Pot Restaurant and Filling Station percolated its last cup in 1960, much as the Frozen Custard Igloo in Lafayette had a dozen years earlier—under the treads of a bulldozer.

Attractions associated with Hoosier factories have not fared well, closing when the industries moved elsewhere. Noble County once manufactured more than half of the world's marshmallows, but the tours stopped when the last of the plants moved to Ohio. Ligonier's annual Marshmallow Festival is now on squishy ground. Seyfert Foods of Fort Wayne had Myrtle Young's collection of 400 famous potato chips. Working as a picker on the chip line, Young discovered likenesses of Tweetie Bird, Mr. Magoo, Bob Hope, Rodney Dangerfield, Yogi Bear, and Ronald Reagan, and had even exhibited them on *The Tonight Show*. But when the plant moved to Missouri, so did her unique collection. And Jeffersonville was long home to baseball's Slugger Park, adjacent to the milling operations for the Louisville Slugger, but the park disappeared when the outfit moved across the river to, of all places, Louisville.

Some oddball sites have fallen victim to bad PR. The American Atheist Museum in Petersburg, which sponsored Dial-an-Atheist and billed itself as "the most ungodly place north of the Mason-Dixon line," was probably doomed from the start. The International Palace of Sports in North Webster crowned a King of Sports each year and reproduced the honored athlete in wax. As bad luck would have it, one of its first Kings was O. J. Simpson.

Who knows what happened to some roadside oddities? Where did the Brazen Serpent of Bedford go? The 21-foot-long, 300-pound, hand-carved snake had 362 wooden ribs and 4,000 metal scales, and would hiss at visitors, powered from within by a small motor. Only one building from Chesterton's 125-structure Littleville survives (in the backyard of a local resident), but the other 124 have to be *somewhere*, don't they? And the Martinsville building that once housed Drake's Midwest Phonograph Museum of more than 600 recording devices is now a church . . . as if there already weren't plenty of those around. But where can you find a machine that records sound on chocolate? Not Martinsville anymore.

Heed my warning, fellow travelers! The evil forces of good taste are wiping out unique and bizarre attractions wherever they find them. Indiana is no exception. There was a time, not so long ago, that the present oh-so-precious town of Nashville had a Serpentarium crawling with venomous snakes and photos of humans who'd been bitten. Just try and find something, *anything*, that wonderful in Nashville today.

So go. GO! The oddballs are out there—but they won't be forever. In a world of round donuts, can you live with the knowledge that you passed up an opportunity to eat a square one? I can't.

ACKNOWLEDGMENTS

ndiana is a wonderful state. I know because I spent four years of my life in South Bend. Some of the nicest folks I've ever known lived there, and still do. But I also had the misfortune of being in South Bend on January 20, 1985, when the wind chill dropped to –80 degrees—a new state record—and I swore to myself that when I left that town I would never return. Ever.

Well, it's difficult to hold a Canadian cold front against an entire state, and when the snow melted that spring, so did my resolve. I did leave, yet the first three-day road trip I ever took in search of oddball sites was through Hoosierland, and I've returned dozens of times over the years for day trips, extended vacations, and to research this second edition.

This book would not have been possible without the assistance, patience, and good humor of many individuals. My thanks go out to the following people for allowing me to interview them about their roadside attractions: Linda Black (Jim Jones's Early Life), "Blondie" (Murat Temple), Michael Carmichael (World's Largest Ball of Paint), Doreen Squire Ficara (World's Smallest Children's Art Gallery), James Henager (Henager's Memories & Nostalgia Museum), Al Hesselbart (RV/MH Heritage Foundation), Andrea Hill (West Baden Springs Hotel), John Ivers (Blue Flash), Keith Kaiser (Dan Quayle Childhood Home), Tony Kendall (Wild Hair Museum), Rick Kiefer (National New York Central Railroad Museum), Yvonne Knight (Howard Steamboat Museum), Lloyd "Tud" Kohn (Big Model Airplanes), Randy Koorsen (Koorsen Fire Museum), Bill Larkin (Bill's Yard), Becky Lindquist (RV/MH Heritage Foundation), Roselyn McKittrick (*Hoosiers*/Milan Station Antiques & Collectibles), Sally Newkirk (Yenawine Exhibit), Betty Palmer (Willard Library), Maria Peacock (Bendix Woods), Mark Racop (Batmobile/Fiberglass Freaks), Susan Richter (Belle Gunness/LaPorte County Historical Society Museum),

DeVon Rose (Bird's Eye View Museum), C. R. Schiefer (Touchables Sculpture Garden), Warren & Jill Schimpff (Schimpff's Confectionery), Allen Stewart (Hall of Heroes Museum), Julia Stolle (Museum of Miniature Houses), Katie Stone (Howard Steamboat Museum), Virginia Terpening (Indiana Medical History Museum), Alan Ray Whitaker (Gassy Garden), Peter Youngman (Diana of the Dunes/Ogden Dunes Historical Society), and Gaby Zimmerman (Bill Monroe's Memorial Music Park & Campground). There are a few people whose names I never got—the kind, young docent at KidsCommons, the sheriff's deputy who took my photo at Hoosier Hill, and the police clerk in Peru who brought me into their offices to see Dillinger's guns.

For research assistance, I am indebted to the librarians in the Indiana communities of Carmel, Chesterton, Crawfordsville, Daleville, Evansville, Freetown, Gosport, Greensburg, Jasper, Martinsville, Monticello, Montpelier, Mooresville, New Carlisle, Odon, Peru, Seymour, Shoals, South Bend, Tell City, Terre Haute, and Winamac. Thanks also to the Visitors Bureaus and/or Chambers of Commerce in Bedford, Bloomington, Columbus, Fort Wayne, Huntington, Indianapolis, Madison, Muncie, Nashville, New Albany, New Harmony, Porter, Richmond, Seymour, Vevay, and Warsaw. I was also assisted by the Santa Claus Post Office and the *Curubusco News*.

Friends and family members willingly volunteered (sometimes after excessive badgering on my part) to act as models for the photographs in this book: Jim Frost, Gianofer Fields, Patrick Hughes, Eugene Marceron, Michael Carmichael, Bill Larkin, James and Naomi Lane, Yoshio and Yukiko Sakamoto, Eriko Sakamoto, and Richard Lane. You were all great sports.

My deep-felt gratitude to everyone at Chicago Review Press (many of whom are Hoosiers!) for supporting the Oddball travel series, especially publisher Cynthia Sherry, Ellen Hornor, Jon Hahn, Allison Felus, and Mary Kravenas.

To the Hoosiers (native, adopted, or temporary) in my life, Olga, Tom, Kyle, Kat, and Taylor Granat, Elizabeth Wangler, and Maggie Gomer, I hope I did your state justice. To my Notre Dame friends through the Center for Social Concerns, especially Kathy Royer, Mary Ann Roemer, Dee

Schlotfeldt, Don McNeill, and Eugene McClory, when I think of Indiana, I think of you, and I forget all about 80 below.

Finally, to Jim Frost, who has driven with me to the moon and back in my Saturn, my deepest gratitude.

RECOMMENDED SOURCES

*I*f you'd like to learn more about the places and individuals in this book, the following are excellent sources.

General Indiana Guides

Indiana: A New Historical Guide by Robert Taylor, Errol Wayne Stevens, Mary Ann Ponder, and Paul Brockman (Indianapolis: Indiana Historical Society, 1989)

Indiana Historical Tour Guide by D. Ray Wilson (Carpentersville, IL: Crossroads Communications, 1994)

Indiana Curiosities: Quirky Characters, Roadside Oddities & Other Offbeat Stuff, 3rd ed., by Dick Wolfsie (Guilford, CT: Globe Pequot, 2010)

My Indiana: 101 Places to See by Earl L. Conn (Indianapolis: Indiana Historical Society, 2006)

Weird Indiana: Your Travel Guide to Indiana's Local Legends and Best-Kept Secrets by Mark Marimen, James A. Wallis, and Troy Taylor (New York: Sterling, 2008)

It Happened in Indiana: Remarkable Events That Changed History by Jackie Sheckler Finch (Guilford, CT: Globe Pequot, 2011)

Indiana Off the Beaten Path, 10th ed., by Phyllis Thomas (Old Saybrook, CT: Globe Pequot, 2012)

Indiana Legends by Nelson Price (Carmel: Guild Press of Indiana, 1997)

Amazing Tales from Indiana by Fred Cavinder (Bloomington: Indiana University Press, 1990)

More Amazing Tales from Indiana by Fred D. Cavinder (Bloomington: Indiana University Press, 2003)

Borderline Indiana by Wendell Trogdon (Mooresville, IN: Backroads Press, 1996)

Indiana Trivia

Awesome Almanac: Indiana by Jean Blasfield (Fontana, WI: B&B Publishing, 1993)

The Indiana Book of Records, Firsts, and Fascinating Facts by Fred Cavinder (Bloomington: Indiana University Press, 1985)

Indiana Trivia by Ernie and Jill Crouch (Nashville, TN: Rutledge Hill, 1997)

Legends and Losers by Andy Jones (South Bend: and books, 1999)

From Needmore to Prosperity: Hoosier Place Names in Folklore and History by Ronald Baker (Bloomington: Indiana University Press, 1995)

Indiana Ghosts

Hoosier Hauntings by K. T. MacRorie (Grand Rapids, MI: Thunder Bay, 1997)

Haunted Indiana by Mark Marimen (Grand Rapids, MI: Thunder Bay, 1997)

1: Northern Indiana

Auburn Cord Duesenberg Museum

It's a Duesy! by Lee P. Sauer (Auburn, IN: Auburn Cord Duesenberg Museum, 1999)

Diana of the Dunes

Diana of the Dunes: The True Story of Mabel Alice Gray by Janet Zenke Edwards (Charleston, SC: History Press, 2010)

The Lincoln Highway's "Ideal Section"

The Lincoln Highway Forum (Tucson: Lincoln Highway Association)

RVs and Motor Homes

Home on the Road: The Motor Home in America by Roger B. White (Washington, DC: Smithsonian Institution Scholarly Press, 2000)

RVs & Campers: 1900–2000 by Donald Wood (Hudson, WI: Enthusiast Books, 2002)

Johnny Appleseed

Johnny Appleseed: The Man, the Myth, the American Story by Howard Means (New York: Simon & Schuster, 2011)

Johnny Appleseed: Man and Myth by Robert Price (Bloomington: Indiana University Press, 1954)

Octave Chanute

Locomotive to Aeromotive: Octave Chanute and the Transportation Revolution by Simine Short (Champaign-Urbana: University of Illinois Press, 2011)

Progress in Flying Machines by Octave Chanute and Adam Frost (New York: Dover, 1998)

Michael Jackson and the Jackson 5

Moonwalk by Michael Jackson (New York: Crown, 2009)

Michael Jackson: The Magic and the Madness by J. Randy Taraborrelli (New York: Birch Lane, 1991)

Michael Unauthorized by Christopher Andersen (New York: Simon & Schuster, 1994)

A Christmas Story

A Christmas Story: Behind the Scenes of a Hollywood Classic by Caseen Gaines (Toronto: ECW, 2013)

Dan Quayle

The Man Who Would Be President by Bob Woodward and David S. Broder (New York: Simon & Schuster, 1992)

Standing Firm by Dan Quayle (New York: HarperCollins, 1994)

What a Waste It Is to Lose One's Mind by The Quayle Quarterly (Bridgeport, CT: The Quayle Quarterly, 1992)

The Dan Quayle Quiz Book by Jeremy Solomon and Ken Brady (Boston: Little, Brown, 1989)

Belle Gunness

Belle Gunness: The Lady Bluebeard by Janet L. Langlois (Bloomington: Indiana University Press, 1985)

The Gunness Story by Madeline G. Kinney and Gretchen Tyler (La Porte, IN: La Porte County Historical Society, 1984)

Lodner Phillips and His Submarines

Great Lakes' First Submarine by Patricia A. Gruse Harris. (Michigan City, IN: Michigan City Historical Society, 1982)

Indiana Circuses

Life in a Three-Ring Circus by Sharon Smith and Stephen J. Fletcher (Indianapolis: Indiana University Press, 2001)

Indiana's Big Top by Don L. Chaffee (Grand Rapids, MI: Foremost Press, 1969)

The First 25 Years by DeLoris Welden (Peru, IN: Circus City Festival, 1985)

Cole Porter

Cole Porter: A Biography by William McBrien (New York: Alfred A. Knopf, 1998)

Elmo Lincoln, the First Tarzan

My Father, Elmo Lincoln, The Original Tarzan by Marci'a Lincoln Rudolph (Rochester, IN: Self-published, Date unknown)

Studebaker

More Than They Promised: The Studebaker Story by Thomas E. Bonsall (Palo Alto, CA: Stanford University Press, 2000)

Studebaker: The Life and Death of an American Corporation by Donald Critch-
    clow (Bloomington: Indiana University Press, 1997)

George Gipp

*The Gipper: George Gipp, Knute Rockne, and the Dramatic Rise of Notre Dame
    Football* by Jack Cavanaugh (New York: Skyhorse, 2010)

One for the Gipper by Patrick Chellan (New York: Arrowhead Classics, 1996)

Orville Redenbacher

Just Call Me Orville: The Story of Orville Redenbacher by Robert W. Topping
    (West Lafayette, IN: Purdue University Press, 2011)

2: Central Indiana

The Battle of Tippecanoe

*The Gods of Prophetstown: The Battle of Tippecanoe and the Holy War for the
    American Frontier* by Adam Jortner (New York: Oxford University Press,
    2011)

Lew Wallace and *Ben-Hur*

The Sword & the Pen: A Life of Lew Wallace by Ray E. Boomhower (Indianapolis:
    Indiana Historical Society, 2005)

Jim Jones and the People's Temple

Raven: The True Story of Jim Jones and His People by Tim Reiterman (New York:
    TarcherPerigee, 2008)

White Night by John Peer Nugent (New York: Rawson, Wade, 1979)

Our Father Who Art in Hell by James Reston, Jr. (New York: *Times* Books, 1981)

James Dean

The Real James Dean: Intimate Memories from Those Who Knew Him Best by
    Peter L. Winkler, ed. (Chicago: Chicago Review Press, 2016)

James Dean: The Mutant King by David Dalton (Chicago: Chicago Review Press,
    2001)

Boulevard of Broken Dreams by Paul Alexander (New York: Viking, 1994)

The James Dean Story by Ronald Martinetti (New York: Birch Lane, 1995)

Levi Coffin and the Underground Railroad

Fleeing for Freedom by George Hendrick (Chicago: Ivan R. Dee, 2004)

Levi Coffin: Quaker Breaking the Bonds of Slavery in Ohio and Indiana by Mary
    Ann Yannessa (Richmond, IN: Friends United, 2001)

Reminiscences of Levi Coffin: The Reputed President of the Underground Railroad
    by Levi Coffin and Ben Richmond (Richmond, IN: Friends United, 2001)

Dan Patch

Crazy Good: The True Story of Dan Patch by Charles Leerhsen (New York: Simon
    & Schuster, 2009)

Larry Bird
Drive: The Story of My Life by Larry Bird (New York: Bantam, 1990)

3: Southern Indiana
General Southern Indiana Guides
Strange Tales of Crime and Murder in Southern Indiana by Keven McQueen
(Charleston, SC: History Press, 2009)
Bill Monroe
Can't You Hear Me Callin': The Life of Bill Monroe, the Father of Bluegrass by Richard D. Smith (Boston: Little, Brown, 2000)
Kinsey Institute
Alfred C. Kinsey: A Life by James H. Jones (New York: Norton, 2004)
Sex the Measure of All Things: A Life of Alfred C. Kinsey by Jonathan Gathorne-Hardy (Bloomington: Indiana University Press, 2000)
Lincoln in Indiana
There I Grew Up: Remembering Abraham Lincoln's Indiana Youth by William E. Bartelt (Indianapolis: Indiana Historical Society, 2008)
Lincoln's Youth: Indiana Years, Seven to Twenty-One, 1816–1830 by Louis A. Warren (Indianapolis: Indiana Historical Society, 1991)
The Real *Hoosiers*
The Greatest Basketball Story Ever Told by Greg Guffy (Bloomington: Indiana University Press, 1993)
The Making of Hoosiers: *How a Small Movie from the Heartland Became One of America's Favorite Films* by Gayle L. Johnson (Self-published, 2010)
Virgil I. Grissom
Calculated Risk: The Supersonic Life and Times of Gus Grissom by George Leopold (West Lafayette: Purdue University Press, 2016)
New Harmony
New Harmony Then and Now by Darryl D. Jones and Donald E. Pitzer (Bloomington, IN: Quarry Books, 2011)
Walker's Guide to New Harmony's History by Janet R. Walker (New Harmony, IN: Historic New Harmony, 1996)
Santa Claus, Indiana
Holiday World by Pat Koch and Jane Ammeson (Mt. Pleasant, SC: Arcadia, 2006)
Santa Claus by Pat Koch and Emily Weisner Thompson (Mt. Pleasant, SC: Arcadia, 2013)
New West Baden Springs Hotel
History of the New West Baden Springs Hotel by Gregory S. Gatsos (West Baden Springs, IN: Self-published, 2001)

West Baden Springs: Legacy of Dreams by Chris Bundy (West Baden Springs, IN: Self-published, 2001)

4: Indianapolis and Suburbs
General
Wicked Indianapolis by Andrew E. Stoner (Charleston, SC: History Press, 2011)
David Letterman
The Letterman Wit by Bill Adler (New York: Carroll & Graff, 1994)
David Letterman by Frances Lefkowitz (New York: Chelsea House, 1997)
Dave's World by Michael Cader (New York: Warner Books, 1995)
Kurt Vonnegut
We Never Danced Cheek to Cheek: The Young Kurt Vonnegut in Indianapolis and Beyond by Majie Alford Failey (Portland, OR: Hawthorne Books, 2011)
Mike Tyson
Heavy Justice: The Trial of Mike Tyson by Randy Roberts and J. Gregory Garrison (New York: Addison Wesley, 1994)
Robert Kennedy
Bobby Kennedy: The Making of a Liberal Icon by Larry Tye (New York: Random House, 2016)
USS *Indianapolis*
Left for Dead: A Young Man's Search for Justice for the USS Indianapolis by Pete Nelson (New York: Delacourt Books for Young Readers, 2003)
In Harm's Way: The Sinking of the USS Indianapolis *and the Extraordinary Story of Its Survivors* by Doug Stanton (New York: Henry Holt, 2001)
Abandon Ship! The Sage of the USS Indianapolis, *the Navy's Greatest Sea Disaster* by Richard F. Newcomb (New York: HarperCollins, 2000)
Indy 500
The Indianapolis 500: A Century of High Speed Racing by Lew Freedman (Indianapolis: Blue River, 2016)
Indianapolis 500 Chronicle by Rick Popely (Lincolnwood, IL: Publications International, 1998)
Indianapolis Motor Speedway—100 Years of Racing by Ralph Kramer (Iola, WI: Krause, 2009)

5: John Dillinger Diapers to Death Tour
Hoosier Public Enemy: A Life of John Dillinger by John A. Beineke (Indianapolis: Indiana Historical Society, 2014)

Dillinger: A Short and Violent Life by Robert Cromie and Joseph Pinkston (Evanston, IL: Chicago Historical Bookworks, 1990)

Dillinger: The Untold Story by G. Russell Girardin and William J. Hemmler (Bloomington: Indiana University Press, 1994)

The Dillinger Days by John Tollard (Cambridge, MA: Da Capo, 1995)

Dillinger Strikes in East Chicago by Richard Smyers (Self-published: East Chicago Public Library, date unknown)

INDEX BY CITY NAME

INDEX BY SITE NAME

OTHER BOOKS IN THE
ODDBALL SERIES

978-1-61374-032-3 | $16.95 (CAN $18.95)

FEATURING:

- Henry's Rabbit Ranch
- America's One and Only Hippie Memorial
- World's First Jungle Gym
- Popeye's Hometown
- The Leather Archives and Museum
- General Santa Ana's two wooden legs
- World's Largest Sock Monkey
- Scarlett O'Hara's green drapes
- The Friendship Shoe Fence
- And many, many more sites

978-1-55652-564-3 | $14.95 (CAN $16.95)

FEATURING:

- World's Largest Cheeto
- Future Birthplace of Captain Kirk
- Iowa's Only Tunnel
- The Hobo Museum
- Matchstick Marvels

- Lovers Leap Bridge
- Mule Cemetery
- *Twister* House
- Pinky the Elephant
- And many, many more sites